Critical Literacy and Urban Youth

Critical Literacy and Urban Youth offers an interrogation of critical theory developed from the author's work with young people in classrooms, neighborhoods, and institutions of power. Through cases, an articulated process, and a theory of literacy education and social change, Morrell extends the conversation among literacy educators about what constitutes critical literacy while also examining implications for practice in secondary and postsecondary American educational contexts. This book is distinguished by its weaving together of theory and practice.

Morrell begins by arguing for a broader definition of the "critical" in critical literacy—one that encapsulates the entire Western philosophical tradition as well as several important "Othered" traditions ranging from postcolonialism to the African-American tradition. Next, he looks at four cases of critical literacy pedagogy with urban youth: teaching popular culture in a high school English classroom; conducting community-based critical research; engaging in cyberactivism; and doing critical media literacy education. Lastly, he returns to theory, first considering two areas of critical literacy pedagogy that are still relatively unexplored: the importance of critical reading and writing in constituting and reconstituting the self, and critical writing that is not just about coming to a critical understanding of the world but that plays an explicit and self-referential role in changing the world. Morrell concludes by outlining a grounded theory of critical literacy pedagogy and considering its implications for literacy research, teacher education, classroom practice, and advocacy work for social change.

Ernest Morrell is assistant professor in the Urban Schooling division, Graduate School of Education and Information Studies, University of California, Los Angeles.

Language, Culture, and Teaching
Sonia Nieto, Series Editor

Critical Literacy and Urban Youth

Pedagogies of Access, Dissent, and Liberation

Ernest Morrell

Routledge
Taylor & Francis Group

NEW YORK AND LONDON

First published 2008
by Routledge
270 Madison Ave, New York, NY 10016

Simultaneously published in the UK
by Routledge
2 Park Square, Milton Park, Abingdon, Oxon OX14 4RN

Routledge is an imprint of the Taylor & Francis Group, an informa business

© 2008 Taylor & Francis

Typeset in Minion Pro by Prepress Projects Ltd, Perth, UK
Printed and bound in the United States of America on acid-free paper
by Walsworth Publishing Company, Marceline, MO

Library of Congress Cataloging in Publication Data
Morrell, Ernest, 1971–
Critical literacy and urban youth: pedagogies of access, dissent, and liberation/Ernest Morrell.
     p. cm. — (Language, culture, and teaching)
  Includes bibliographical references and index.
  1. Literacy—Social aspects—United States. 2. Urban youth—Education—United States. 3. Critical pedagogy—United States.
  I. Title.

LC149.M614 2008
370.11′5—dc22
               2007023902

ISBN 10: 0–8058–5663–3 (hbk)
ISBN 10: 0–8058–5664–1 (pbk)
ISBN 10: 0–203–93791–0 (ebk)

ISBN 13: 978–0–8058–5663–7 (hbk)
ISBN 13: 978–0–8058–5664–4 (pbk)
ISBN 13: 978–0–203–93791–4 (ebk)

To my grandfathers

Upperton Livingston Hurts (1919–1960)
and Preston Davis Coats (1910–1952)

and to my second son

Antonio Kiyoshi Morrell (b. 2004),
welcome to the world!

Contents

Foreword

Aside from the sentimental and romantic public schools documented in Hollywood movies or first-person non-fiction accounts (often written by teachers who leave the classroom after only one year), it is difficult to find texts that genuinely champion public schools and those who inhabit them. Just the opposite, in fact, is the case: many schools, particularly urban public schools, are depicted as joyless and regimented places where unruly youth rule and little learning takes place. Given this context, writing a book that celebrates urban public school students is not only a creative endeavor but indeed an act of hope. The book you are about to read is just such a book.

Critical Literacy and Urban Youth takes us on a remarkable journey of theory and practice in classrooms and schools as few books have been able to do. Ernest Morrell was a high school English teacher at an urban public school and, later, a doctoral student and now faculty member in literacy education. Drawing on his experiences as both a high school teacher in urban schools, and his theoretical training as a researcher and faculty member at elite universities, Morrell demonstrates what it means to have *praxis* (i.e., reflection plus practice) at the core of teaching. This is a profoundly theoretical (and, at the same time, enormously accessible) text that places the voices and writings of high school students in the forefront. More importantly, it demonstrates in graphic detail the brilliance of urban high school students who have been all but abandoned by our society.

In this text, Morrell challenges preservice and practicing teachers to embrace complex ideas in order to improve their classroom practice, especially if they want their students to become critical and engaged citizens of our nation and world. From Plato to hip-hop, from the philosophy of the Frankfurt School to the poetry of Pablo Neruda, he explores the most important theoretical contributions to education today, all the while encouraging teachers and students to become theoreticians in their own right. Weaving theory and practice throughout, he describes methodologies from critical textual production to cyberliteracies to "guerrilla filmmaking" as grist for the mill of literacy teaching.

Critical Literacy and Urban Youth is a passionate book, elegantly written and beautifully developed. It is also an unabashedly political book. Drawing on the ideas of Paulo Freire, Morrell makes no apologies for believing in and trusting both students and teachers. For him, writing, and indeed all literacies, are practices of freedom. Confident that teachers can create classrooms and schools that are critical, lively, and hopeful spaces, he provides teachers and those about to enter the profession with inspiration.

Sonia Nieto

Preface

This book represents a five-year labor of love. While I have thoroughly loved every minute of its conception and production, I am also well aware that it has been labor. I feel that there is so much to say about critical theory, about critical literacy, about the worlds of schools, and classrooms, and teachers, and about the potential of young people, and of words, and images, and revolutionary moments. But, alas, it is only one book and one book can only do so much. So ultimately I had to decide when enough was enough and I had to send these words from my computer screen into the world and, as it seems, into your hands.

There is so much to say, I feel, because there is so much to do and so much at stake. Literacy, well at least critical literacy, is fundamentally tied to the realization of our full humanity, especially in times like these. For our children, literacy determines their ability to engage the world as citizens, as intellectuals, as workers, and hopefully as the artists, filmmakers, and writers of the next generation. The possibilities are humbling and, yet, the consequences of failure are unthinkable at the individual and societal levels. As has been the case with all of our predecessors, we stand at the threshold of our destinies; the world and the future are ours to make.

Which means that we have to get smarter, we have to do better, and we have to know more if we are truly to accomplish our aims. That, for me, is what this book represents: my own labor to become the educator and scholar that I need to be in order to do the work that I feel needs to be done. And it represents my simultaneous engagements with theory and with young people who live and act and are acted upon by the world in real time. My engagements with theory challenge my worldviews, and my assumptions about pedagogy, knowledge, learning, and textual consumption and production. My engagements with young people remind me that time is of the essence and that pedagogy is the ultimate tool of revolutionary change.

I began (and remain) convinced that substantive and sustained engagement with critical theory can result in the development of frameworks and practices that lead to empowering outcomes for youth in the world today. As an educator (and not a philosopher) by training, that meant taking a lonely walk of trepidation through the unwieldy streets of critical theory. It meant reading texts first and asking questions about their immediate relevance later. It meant reading an entire page written in my native language and admitting to myself that I didn't understand a word of it, and it wasn't attributable to some flaw with the author's ability to construct text. Critical theory consumed me and changed me; changed the very way that I approach text and the world. In this book I have attempted to retrace some of that initial voyage as I advocate for the continued significance of critical theory to our task; that is, I believe that those interested in critical literacy need to engage critical theory.

At the same time, I also understand that the narrowness of the construction of the canon of critical theory is an issue that requires confrontation. My voyage into the Western canon alerted me to other texts, "Othered" texts that had much to offer to my growth and development. As I became more familiar with the pillars of critical theory I also began to reinvent my own critical canon to include women, people of color, the young, and other groups who do not adorn shelves with the likes of Adorno or Marcuse. Ultimately critical theory is about a way of being and knowing and acting in the world; it is not about canonized authors. So in this text I have taken a very liberal approach to my use of the term and I have constructed a rather large tent under which my family of critical mentors can roam free and mingle with one another. After all, our purpose is to mine the theory as we develop our practice, which will in turn produce better theory and practice. Our purpose is not to preserve the purity or sanctity of a set of texts. Critical theory loses its potency and its purpose when left to gather dust on the shelves of libraries and college bookstores; and critical theory left uninterrogated by the world ceases to act as critical theory and becomes something akin to dogma.

We interrogate critical theory through our practice. In this book I have attempted to interrogate critical theory through my practices with young people in classrooms, and neighborhoods, and institutions of power. What I offer, hopefully, are a few humble cases, an articulated process, and, yes, more theory; a theory of literacy education and social change.

OVERVIEW OF THE BOOK

I begin by arguing for a broader definition of the "critical" in critical literacy—one that encapsulates the entire Western philosophical tradition as well as several important "Othered" traditions ranging from postcolonialism to the African-American tradition. Next, I examine four cases of critical literacy pedagogy with urban youth: teaching popular culture in a high school English classroom; conducting community-based critical research; engaging in cyberactivism; and doing critical media literacy education. Lastly, I return to theory, first considering two areas of critical literacy pedagogy that are still relatively unexplored: the importance of critical reading and writing in constituting and reconstituting the self, and critical writing that is not just about coming to a critical understanding of the world but plays an explicit and self-referential role in changing the world. I conclude by outlining a grounded theory of critical literacy pedagogy and considering its implications for literacy research, classroom practice, and advocacy work for social change.

ACKNOWLEDGMENTS

As always, I acknowledge the students who inspired these words and who make the work that I so dearly love possible. In a world where it is so easy to lose hope, my students continue to surprise and amaze and inspire me and, for that, I am eternally grateful. Additionally, I would like to acknowledge my graduate students at Michigan State University and UCLA, whose wonderful questions about critical theory and critical literacy also serve as inspiration for this writing. I would be remiss if I didn't thank my colleagues on the faculties at these universities; they have shown nothing but confidence and support in this work. Especially I am grateful to John Rogers and Jeannie Oakes, my colleagues at the Institute for Democracy, Education, and Access (IDEA) at UCLA who have also been my collaborators on these many projects over the past eight years. Thanks to Naomi Silverman and Sonia Nieto, my editors, for their wisdom and patience. An extra special thanks to my comrades in pedagogy Jeff Duncan-Andrade and K. Wayne Yang; we have spent now half of our lives in this beautiful struggle and there is so much more yet to do. Thank you to Jodene for this fifteen-year walk and for still believing and being willing to dream; true friendship is a lifelong journey, and it doesn't matter where we're headed anyway, if we're traveling in the company of friends. And, finally, to my boys Amani and Antonio, for nudging me gently into adulthood, and for going to bed early enough to give me some brief moments to write.

1

Introduction

GIVING THEM BACK THEIR BOOKS

It is Friday August 1, 2003, and I, along with the teachers and students, am in the pool table room adjacent to the California room at the university's Faculty Center. We have been here before, huddled together in our final moments before the presentations; where I tell the students that I love them and that the presentations, though important, are post script to the seminar. That being the case, the charge is still to give the crowd a show. The final student presentations are the first step toward the distribution of the critical research that the students have generated throughout the seminar. It is an anxious, yet exciting time; I can feel the palpable tension in the room.

On this occasion, I am reminded by a research colleague to try to gather the students' notebooks for analysis. I think to myself that the notebooks belong to the students and not the research team. The 100+-page philosophical, social, and analytical texts that the students have created over the preceding five weeks are mementos of a prolific time and will serve the students well as reminders of the past and predictors of a future of possibilities for writing and action. So, as an addendum to the annual pep talk, I ask who's willing to give up the notebook and a couple volunteer and hand them over to a pair of research assistants who will promise to return them as soon as possible.

Now, my co-director and I could demand access to the notebooks and the students would comply with our demands against their wishes; largely out of respect. The notebooks would certainly provide great data for analysis and what researcher would not want to have access to data like that? But we understand that we have to give the students back those notebooks. What rhetorical guides for future lives as researcher-activists; what testaments to the possible, reminders of our short, yet significant time together; verbal memory books. Self-writing. Hopefully these texts represent the first, for these scholar-activists, in a long succession of filled black composition notebooks containing subversive, liberatory prose.

Some of our colleagues in the academy will think that we are just sloppy researchers letting golden data slip right through our fingers like that. Are we crazy? Incompetent? Disorganized? These critics wouldn't understand what it means to have trust and love for and from the "research subjects" who leave indelible imprints on our lives forever; subjects who become embedded in our lives and in our work. And, so, these students walk out of the Faculty Center and into the world with a great deal of our data, most of which we do not have in any other place; data that cannot inform the manuscripts of research articles, but will undoubtedly buoy those first few steps into life beyond. That is because our data are also their critical texts; texts that will be the first of many, texts of power and of the empowered; notes to the self and to the world; announcements of sorts of young writers on the critical edge; writers whose words will change the world. And, as an educational scholar, I feel fairly confident that this is as it should be and that, maybe, we are learning a thing or two about this project of critical literacy. At least that is what I hope.

CRITICAL LITERACY MATTERS

Critical literacy matters.

A consensus seems to be emerging among educators, researchers, policymakers, politicians, and business leaders across the political and ideological spectrums that *literacy* matters. Whether we are talking about balanced literacy instruction, teaching literacy through literature, or mastering digital and virtual technologies, there is some agreement that an ability to consume and produce academic language is a prerequisite for personal and professional success. The United Nations has gone so far as to declare the decade of 2003–2012 the "Decade of Literacy." Toward these ends millions of dollars and millions of people hours are being devoted to research, program development, and implementation in settings as diverse as refugee camps, community centers in developing nations, and urban classrooms in the "First World" nations of the West, like the United States.

And this makes sense. There exists a host of research that correlates (dominant/functional/informational) literacy development with positive social and economic outcomes (UNESCO, 2005). Those students who are able to acquire and master dominant literacies have a greater likelihood of attending universities and earning higher paying jobs. Parents who have acquired dominant literacies are also better able to advocate for and tutor their own children, thereby increasing the likelihood of them experiencing academic and economic success themselves (Laureau, 2000). Further, everyday citizens who have acquired dominant literacies are more inclined to participate in civic life as voters, activists, public intellectuals, and even as holders of local, state, or national office (US Department of Education, 2005).

There are also, however, gross disparities in dominant literacy development and negative economic and social outcomes associated with the failure to acquire dominant literacies ranging from poverty and unemployment to incarceration and teen pregnancy rates. The National Assessment of Adult Literacy Surveys (NAAL) of 1992 and 2003, for example, suggest gross differences in dominant literacy development along lines of class and race (Greenberg *et al.*, 2007). A report published by the Department of Prison Statistics claims that as many as 84 percent of the more than two million prisoners in the United States lack basic functional literacy skills. These negative outcomes also have a higher incidence among urban populations, where the disparities in income, dominant literacy development, and academic achievement are the most glaring (Kozol, 1991; Ladson-Billings, 1994; Noguera, 2002; US Department of Education, 2002). These urban and impoverished populations (and rates of poverty are twice as high in urban districts as in the nation at large) are also the frequent objects of literacy education reform, most notably exemplified in the recent federal Elementary and Secondary Education Act (known as *No Child Left Behind*) legislation intended to "improve the achievement of the disadvantaged."

There is little argument that members of our most disadvantaged populations need to acquire dominant literacies in order to participate fully in economic and civic life in the new world order. The diligent work of researchers, policymakers, and development agencies in this vein should be admired, at least in principle. Many scholars, however, who hail from the multicultural and critical traditions, are justifiably concerned with the unintended consequences of an exclusive focus on a narrowly defined and conceived dominant literacy agenda.

For example, multiculturalists (Ladson-Billings, 1994; Nieto, 1992) have argued that traditional academic instruction can alienate and exclude members of culturally marginalized groups. Even though these students may acquire literacy, they do so at a great cost of losing the opportunity to learn about their own culture or the cultures of other marginalized groups. This lack of representation can decrease motivation and achievement while leading to resistance, apathy, and dropping out. Fine (1991) has argued that schools that disrespect and alienate students conspire to "push out" students who are members of historically marginalized schools. This change in terminology appropriately places the onus of responsibility as much on the institution and its explicit and hidden curricula as on the students who, one way or another, prematurely exit the system.

Further, little of the research practice in formal pedagogical settings takes into account that students who are labeled by schools as illiterate or semiliterate partake in vibrant and sophisticated language and literacy practices that they learn and utilize in non-school settings as they participate in everyday sociocultural activity (Gee, 2000; Heath, 1983; Street, 1984). As such, these students are treated as pathological and as deficits when educators would be better served to brainstorm how to make meaningful links between their local language and literacy practices and the literacies needed to more effectively navigate discourses of power.

Finally, the dominant discourses surrounding literacy instruction usually treat literacy as an autonomous and, therefore, neutral entity or skill set, namely the ability to read and write. These discourses fail to take into account that literacies are multiple (New London Group, 1996), situated (Barton and Hamilton, 1998), ideological (Street, 1984), and tied to power relations in society (Freire and Macedo, 1987). It is a given that the acquisition of dominant literacies is crucial to creating more equitable spaces in the world; but it is also true that literacy instruction does not need to occur in a social, cultural, and political vacuum. Nor should dominant literacies be the only focus of interventions in schools and other pedagogical spaces. This book makes the argument that a more thorough, encompassing, and theoretically grounded approach should center upon the acquisition and demonstration of critical literacies. The remainder of the book is dedicated toward providing this theoretical foundation along with examples of what courses critical literacy education might take with urban adolescents in the United States. The lessons from the empirical research, I argue, have applications across the spectrum of primary and secondary education (K-12).

WHY CRITICAL LITERACY?

The Soviet psychologist, educator, and social theorist Lev Vygotsky rightly claimed that all thought is mediated through language (Vygotsky, 1962). His fellow Soviet and philosopher of language Mikail Bakhtin also sought to understand the role of language in the social construction of reality. According to Bakhtin, at any given moment a language is stratified into socio-ideological languages: languages belonging to professions, to genres, and to particular generations (Bakhtin, 1981). It was Bakhtin's desire to understand how social processes operated to determine how maximal mutual understanding or language occurred when the natural tendencies of speech tended toward *heteroglossia*, or distinct and disparate utterances. He attempted to use philosophical analysis to understand the social and ideological forces that allowed fragmented speech to become constituted as language. It became clear that dominant forces would have the potential to shape language, and thus meaning, even though language could work to resist and contend against these pressures, but any ultimate meanings of language are nevertheless constructed within these social and political contexts.

Proto-structuralist Swiss philologist and linguist Ferdinand de Saussure (1915/1966), attempted, in the early twentieth century, to demonstrate the arbitrary relationship between sign systems in language and their socially determined meanings. Semiotics drew upon the work of Saussure to contend that ideology intervened in this relationship to determine the meanings of signs in ways that supported the dominant modes of thinking and being (Barthes, 1967). In short, these theorists and social scientists all contend that we are socially constructed, linguistically mediated beings. We are defined and we define ourselves largely through our interactions with ideologically laden language and texts. If, as these theorists and researchers contend, language is a constructed and non-neutral entity, then those who teach (and learn) language and literacy must also work to make themselves aware of the various social, ideological, cultural, and political contexts in which the languages and literacies of power operate. This is one primary intention of the critical literacy education I advocate.

Critical theorists and education scholars know and understand that the general population is receiving a great deal of "bad" information via social institutions such as the media, corporate America, and public schools. Daily, these institutions commit a linguistic and semiotic violence that leads to alienation, obesity, depression, low self-esteem, academic failure, and a dependency on consumer goods. Information brokers control the world via their power over the knowledge that is produced and sanctioned through these cultural institutions. Any citizen who aspires to live an independent life will need to confront and counter the ideologies latent in language and texts in our postindustrial, postmodern society in which information is the ultimate capital of exchange (Gates, 1996). In order to define ourselves on our own terms, we must understand the role of language and texts in the construction of the self and the social.

Not only must these citizens understand these constructions, but they must also intervene in them; they must speak back and act back against these constructions with counter-language and counter-texts. Critical literacy, therefore, is necessary not only for the critical navigation of hegemonic discourses; it is also essential to the redefining of the self and the transformation of oppressive social structures and relations of production. Confronting ideological language and texts is a requisite activity, but resistance and transformation are also textually based practices for the critically literate citizen.

Whether we are talking about reading the newspaper, watching television commercials, consuming texts in preparation for an election, organizing a demonstration, writing a letter in protest of a faulty product, or interrogating our child's standardized test scores, our actions as critical citizens in the postindustrial new world order demand a certain set of critical textual practices. These critical textual practices incorporate, even subsume traditional textual practices. That is, people need to read, write, and speak in certain sorts of socially sanctioned ways if they have any hopes of confronting problematic texts or producing informative and empowering ones.

And no population requires critical literacy more than today's urban youth. As young people, they are targeted by corporations that want them to feel self-conscious, even self-loathing if that will lead to the purchase of certain products. Corporate advertisers spend billions of dollars annually encouraging our youth to crave cigarettes; to spend too much money on basketball shoes; to drink too much pop; to eat too many potato chips; and to demand constantly updated video gaming systems. Mainstream media advertising achieves its intended outcome of encouraging its young audience to desire its products; to desire to be cool; to desire to be desired; even to desire to be sexy at increasingly younger ages. These young people are also daily bombarded with racist, sexist, classist language and texts that threaten to circumscribe their worldview and to encourage them to participate willingly in preserving a status quo that may be problematic and oppressive toward others that do not look or act or think like the "norm"; a status quo that may ultimately serve against the self and collective interests of youth in urban America.

Many of those adolescents who find themselves attending schools in urban America are also less likely to have libraries, bookstores, and newspaper stands within easy reach. Unfortunately, they may be far more likely to have liquor stores than bookstores in their neighborhoods. In one of the summer seminars in which urban teens learned to conduct critical research, the students once mapped a census tract in their inner city neighborhood where there were fifty-eight liquor stores and no libraries! Urban adolescents must also confront the languages of ghettoization and criminalization (Giroux, 1996). They will be forced to inhabit linguistic and semiotic symbol systems that have cast them as the "Other" (Said, 1979); an "Other" to be feared, exoticized, and ultimately kept in check, even kept behind bars. They will constantly be forced to interpret (and will need to critique) popular texts that could make them feel badly about themselves or others who share their phenotype or lived experience. One only need to browse the newspapers of any major city, or watch popular television shows or major new film releases to gain a sense of the popular messages circulating about the urban poor and people of color. Todd Boyd (1997), for instance, examines the multiple problematic representations of African-Americans in popular culture and the multiple problematic readings African-Americans themselves have of these same popular cultural artifacts. Additionally, higher concentrations of poverty, disappearing jobs, underfunded schools, toxic playgrounds, and lack of safe, clean public spaces will require, even demand, a vigilant form of textually and linguistically mediated political activism much greater than that required of the general population.

At the same time that urban youth find themselves in these constraining conditions, they are also uniquely positioned to enact a critical literacy praxis that would promote meaningful societal change even as they set in motion a life of personal freedom. As young people, they inherit a tradition of activism and dissent that has fostered countless cultural and social revolutions in the United States and abroad (Kurlansky, 2003). Their demonstrated willingness and ability to act, their unique social vantage point and their openness to alternate possibilities make America's urban youth perfect candidates to make the world a more humane planet for people who look and live like them.

This sort of youth-initiated pedagogy, however, requires the development and use of conceptual and technical tools that are not acquired naturally through indigenous cultural practices. Even young people who possess "critical instincts" will need to learn those essential literacy skills that enable them to powerfully navigate socially sanctioned language systems as they also attempt to speak the truth to power. In short, there is no model of critical literacy praxis that can evade a critical literacy education. Given that critical literacy incorporates and subsumes traditional literacies that are frequently taught in schools, the urban literacy classroom becomes the ideal location for a critical literacy education that will lead toward engaged citizenship and personal emancipation: outcomes that so many of us feel are crucial to the type of world we imagine. When we invoke the term "critical literacy" as educators or scholars, we implicate ourselves in this pedagogical and revolutionary task of fostering in our youth skills with and attitudes toward language and texts that are essential to remaking the planet. Recognizing our implication, though, is important because it means that change is possible; it also means that there is something that we can do to precipitate that change. This book will offer a few cases that I offer as evidence of what shapes this change may take in praxis-oriented literacy work with youth.

I would now like to turn toward three conceptual and methodological strands that are woven together throughout the book: grounded theory, poststructural ethnography, and critical teacher research. Taken together, these strands offer an interesting and innovative approach to critical literacy research and practice: an approach that, I argue, leads toward a transformational model of the scholarship of teaching; one that breaks down fundamental divisions between theory and practice, between researchers and research subjects, and between scholars and practitioners. It is also an approach that ideally facilitates more collaboration and collective engagement between K-12 practitioner-scholars and university-based educators, and one that promotes achievement and educational and social justice. I will cover, in greater detail, these concepts of fusion, intersection, and change throughout the book. For now, I begin with a brief description of each of the major theoretical and methodological strands that have informed this study.

GROUNDED THEORY

This book is largely shaped conceptually by the grounded theory as originally explained by Glaser and Strauss (1967) and later rearticulated by Strauss and Corbin (1997). According to their constant comparative method, research should exist as a dialectic interaction between existing theories and contemporary experience. Rather than take existing theory ipso facto and apply deductive measures to test theory, the authors argue that grounded theorists believe that knowledge is created through actual experience in the world. This experience is not atheoretical by any means. Instead, grounded theory begins with nascent theory that is tested in real world situations with the goal of producing better theory. This process is consonant with Hegel's (1999) conceptualization of dialectic as a juxtaposition or contestation between competing forces—what he labeled as a thesis and antithesis—that ultimately leads toward a synthesis or greater truth. Hegel's nineteenth-century enlightenment ideals concerning historical development have been incorporated and expanded upon by many Marxist and post-Marxist scholars including the twentieth-century Brazilian educator-philosopher-activist Paulo Freire, who articulated and enacted a dialectic (and dialogic) pedagogy whereby reflective-action would lead to greater active-reflection and informed reflective-action, what he termed praxis.

Freire's (1970) theory of critical pedagogy, as articulated in *Pedagogy of the Oppressed*, is a powerful example of grounded theory. From his reading of Marxist and existential philosophy Freire imagined a model of humanizing literacy pedagogy that he began to implement with Brazilian peasants during the 1940s and 1950s. From his practical work with people, he was then able to coalesce, refine, and push back against these various theories about knowledge, humanity, action, and freedom to develop a grounded theory of revolutionary literacy pedagogy that has informed so much critical scholarship around the world, including this author and this text!

That is where I have begun with this book. I acknowledge that I am drawing upon 2500 years of "critical literacy theory" that inform, at some level, how we think about the terms "critical", "literacy", and "theory" and their possibilities for revolutionizing urban educational practice and specifically, for the purposes of this work, literacy instruction. But I am not hypothesis-testing these theories; rather I am attempting to show how I developed a metatheory of critical literacy pedagogy from my experience with the philosophical and non-Western traditions that informed my literacy teaching and teacher research with teens at two major urban centers. In addition to spelling out that metatheory, this book attempts to show instantiations of that theory in practice. It is important to understand how this theoretically informed practice translated into powerful learning outcomes for students. But I argue that it is even more important to understand how an analysis of this theoretically informed classroom practice can help us to develop better, grounded theories of critical literacy praxis with urban youth that may inform literacy research, teacher education, professional development, and curricular policy for literacy instruction at every level. It is my belief that grounded theory is important not only for this work on critical literacy; it also serves as an important model for activist research in general.

POSTSTRUCTURAL ETHNOGRAPHY

Another conceptual strand that informs this study is that of poststructural ethnography. The theorist of qualitative research Norm Denzin (1997) addresses a triple crisis of representation, legitimation, and praxis that confronts researchers in the human disciplines. In his work *Interpretive Ethnography: Ethnographic Practices for the 21st Century* he argues:

> Traditional ethnographers have historically assumed that their methods probe and reveal lived experience. They have also assumed that the subject's world is always final, and that talk directly reflects subjective and lived experience. The literal translation of talk thus equals lived experience and its representation. Critical poststructuralism challenges these assumptions. Language and speech do not mirror experience. They create experience and in the process of creation constantly transform and defer that which is being described. The meaning of a subject's statements are, therefore, always in motion . . . There can never be a final accurate representation of what was meant or said—only different textual representations of different experiences. (p. 5)

Denzin promises that the new language of ethnography, heavily influenced by poststructuralism, will be personal, emotional, biographically specific, and minimalist in its use of theoretical terms. The twenty-first century, he claims, will witness ethnographies that take the shape of: new journalism, narratives, autobiographies, documentaries, and performance texts. Denzin further claims that:

> qualitative research in the (sixth) moment discovers what has always been known: we are our own subjects. How our subjectivity becomes entangled in the lives of others is and has always been our topic. (p. 27)

All of this raises a logical and valid question for educational researchers: if all meaning is constructed through language, what is the purpose of doing ethnography? Denzin and others have referred to such questions as a crisis of legitimation, which stems partly from our desire that texts have authority, that they be judged as valid, and that they be generalizable to a larger context beyond the specific site of research. If, as the poststructuralists claim, neither ethnography nor any research in the human sciences can do this, what can they do?

If there is not a method or status of the researcher that confers authority on a text, poststructuralists argue, then the authority must emerge from the content of the text itself. This frees the ethnographers to simply tell their stories. As with other genres of writing, the readers will convey ultimate authority on a text. This provides a space for critical poststructural ethnographers to construct ethnographic narratives fully invested with themselves as emotional and ultimately fallible beings. These ethnographers can eschew claims to impartiality, distance, or objectivity that interfere with the telling of the only narrative they have ownership of: that of their own relationship to the stories they present; stories that they ideally present with all of their honesty, with all of the facts that they can remember or reclaim, with wit, with creativity, and with passion. They simply tell the stories as best they can and, in telling honest, accurate, and compelling stories, add to collective conversations and play a small role in illuminating the human condition in a time of interfacing and border crossing in which such illuminations are badly needed (Geertz, 2000).

Another tradition of anthropologists and critical theorists conceptualizes ethnography that informs, and is itself, social change. Kincheloe and McLaren (1998), for example, define a criticalist as a researcher or theorist who attempts to use her or his work as a form of social or cultural criticism and who accepts certain basic assumptions: that all thought is fundamentally mediated by power relations that are socially and historically constituted; that facts can never be isolated from the domain of values or removed from some form of ideological inscription; that the relationship between concept and object and between signifier and signified is never stable or fixed and is often mediated by the social relations of capitalist production and consumption; and that the oppression that characterizes contemporary societies is most forcefully reproduced when subordinates accept their social status as natural, necessary, or inevitable (p. 263). In the process of articulating the politics, purposes, and practices of critical research, they offer the following:

> To engage in critical postmodern research is to take part in a process of critical world making guided by the shadowed outline of a dream of a world less conditioned by misery, suffering, and the politics of deceit. It is, in short, a pragmatics of hope in an age of cynical reason. (p. 294)

This criticalist tradition advocates a public, civic, or everyday life ethnography that draws on the legacies of the new journalists, that evidences a desire to connect with people and their concerns, and writes ethnographies that move people to action and:

> answers to a new readership—the biographically situated reader who is a coparticipant in a public project that advocates democratic solutions to personal and public problems. (Denzin, 1997, p. 146)

It is from this emergent tradition that I offer these narratives of critical literacy practice from data that were collected over a twelve-year period across two urban settings: one in southern California and the other in northern California. (I will say more about these two sites of engagement later in this chapter). Though I borrow methodologically from cultural anthropology I agree with Denzin that there are some key differences between the ways that ethnography has been interpreted for educational (and other cultural) settings and what I have attempted to do. I have not attempted to distance myself from the students with whom I worked. I am fond of saying that I loved the participants who have informed my data sets. I feel I stand on firm conceptual grounding when I say that that is not a problem, but an advantage in my work. I work from the critical tradition of ethnography that envisions proximity, intimacy, and trust as important, if not essential, to the relationships between researchers and their subjects. I have also not tried to take a distanced perspective from the data or separate myself from these stories that I represent. To the contrary, what I offer here is but a small portion of my story as an educator and a researcher who had the privilege of working for over a decade with students as they engaged with a secondary English curriculum that linked literacy with popular culture and as they participated in a summer research seminar where they designed and carried out studies of the material conditions of the schools within their communities.

CRITICAL TEACHER RESEARCH

The third conceptual strand that informs this work, critical teacher research, emerges in response to a series of related crises in urban schooling: student dropout rates (Darling-Hammond, 1998) and teacher attrition rates (Darling-Hammond, 2000). The school exodus numbers for urban teens and their teachers are both alarming, even tragic, and both, I argue, stem from similar sorts of issues that I will explain further.

In many urban schools, the four-year completion rate (as measured by the percentage of incoming ninth graders who graduate with a diploma in four years) is less than fifty percent. The completion rates are a far more accurate measure of dropouts than the actual dropout rates, which generally measure the percentage of incoming seniors who graduate. These completion numbers converge to tell a chilling story about our urban high school students: more are dropping out than are completing this now basic and essential level of education. The University of California All-Campus Consortium on Research for Diversity (UC/ACCORD) created College Opportunity Ratios (COR) to help educators and policymakers understand how successful (or unsuccessful) the state's high schools are at moving hopeful ninth graders into positions of college readiness over their four-year high school tenure. They found that startling differences exist for students in variously situated schools across the state; differences largely determined by race and socioeconomic status (UC/ACCORD, 2004). These numbers from the nation's most populous state are by no means unique.

Related to the exodus of students is an exodus of teachers. It is no coincidence that the schools with the lowest completion rates are also the schools with the highest teacher attrition rates. In our most impoverished urban centers, these numbers are quite high. The National Commission for Teaching and America's Future estimates that nearly thirty percent of new teachers leave the profession within five years; this percentage is much higher in urban districts (Darling-Hammond, 2000). There are many hypotheses attempting to explain why teachers leave the profession. Most popular explanations point to low wages, long hours, classroom management, and a lack of preparation or training. All of these explanations have merit. However, in a series of interviews and surveys of their program's alumni, teacher educators at UCLA learned that graduates did not feel as though they were treated as intellectuals, nor did they feel there were authentic spaces for intellectual development (Quartz *et al.*, 2003).

These teachers' attitudes resonate with the work of scholars such as Giroux (1988) and Apple (1988) who have examined and critiqued the phenomenon they label as the de-skilling of teachers. Since this writing began in earnest during the late 1980s, these trends have been only exacerbated with the proliferation of standardized tests as assessments and "teacher-proof" curricula. Linda McNeil, for example, in her 2000 book *Contradictions of School Reform: Educational Costs of Standardized Testing*, examines how the testing climate inhibits the freedom of teachers and leads to regressive drill and kill pedagogy under the guise of test preparation. Hughes (2004) discusses the impact of "teacher-proof" curricula on the training of teachers and ultimately on student learning. As with McNeil, Hughes' article discusses regressive reactionary pedagogies that limit the quality of instruction for students and lead to the disillusionment of teachers.

In a time of real or perceived educational crisis, the two populations most affected (teachers and students) are also de-skilled and de-intellectualized in the practices of traditional urban education. These practices send them out of the schoolhouse doors in epidemic numbers. It is my contention that critical teacher research can work as a foundational practice that counters each of these disturbing trends. During the decade and a half since Cochran-Smith and Lytle (1993) published their text on teacher research, there has been a growing interest in the idea of teachers conducting research in their own classrooms. Although the idea of critical teacher research is not without its detractors, the movement is important for several reasons. First, it is a conceptualization of educational research that respects teachers as agents and intellectuals that have something to offer to the educational discourse. Second, teacher research grants a voice to those practitioners who have the greatest proximity to and intimacy with the very students that are opting out of public education. Third, a model of teacher research can create networks for teachers to work together and share relevant knowledge that can be used to develop informed practices that increase student achievement and engagement while also serving as the core of supportive intellectual communities that can help to lower the teacher attrition rates.

There are at least three aspects of this research that make critical teacher research "critical." Part of "critical" implies the who: usually members of marginalized groups. In different contexts in education, both teachers and students are marginalized groups. This is definitely the case within the field of educational research. Critical teacher research challenges the "who" (classroom teachers in addition to university researchers) of educational research. By sanctioning teachers as researchers and intellectuals, critical teacher research provides an explicit and much needed critique of traditional research paradigms in education and the social sciences. This is not to suggest that basic traditional research has no place within educational research. I merely argue that critical teacher research provides an important complement to the important research conducted by professionally trained university-based researchers who bring their various social science research methods from linguistics, sociology, psychology, and anthropology to bear on the most significant challenges that confront our most impoverished schools.

Critical teacher research is also critical because of its "how." Traditional research is often defined by its distant and objective stance toward research subjects and data; critical research, on the other hand, is defined by its closeness, its engagement, and its interestedness. The intimacy between teachers and students allows for different and unique methods of data collection and analysis that would add to the existing body of research. This intimacy also leads toward empathy and compassion and, as I mentioned earlier, love. This also means that teachers are not equally satisfied with any outcome where their students are concerned and, when problem schooling environments are challenged to provide structures of participation that lead to academic success, being a critical teacher-researcher also entails being an agent for social justice.

Finally, and most importantly, critical teacher research differs in its "why." The purpose of most traditional basic research is to add to our knowledge of a particular subject such as the way that language works or the levels of poverty in particular societies. Certainly obtaining this type of knowledge is important for society and critical teacher research does add to knowledge and theories of teaching and learning. Its primary purposes, however, are to increase academic achievement and to facilitate educational and social justice. In this way it is activist research, interventionist research, and a potentially transformational research, which makes it different from research as it is usually conceived.

This becomes an important topic of discussion with educational research being under siege on all sides and in places like Washington DC and from others in the social sciences for being irrelevant or for lacking in sufficient rigor to affect educational change. The recently published book *Advancing Scientific Research in Education* (Towne *et al.*, 2004) from the National Academies Press explicitly critiques educational research for lacking scientific rigor; it further critiques graduate training programs in education for not sufficiently preparing future research scholars.

Along similar lines the 2004 Report of the National Research Council also explicitly critiques many of the research methods that have become prevalent in educational scholarship. Rather than embracing a defensive posture, educational researchers need to confront these challenges head on. Although it is important and necessary to draw research tools and methods from the social sciences such as anthropology, linguistics, sociology, and psychology, I challenge educational researchers to consider and to develop other research tools and methods that are unique to our discipline, our disciplinary questions, and our disciplinary contexts. Rather than take our cue from others in politics or competing disciplines, I argue that we need to develop our own definitions of quality research that make sense for our field. Certainly, critical educational research is one approach that can stand as a focal tradition of inquiry in education.

We need more grounded theory research in classrooms and schools, and more research that comes out of the critical educational tradition that opens up spaces for students and teachers to function as researchers and intellectuals. Further, we need more formative experiments and other educational research traditions that theorize interventions and develop various tools to assess the quality of those interventions. This is the type of research that is needed to distinguish the discipline from its social science neighbors. It is in this spirit that I conducted the research for this book. With that, I transition to a brief discussion of the sites of research and the participants who have been involved in the research process.

SITE AND PARTICIPANTS

Data for this book were collected over a twelve-year period across multiple educational contexts including English and social studies courses at two urban high schools (called North High and South High respectively) and a summer research seminar that, for six consecutive summers, convened teens from local neighborhoods throughout Greater Los Angeles to draw upon theory and existing educational literature to design and conduct critical research in schools and communities for social and educational justice. I will now introduce the sites and, while introducing each site, also talk in more detail about the participants and my role as educator and researcher.

North High 1993–1999

Located in northern California, North High School[1] is an urban school of approximately 3100 students inhabiting a campus space that is better suited

---

[1] All of the names of the schools, the students, and the teachers in this book are pseudonyms used to protect the privacy of the people and institutions involved in these studies.

for a population half that size. All of the city's high schools are notoriously small. In fact, the smallest (in terms of space) high school in the state of California is located in this city. That school, however, houses 1300 students! I mention the overcrowding of the school because that is one of the lasting memories of my six years of teaching at North. During my fifth year of teaching the school switched from a tenth–twelfth grade high school with 2200 students to a ninth–twelfth grade high school serving 3100 students. The existing faculty and student body inherited a freshman class of nine hundred students without inheriting any additional space to house them. So the already cramped campus became impossible to navigate. I remember the jostling and the swaying to and fro of large masses of people during passing periods; all of these inhabitants putting in a great deal of effort and not getting anywhere.

That visual image of the halted bodies and the cramped hallways provides a suitable analogy to talk about academic achievement at North High School. I witnessed students and teachers who were all putting in a great deal of effort without "getting anywhere" in terms of academic achievement. During the years that these studies were conducted fifty-eight percent of the students lived in homes where their families were eligible for AFDC (Aid to Families with Dependent Children). The average SAT score of seniors taking the test was 845 (which would place an individual student at about the tenth percentile) compared with 1011 for the state of California and 1016 for the nation (www. ed-data.k12.ca.us). On the STAR test, the National Percentile Rankings for tenth graders were twenty-first percentile for reading and twenty-ninth percentile for language. During the years of the study, the state of California instituted an Academic Performance Index (API) that rated the state's schools on a range of 1 to 10, with 10 being the highest. According to the API, eighty percent of the state's high schools were "superior" to North. By all accounts, North High was an underperforming school serving impoverished students of color.

Alongside the culture of underachievement, however, there existed a vibrant and ethnically diverse high school with a culture of student activism and a small cadre of committed teachers, who were also activist in orientation. All of this activity occurred with the tacit approval of the administration, which certainly didn't bolster these efforts, yet did not sabotage them either. The student body, approximately forty-five percent Asian and Asian-American, thirty percent African-American, and fifteen percent Chicano/Latino, was one of the most diverse schools in the region. These students initiated clubs for ethnic pride and social justice, and a general ethos of empowerment and resistance existed within a context of police, security, poor material conditions, lack of resources, and a culture of failure. As a young teacher coming into his own understanding of critical pedagogy, I thought the environment was ripe for a dialogic pedagogy and for social praxis. I wanted to tap into the pride and activism that had been at the heart of the school and the city's culture for a generation to make connections to academic literacies that were needed for success in school, in the professions, and in civic life. To accomplish these goals I instituted a critical pedagogy of popular culture (Morrell, 2002) that I will briefly discuss in chapter 4 through the explanation and analysis of several units that utilized popular culture to develop critical literacies amongst urban adolescents.

South High 1999–2001

By contrast, South High remained an extremely diverse school economically and ethnically. In a city that had managed to become seventy-five percent white, the high school remained nearly sixty percent non-white. There are a host of explanations for this disparity; the bohemian upper middle class (mostly white) in the city is largely a childless one, and in order to retain enrollment figures (and, consequently, state monies and jobs) the district accepts a large number of students on transfer. These transfer students, as would be expected, are more reflective of the demographics of the metropolitan area and thereby contribute to the racial, ethnic, and socioeconomic diversity of the school.

These contrasts within the school and the city make for an interesting and provocative site for analysis and intervention. Whereas North High classrooms had no windows, the room at South High looked out onto a quad area with palm trees; other classrooms had a faint view of the ocean, which was only blocks away. The entire campus was open, filled with light and color and vegetation; it was an architectural wonder where a seeming rainbow of humanity co-existed in relative peace. The vista, however, could easily lead students, parents, and faculty into a false sense of accomplishment; like an iceberg, the surface utopia hid a much larger mountain of tensions and inequities resting not too far beneath.

Even the aggregate data for South High are impressive. Standardized test scores, college-going rates, and college eligibility rates are well above state averages. It is only when one takes a closer look—when one employs Mills' (1959) sociological imagination—that the portrait of this divided school becomes clearer. Armed with the language and tools associated with this sociological imagination one begins to ask difficult questions about South High. Why are the classrooms so segregated? Why do so few of the classrooms reflect the rich diversity of the school? Why is it so easy to peer into a classroom and guess immediately the level of instruction, simply by taking stock of the ethnic composition of the room? To spell this out more bluntly, why are all of the students in the Advanced Placement courses white or Asian-American? Why are African-American and Latino students over-represented in most "basic" classes?

The hunches informed by this sociological imagining are very much corroborated by the collection and analysis of sociological data. Researchers working in the district, for instance, have been able to quantify enrollment in Advanced Placement courses by ethnicity (see Table 1–1).

In the 1999–2000 school year, for instance, only 6.8 percent of African-American students at South High had a grade point average (GPA) over 3.5 while 79.2 percent held less than a 2.9 GPA and 40.1 percent held less than a 2.0 GPA. With respect to the Latino population, only 9.1 percent held a grade point average over 3.5 while 74.1 percent held less than a 3.0 GPA and 43.9 percent held less than a 2.0 GPA. A comparison of the grade point average distribution from the 1993–1994 school year reveals that these numbers have held relatively consistent over a lengthy period of partnerships with local universities and an administrative climate of educational reform.

South High boasted a high rate of acceptance to the most elite colleges in the state and across the country. When the data were disaggregated, however, they once again revealed that the wealth is not being shared equally. For example, whereas African-Americans and Latinos comprised nearly fifty percent of the school's population, they made up only slightly more than twelve percent of the school's acceptances to the University of California system for the 1999–2000 school year.

TABLE 1–1

1997–1998 Advanced Placement Course Enrollment for African-American and Chicano/Latino Students, South High School

Course	% African-American	% Chicano/Latino
AP English 12	4.8	8.1
AP Calculus AB	2.5	10.0
AP Chemistry	3.6	3.6
AP Physics	0	6.7

Source: From Family Report for South City 1998–1999: "a report prepared for faculty, administration, and citizens of the South City community." African-Americans comprised roughly fifteen percent of the student body and the Chicano/Latino population was roughly thirty-two percent.

There was also a large discrepancy between the test scores of African-American and Latino students on the one hand and white and Asian-American students on the other. Data from the state-mandated Stanford 9 Reading Tests indicated that, whereas 13.0 percent and 11.1 percent respectively of African-American and Latino students scored in the top quartile on the test, 44.1 percent of white students and 41.0 percent of Asian/Asian-American students reached this standard. Conversely, only 16.7 percent of Asian-American students and 7.5 percent of white students scored in the lowest quartile while these percentages were 31.5 percent and 30.5 percent for African-American and Latino students

Another traditional measure of academic achievement and college readiness is the SAT, offered several times annually to high school juniors and seniors and required by virtually every major university in the country. Once again, a look at these aggregated data indicates that South High scored well above the state and national averages with a median score of 1048. The disaggregated data, however, show that African-American and Latino students scored approximately 200 points below the school mean and well below the state and national averages.

All of these numbers revealed the serious problem that we all understood at South High to be the "two-school phenomenon." That is, whereas the outside public saw one South High, we saw two. One that sent the wealthiest white and Asian-American students to the most prestigious universities throughout the country and another that, for poor and working-class African-American and Latino students, functioned like another urban school replete with low test scores and low high school completion rates. Our intervention at South High, the "South High Futures Project," focused on this second population and used critical pedagogy, youth research, and popular culture to increase achievement and consciousness while also entering into larger conversations with teachers, school and district administrators and, through the research, critical literacy scholars around the country.

To be more specific, in the autumn of 1997, the South High Futures Project enrolled a randomly selected ninth grade cohort of working-class students who were targeted for a larger program aimed at students who were considered "at risk." Over the course of their four years in high school the Futures Project, a collaboration between a major university and a local school district, offered special coursework in the humanities, a summer internship program (which became the Summer Seminar), and opportunities for research and presentation. The program experienced a great deal of success; in the spring of 2001, all but one student who stayed with the program graduated from high school. Over eighty percent (twenty-one of twenty-seven) of the students received offers to attend four-year universities, and all but two (one went to the military and one pursued a music career) of the high school graduates enrolled in some form of postsecondary education the following fall. I joined the project in the spring of 1999, the end of the sophomore year, and participated with the students and the project's lead teacher, Mr. Genovese, through two summer seminars and two school years at South High.

The Summer Seminar 1999–2004

Beginning in 1999, several colleagues at the Institute for Democracy, Education, and Access (IDEA) began convening a summer seminar at the University of California, Los Angeles. Initially the seminar targeted the South High participants in the Futures Project, but by the summer of 2000 the seminar expanded to include students from other high schools around the metropolitan area. The seminar brought together students, teachers, and parents from urban schools and communities to design and carry out critical research projects on issues of immediate concern to these schools and communities. The students worked in groups of four or five on research teams led by teachers in the local schools. Throughout the five weeks of the seminar the students read seminal works in the sociology of education and critical methods of educational research; they developed research questions, read relevant literature, collected data, analyzed data, and created research reports; and they presented these reports to university faculty, policymakers, and, on occasion, regional and national conferences of educational researchers and practitioners. Students also wrote individual papers in which they contemplated the practical applications of their research to the issues in their own schools and communities.

There were multiple goals of the seminar, but two emerge as primary. We desired to use the seminar space to help students acquire the language and tools they need to function within the academy, what we have called *academic literacy* (Morrell, 2004a). Customarily, the student populations that we worked with had not been well represented within colleges and universities throughout the state. We wanted to demonstrate to the schools and universities that dismissed these students that the students were indeed capable of college-level work. At the same time, we wanted to use the context of critical, community-based research to help the students gain the literacy tools they would need in order to be successful at these universities.

A second goal of the seminar relates to the research itself. We held the sincere belief that teachers, students, and parents were the most legitimate collaborators for the kind of community-based praxis-oriented research that we ourselves were interested in. In other words, the research studies were not merely a context for literacy learning; the products themselves were important to the struggle for educational justice within the teacher education program, with the local districts, the greater metropolitan area and even statewide. The student participants and their work would influence policy and practice across all of these settings.

The seminar met at UCLA for six summers in the Graduate School of Education and Information Studies and the Law School. Over the course of the six summers, the seminar served 127 students (the Futures students participated for two summers) from thirty-four schools in the Greater Los Angeles Area. Each summer, the twenty-five or so student participants attended all-day sessions for five weeks to earn a semester credit for a university course. As a part of the seminar, students were exposed to critical theory, cultural studies, educational sociology, legal history, social theory, and critical qualitative research methodology as they worked, in small groups, to design and conduct research projects related to issues of equity and access in urban schools and communities. Given its focus on urban education, its academic rigor, and its status as a university course, the seminar sought to address the issues of access both in terms of course content and desired outcomes for its students.

In the summer of 1999 the seminar focused on *Language, Youth Culture, and Transformational Resistance in Urban Schools*. The four research groups investigated: the potential of hip-hop music and culture to transform high school literacy curricula; the different manifestations of student resistance in urban schools; the impact of teachers' attitudes towards students' home languages on student achievement; and differences between home and school attitudes of well-educated citizens in the African-American and Latino communities.

In the summer of 2000 the seminar focused on *Youth Access and the Democratic National Convention*. We took advantage of the fact that Los Angeles was host to the Democratic National Convention to provide the students with the opportunity to participate in the DNC as researchers and as interested community citizens. Students attended formal meetings and organized protests and met with elected officials, media personnel, delegates, and representatives of activist organizations. The youth probed the Democratic National Convention to explore provocative political, social, and educational issues around which students formulated research questions, collected and analyzed data, and presented their findings to a panel of university faculty and community activists. In the context of the DNC, research teams investigated youth access across five domains: youth access to the media, youth access to a livable wage, youth access to community learning resources, youth access to learning resources in schools, and youth access to civic engagement.

In the summer of 2001, the seminar focused on an *Educational Bill of Rights*. The seminar theme was chosen in response to survey polls at the time, which revealed that education remained the number one priority for most Californians. Regardless of political affiliation and belief, most citizens recognized the importance of a quality education to social, economic, and political empowerment. That being said, most citizens, particularly those affiliated with the urban poor, realized that not all children in California were provided fair and equal access to a quality education. Our research staff understood that one's race, class, and geography often determine access to postsecondary education. Unfortunately, students whose families have the least financial resources often receive the least educational resources. To examine and challenge these inequities, we convened our third summer seminar to articulate an Educational Bill of Rights that outlined the basic entitlements of all students in California. The students selected for this seminar, along with university faculty from the Graduate School of Education and Information Studies and the Law School, parents, and community leaders, engaged in research that examined these rights in the context of urban schools across Los Angeles. The seminar sought to answer the following questions:

• What does every student in California deserve?
• What inequalities arise in the experiences of California's students?
• Why do these inequalities arise? (What is our explanation for the inequality?)
• What can youth do? How can they use research to play a part in legal advocacy?

The 2002 Summer Seminar focused on *Equity and Access in California's Public Schools*. The central question of the seminar dealt with how students (and parents) could contribute information about school conditions to the state-mandated School Accountability Report Cards (SARCs).[2] This question embodied three sub-questions:

a) What are the conditions of learning in urban schools across Los Angeles?

---

[2]The state mandates that each school develop and provide a SARC that includes required elements (e.g., standardized test scores, teacher certification information, etc.), but that can be supplemented with locally generated information.

b) How can students access and contribute information about these conditions?

c) How can students, working in conjunction with parents and community advocates, pressure their schools and districts to include student-generated data in the official SARCs?

The seminar divided students into four student research teams, each focused on one core condition of schooling—quality teachers, a rigorous curriculum, adequate learning materials, and a positive physical and social school environment. Under the guidance of local K-12 schoolteachers, the research teams conducted field research in several Los Angeles area schools. The students explored various research and pedagogic tools (GIS mapping, audio tape recording, video and still digital photography, and theater of the oppressed) for gathering and representing this data. The research teams were asked to report both results and methods so their example might guide other students and teachers interested in developing their own action research projects. Throughout the five-week seminar, the students also interviewed and met with educational researchers, community organizers, parent advocates, school administrators, civil rights attorneys, and elected officials to investigate how student research might become a standard part of the SARC process. On the final day of the seminar, the research teams presented their findings, methods, and analysis of the politics of implementation to a public audience of university faculty, civil rights attorneys, educators, community advocates, and parents.

In the summer of 2003 the fifth summer seminar focused on *Oral Histories of the Educational Experiences in Post-Brown Los Angeles from 1954–2003.* We were intrigued by the possibility of apprenticing young people as critical public historians of schooling in urban Los Angeles for several reasons. As the seminar convened, the looming fiftieth anniversary of the *Brown* decision forced the nation to look at the progress it was making toward racial and economic equality. As many of our students attended schools that many would consider inequitable, we thought that we could use the context of *Brown* to encourage students to explore the colorful past of schools in their own district as a strategy to acquire relevant historical knowledge, but also as a strategy to ultimately use youth-generated historical research as a tool to lobby for change in the present. When students make public history— when they conduct interviews, examine historical records, visit archives, and analyze census and school demographic data—they see what it means to construct an historical narrative. It lets them look at how the lived experience of everyday people is shaped by and in turn shapes structural conditions in the economy and legal system. As young people place themselves and their families in this historical narrative, they forge a deeper understanding of who they are and the society they live within. And when this history calls on them to study people like themselves who have joined the struggle for education on equal terms, they begin to imagine an identity as historical agents. By writing public history, young people could come to see themselves as *authors* of the future as they also develop sophisticated academic literacies (Morrell and Rogers, 2007). Toward these ends, each research team focused on one of the five post-Brown decades in Los Angeles and coalesced multiple forms of interview, archival, and statistical data into research reports, PowerPoint presentations, and short digital documentary films.

In the summer of 2004, the seminar focused on *Urban Youth, Political Participation, and Educational Reform.* Students explored: a) what it means for urban youth to participate powerfully in civic life; b) how urban youth can learn to participate in such ways; and c) what civic lessons young people now learn in and outside of urban schools. The students were placed into four small research teams, determined by geographic area, and asked to conduct a case study surveying the various forms of civic education offered in these particular communities. Students focused particularly on civic education in the formal and hidden curricula of schools, civic education in communities and in community organizations, and the civic education afforded youth via the media. As part of these case studies, student research groups talked with other youth and with educators, community leaders, and elected officials about: a) issues facing young people in the local community; b) how young people should participate in civic life; and c) what (leadership and literacy) skills are needed for such participation. Each team conducted research at a high school site and a community center in a local neighborhood. The teams also developed research tools for examining civic education in a school. These tools included survey instruments, interview and focus group questions (or protocols), and rubrics for examining books and other curriculum materials.

In each seminar students produced individual texts and group texts. These texts ranged from standard written documents to short documentary films and PowerPoint presentations. Individually, students produced 1500–2000-word essays dealing with their journeys to becoming critical researchers and the implications of their seminar work for engagement in their schools and communities. Student research teams produced PowerPoint presentations, research reports, and a public presentation that showcased the tools that they developed along with their research findings. Further, the students produced iMovie documentaries and materials for an electronic journal targeted toward urban teachers and parents. Having outlined the conceptual–methodological frameworks and introduced the site and participants (for a description of the data collection and data analysis procedures, see Appendix A), I would like to briefly introduce the chapters that will flesh out the remainder of the book.

OUTLINE OF THE BOOK CHAPTERS

Chapter 2 takes the reader on a journey through Western philosophy to understand how theorists from Plato to the poststructuralists have conceptualized literacy, particularly literacy practices that are enabling of the individual or of the social. It also examines the revolutionary work of Brazilian educator Paulo Freire and his influence on critical education in the United States. The chapter begins by examining the relationship between critical literacy the work of the classic Greek philosophers. It then moves through the Middle Ages toward the Enlightenment highlighting the contributions of Kant, Hegel, and Karl Marx to critical literacy.

From Marx it then shifts to a focus on twentieth-century philosophical movements that have shaped critical approaches to the study and teaching of language and literacy through the work of Gramsci, the Frankfurt School, existential phenomenology, feminism, structuralism, and postmodernism. The chapter concludes by fleshing out Freirian theories of critical literacy, paying particular attention to how these theories have been translated into mainstream American discourse and research that has embraced this language. Chapter 2 also seeks to understand the influences upon Freire's conceptualizing of critical literacy to consider how critical literacy might be interpreted differently when other critical theorists are considered as well as different ways of looking at the same theorists who influenced the work of Freire.

Chapter 3 considers how "Othered," non-Western or marginalized Western traditions might add to conversations of critical literacy. Some of these other sources include the African-American tradition, indigenous voices, ethnic studies, subaltern/third world studies, and postcolonial studies. I argue that these voices have existed in parallel trajectories to the dominant Western philosophical tradition and have much to add to conversations regarding the relationships between language, literacy, and emancipation. Examples include the work of African-American scholars such as Frederick Douglass, W. E. B. DuBois and Theresa Perry, who make the connections between literacy and freedom for African-Americans. The postcolonial scholar Frantz Fanon, in *A Dying Colonialism* (1965), describes the changes in Algerian culture from a colonial to a postcolonial identity during the five years of revolution against

France. This identity change included a critical literacy in that it encouraged counter-readings to French cultural practices, but these readings subsumed a traditional literacy as well. Further, the Algerian critical literacy entailed a production of new meanings, new language, and new texts. Other postcolonial scholars I represent include Edward Said, Homi Bhabha, and Gayatri Spivak.

Chapters 4 through 7 of the book provide a comparative ethnography of language and literacy practices and are intended to evolve a grounded theory of critical literacy praxis. Chapter 4 examines critical reading and critical textual production through the analysis of data collected through six years of instruction at North High. I look at classroom units that explore hip-hop culture, popular film, violence in society, attitudes toward AIDS, and the ills of urban education. Chapter 5 looks at critical textual production during our summer research seminar. Chapter 6 begins with a unique perspective of cyberactivism as a critical literacy practice; that is, as the production and distribution of critical texts via mainstream and alternative media. Toward this end, it examines the development of a virtual community of urban adolescents dedicated to using Internet tools to promote social justice. Chapter 7 looks toward the discipline of critical media and cultural studies for guidance in developing a set of analytic tools that can be used by urban adolescents to make sense of their own relationship to mainstream media as well as the role that media industries play in the production of knowledge. The chapter will also briefly describe several activities that engaged youth in critical examinations of the workings of the media using a combination of critical social theory and critical qualitative research. The chapter then turns to consider media production as an enacting of critical literacy. Specifically, I will focus on digital video production and distribution as a form of critical literacy praxis. I will conclude this chapter by considering where educators, researchers, and activists need to be heading in relation to critical media literacy.

In chapter 8 I draw upon Foucault's discussion of the *hupomnemata* (Foucault, 1997), Sartre's conception of committed writing as an exercise of freedom for the author (Sartre, 2001), and bell hooks' idea of *self-actualization* (hooks, 1994) to consider how critical literacy can promote important transformations of the self. In contrast to most of the work on critical literacy that examines larger social outcomes, I think about how critical literacy, most importantly, can be about repositioning oneself with oneself.

Chapter 9 examines the role that literacy has played in major social movements such as the Freedom Schools of the Civil Rights Movement or the Cuba Literacy campaign in order to articulate a theory of critical literacy as social praxis. This chapter also examines research conducted by urban teens as an example of how this social praxis may take shape in work with urban youth. For example, I examine work in which high school students used oral history interviews in order to understand the experiences of students in Los Angeles schools in the post-Brown era. I examine another intervention in which students investigated youth participation in civic engagement. The students theorized what youth critical civic literacies were associated with political engagement. They then developed case studies in which they visited schools, neighborhoods, and community-based organizations in search of civic curricula. This example of students engaging in participatory action research is also an example of social praxis as students are engaged in research as an act of resistance and also to promote social and educational justice. The students used their data to inform teaching practices, to lobby district and state officials, and to inform the educational research community on these important issues.

I ultimately conclude in chapter 10 with a vision of urban education permeated by the ideals of critical literacy. I also issue a call to literacy educators and researchers to function as activists and political agents. If the acquisition and use of critical literacies are as important to the life chances of urban youth as we believe, then it is incumbent upon us to do more than teach classes or write papers or books. The real struggle may involve marching or protest; losing our jobs and livelihoods. The literacy revolution that I envision may demand of us everything. In return, though, we may have everything to gain in taking important steps toward remaking the world in a way that is more livable, more just, and more human. If that is not a worthy life's work, I don't know what is.

Ultimately I hope this work helps us to think more substantively about the interrelationship between critical literacy and pedagogies of access and dissent for urban youth. In today's schools, I argue, we need to help urban youth to acquire the literacies they need to navigate the very schools they should critique and deconstruct. At the same time we need to revisit the multiple goals of schooling within a Deweyan (Dewey, 1900/1990) framework of creating spaces for participatory social inquiry (Oakes and Rogers, 2006) and the development of critical citizens and authentic participants in a democratic society in addition to creating future workers to sustain the capitalist mode of production. We live and work in an age when there may not be a job waiting for every student in America's public schools; when the prison track seems more prevalent than the honors track (Davis, 2003). It behooves us, then, to think about literacies for social and educational justice even as we honor our commitment to do all that we can to help students to compete for the fruits of society: entrance into elite universities and well-paying jobs.

Further, we must remember our artists and wordsmiths who have used critical literacies to bring us tomes and tracts that have continually forced us to evaluate our status as humans on the planet. For these reasons and more we need educators and researchers dedicated to understanding and creating spaces in urban schools for the proliferation of critical literacies. For these reasons and more, I have written this book.

2

From Plato to Poststructuralism: The Philosophical Foundations of Critical Literacy

In order to historicize and theorize critical literacy education, it is important to have some knowledge of the critical tradition in Western philosophy, one that I argue goes as far back as the classic Greek philosophers. Too often, I contend, scholars and practitioners in education employ "critical" as a modifier without an understanding of how the term has evolved within the philosophical tradition. Historicizing the term, I argue, gives us more firm grounding to stand on; it also allows for more breadth when contemplating the myriad possibilities for critical literacy education with urban adolescent youth.

This chapter takes the reader on a journey through the Western tradition of philosophy to consider how theorists and thinkers from Plato to the poststructuralists have conceptualized literacy; particularly literacy practices that foster individual or social transformation. It also examines the revolutionary work of the Brazilian educator Paulo Freire and his influence on critical education in the United States. I begin with the antecedents of critical theory, because I believe that a strong argument can be made that critical "sensibilities" about the nature of knowledge production and the role of language and literacy in constituting the self have been at the heart of Western philosophy throughout its 2500-year history. Most associate the beginning of critical philosophy with the work of the late eighteenth-century German philosophers Kant and Hegel. And, if critical theory is associated most closely with one philosopher, it would be the nineteenth-century writer Karl Marx, who was at one time considered a young Hegelian. It is important, however, for emergent critical scholars in literacy education to have some sense of the 2500 years of philosophical tradition before and after these philosophers throughout Europe and the Americas in the nineteenth and twentieth centuries (the following chapter will deal exclusively with "Othered" critical philosophers that are not necessarily associated with the Western canon).

The chapter begins by examining the relationship between critical literacy and the work of the classical Greek philosophers Socrates, Plato, and Aristotle. I then examine the work of the German philosophers of the eighteenth century, Immanuel Kant and Georg W. F. Hegel, the architects of critical philosophy. Next I transition to the subsequent generations of continental philosophers paying close attention to Marx, Engel, Husserl, Heiddeger, and the Frankfurt School of Social Research. The chapter then shifts to a focus on how later twentieth-century philosophy has shaped critical approaches to the study and teaching of language and literacy through the work of existential phenomenology, structuralism, and postmodernism. The chapter concludes by fleshing out Freirian theories of critical literacy, paying particular attention to how these theories have been translated into mainstream discourse and research. This chapter also seeks to understand the influences upon Freire's conceptualizing of critical literacy to consider how critical literacy might be interpreted differently when other critical theorists are considered, as well as different ways of looking at the same theorists who influenced the work of Freire.

THE CLASSICAL PHILOSOPHERS

Though our contemporary use of the term "critical theory" is usually traced back to the work of the Frankfurt School philosophers in the 1930s, theorists, thinkers, and activists have understood, talked, and written about the role of language and critical thought in the consumption, production, and distribution of knowledge and the consciousness-raising of emancipated citizens throughout the entire history of the Western civilization. For our purposes, we will start at the beginning of this 2500-year tradition in theorizing the critical language and literacy praxis that is articulated throughout the remainder of this text.

Debates about language, literacy, and power are at least as old as the Western canon and it is there that I will begin. Serious conversations relating to "critical literacies" date back to Greek philosophers' concerns with the critical use of language (rhetoric) to convince and persuade in the context of social and political discourses. Among the first classical Greek philosophers were the Sophists, who were known for their mastery of language and, as such, were well-known and wielded considerable power in the Athens of Socrates, Plato, and Aristotle (500–300 B.C.E.). The Sophists envisioned themselves as both philosophers and rhetoricians; they tended to view all language as rhetorical. Through language, they believed, people collectively construct a worldview. Similar to current poststructuralists, the Sophists of classical Athens believed that there existed no privileged non-rhetorical discourses and no privileged non-rhetorical knowledge (Bizzell and Herzberg, 2001). Through Plato's dialogues we know that Socrates was quite skeptical of the Sophists and their uses of rhetoric to cloud the search for ultimate truths (it is important to note that Socrates, Plato, and Aristotle all believed in absolute truths). In *Gorgias*, the most famous and polemical of Plato's dialogues on rhetoric, Plato recounts Socrates' debate with the famous Sophist in which he critiques Gorgias and his associate Callicles for their misuse of language to persuade people to, in his opinion, manufacture truth. Socrates, nevertheless, conceded the power of language in the production of meaning, but felt that rhetoric should only be used in the service of good for humankind.

Ironically, Socrates himself used his critical language to convince the youth of Athens to be skeptical of the practices of government and of Athenian society in general. It was his successes with young boys of Athens (among them Plato) that led to his being placed on trial for subversion of the gods and seducing the ambitious young men of Athens by arousing desires in them that would have better been suppressed. It was Socrates' condemnation via this trial that ultimately forced his suicide by drinking hemlock (O'Connor, 1999). Nonpartisan contemporaries saw more in common between Socrates and the Sophists than either side would care to admit. Aristophanes, in his comedy *The Clouds*, contends that Socrates is just another Sophist. Regardless of how we characterize the nature of their disagreements or their statements about the role of language in the production of knowledge, both sides seemed to implicitly understand that language was a powerful tool and the ability to manipulate oral language made one a more powerful citizen (Robinson, 1999).

Plato recounts Socrates' defense in his dialogue *The Apology*. According to Plato's rendition, Socrates remains unapologetic about his right to expose young citizens to the truth and to help them to think for themselves. There are several important points for contemporary literacy theorists, scholars, and practitioners to take away from these Platonic dialogues. We know that an acute awareness of the power of language and literacy lay at the heart and foundation of the 2500-year-old Western tradition; leading intellectuals have been debating these issues for some time. Further, those who were able to manipulate language have held great power, and they have also been considered as dangerous. Those who have been able to use language, literacy, and pedagogy as tools of critique and resistance have always been considered as threats to the status quo.

Socrates was also well aware of language's ability to mask truth or even to create it. He saw it as his mission to develop in the young a set of faculties and tools that would allow them to resist dominant ideals that were peddled through the linguistic and textual practices of articulate spokespersons and civil servants; the dominant "media" outlets of his day. Though Socrates did not use (or have access to) terms such as ideology, power, or critical language awareness, they were scarcely beneath the surface of his ideals or his arguments. In fact, I would argue that, in the example of Socrates, we have all of the antecedents of the discourse of critical literacy that would continue to develop over the subsequent two and a half millennia.

It is important to note also that Socrates was skeptical of the technology of writing. He saw it as a deterrent to the critical language faculties he sought to develop. The only reason, though, that we have access to the ideas of Socrates is that his pupil Plato saw it as necessary to memorialize his teacher by setting his story down on paper and developing him as the protagonist of all of his major dialogues. Print literacy may be ideological and even limiting, but written texts are also portable and distributable through time and space. Socrates would not be the last great thinker to question the relationships between critical literacies and traditional literacies of the day. These debates about the uses, the powers, and the consequences of traditional literacy continue to this very day.

Socrates' critiques and the conversations they engender about the nature and functions of literacy are important for a few reasons. During most of the era of alphabetic literacy a great primacy has been placed on oratorical proficiency. I will say more about this throughout the chapter and the book, but I bring it up at this point to make clear that my definition of literacy as encompassing oral language abilities is an historically and conceptually justifiable one. Over the 2500-year history of Western civilization, literacies have encompassed everything from oral arguments and written texts to digital film productions.

It is also important to note that our access to Socrates is mediated through Plato, who took it upon himself to write down the philosophies of his mentor. Although Socrates was wary of writing's tendency to erase memory, literacy scholars have pointed towards the permanency of written text as one of its more important characteristics. We might still have access to Socrates without the writing of Plato, but certainly not in the form that we now possess.

Some historical scholars, for instance, have claimed that historical research was not possible prior to the written record. Plato's preservation of Socrates' philosophies via his written dialogues is an important example of the significance of "textual production" to the critical literacy enterprise.

In addition to developing critical thoughts and critical language, it is also important to commemorate these thoughts through written words, digital texts, and still and moving images. I will say more about critical literacy as a synthesis of critical language awareness and critical textual production throughout the text, but suffice it to say that both aspects of critical literacy have been present since the very beginning of the Western tradition.

Aristotle, the last of the great three classical philosophers, offers two texts (*The Art of Rhetoric* and *Poetics*) that are central to classic and contemporary discussions of critical literacy. Whereas Plato and Socrates engaged in arguments over the relative merits or faults of rhetoric, Aristotle set out to theorize, document, and describe the nascent art of language manipulation. Aristotle defines rhetoric as the art of discovering the means of persuasion available for any occasion. He charges the rhetor with investigating the situation that she or he faces and the resources available to handle the situation. Aristotle identifies three speech categories; political or deliberate oratory, which is to recommend a future course of action; epideictic or ceremonial oratory, intended to praise or blame a current state of affairs; and forensic or legal oratory, intended to provoke judgment concerning a past action (Bizzell and Herzberg, 2001, p. 30)

The key components of Aristotelian rhetoric (later elaborated by the classical rhetors Cicero and Quintilian) concern the preparation of a speech. Classical rhetoric divides the process of preparing a persuasive speech into five stages:

1. *invention*, the search for persuasive ways to present information and formulate arguments;
2. *arrangement*, the organization of the parts of a speech to ensure that all of the means of persuasion are present and properly disposed;
3. *style*, the use of correct, appropriate, and striking language throughout the speech;
4. *memory*, the use of mnemonics and practice of the speech;
5. *delivery*, the use of effective gestures and vocal modulation to present the speech (Bizzell and Herzberg, 2001, p. 3).

The arguments presented by the rhetor appeal to reason (logos), emotion (pathos), or trust in the speaker's character (ethos). Aristotle felt that the appeal to reason was the most important, though he understood that appeals to ethos and pathos were almost always necessary. Though Aristotle regarded scientific inquiry as the ideal pathway toward absolute truth, he also considered that rhetoric could aid in reaching agreement on questions of value or preference that demand immediate action in everyday life. Rhetoric could also be used to arrive at probable truths when demonstration was not possible.

Aristotelian rhetoric is still with us to this day. We see evidence of rhetorical appeals in the legal arena, in sermons, and in television commercials. In his history of English teaching, Robert Scholes (1998) points out that rhetoric occupied the dominant role in language instruction from classical times until the turn of the twentieth century, when humanistic approaches to literature took precedence. Even so, there are many applications of classical rhetoric to a discussion of critical literacy praxis. At a basic level, it is important to re-theorize the role of orality and oratory in contemporary literacy instruction. Although it is important to communicate through the written medium, many of the everyday decisions are still negotiated orally. In watching a recent round of presidential debates, I was reminded of how impossible it would be to secure an elected leadership position without acquiring oratorical skills. It's not only elected officials or attorneys who need oratorical power, however. Schoolteachers need to use oratorical power in their pedagogy; academicians and business professionals use rhetoric when making presentations to sell products or ideals. Everyday citizens require these skills when advocating for a cause or for children. At present, however, there is very little attention paid in the secondary (or postsecondary) curricula to oratorical rhetoric. Any theory of critical literacy praxis needs to revisit Aristotle's *Rhetoric* in thinking through a strategy for developing oratorical power.

Rhetoric is also important for understanding how to organize arguments in general. In moving from a notion of critical literacy as consumption to critical literacy as production and distribution of countercultural ideas, it becomes important to theorize the production and distribution of these ideas. Aristotle's *Rhetoric* provides guidance for pedagogues who are interested in helping speakers and writers to understand audience and purpose when preparing to engage in public discourses.

Poetics, by contrast, offers the first major analysis of Hellenic literature as well as the first attempt to distinguish between literary genres. This text lays the groundwork for a literary classification and analysis that has influenced literary scholarship up until the present day. Aristotle (1997) begins the treatise by addressing epic and dithyrambic poetry and the music of the flute and music of the lyre. Poetry, for instance, appeals to the fundamental human instincts of imitation and rhythm. Aristotle further outlines the structures of dramatic tragedy, which involves members of great stature or renown and a transition from stability to chaos. This negative transition is normally precipitated by an act of hubris, a mistake, or an error in judgment on the part of the tragic hero, a person who is eminently good; whose downfall causes an audience to feel pity or fear. Dramatic comedy, by contrast, involves everyday persons of lower rank and a transition from chaos toward stability. These definitions not only apply to Greek literary genres of the time, but are also helpful in understanding Shakespearean drama and even contemporary music, plays, and film.

Most notably, however, Aristotle in *Poetics* offers the perspective of literature as revealing something latent, yet fundamental, about the human condition. Aristotle also saw poetry as expressing human universals and revealing human possibilities. Whereas history relates what has happened, poetry relates what is possible. For this reason, Aristotle saw poetry as a higher form of knowledge production than history, likening artistic production to philosophical production. Aristotle charged the artists of his time to disregard incidental facts in search for deeper truths, which they would reveal to audiences via available literary structures. The experience of music, poetry, or tragedy, in Aristotle's view, produced a catharsis, or a purgation of the emotions of pity and fear. When the experience of an epic poem or a tragedy had culminated, the soul would be lightened and delighted (Richter, 1998, p. 41). By imitating life, art could help people to deal with their innermost fears and anxieties. Art could serve as a mirror allowing everyday humans to see, understand, and ultimately transcend themselves. There is certainly not universal agreement with Aristotle's hypothesis concerning the ultimate effect of the literary experience. Marxists, for instance, would look at the role of literary texts in legitimizing the capitalist mode of production; feminists and postcolonialists would contend that dominant texts attempt to enforce passive subjectivity and ideologies that legitimize an inequitable status quo and uphold dehumanizing norms while alienating those delineated as the "Other." However, it is taken for granted by litigants on all sides that literary texts produce profound emotions in their audiences for good or for ill. Robert Scholes (1986) would argue that literary texts have power as do the potential readers of these literary texts. Aristotle's *Poetics* would certainly corroborate this suggestion.

Any contemporary theorizing of critical literacy must confront classical, modern, and contemporary literary and cultural texts as sociohistorical markers of society's aims, goals, and values and ongoing commentaries of the universal human condition. As the Nobel Laureate Toni Morrison states (1993), "National literatures reflect what is on the national mind." More than providing a framework for classifying and making meaning of these literary and cultural texts, though, a critical literacy must encourage expression through fictional genres, literary explanations of the human condition that also serve as reminders of human possibility. In other words, a pedagogy of critical literacies must allow for the possibilities of the emergence of a Joyce, a Shakespeare, or a Zora Neale Hurston. The textual products that accompany a critical literacy curriculum should include novels, plays, poems, music, and films in addition to critical essays and other non-fiction texts.

The next section picks up with the Enlightenment philosophers of the eighteenth century, but before making that transition it seems necessary to say something about the intervening 2200 years of Western philosophy between Aristotle and Kant. Immediately following the classic Greek philosophers came the Romans. The leading Roman intellectuals were primarily guardians of the Greek tradition; they did little to tarnish or add to the ideas proliferated by the Sophists, Socrates, Plato, and Aristotle. The Romans translated and preserved many of the classic texts that we access to this day. It's also significant that the Romans have given us the basic alphabet that we use in most Western and European nations today.

The period between the fall of the Roman Empire (476 A.D.) and the Italian Renaissance is generally known as the medieval period or the "Dark Ages." The mega churches of the West dominated this period and, as a result of this hegemony, the church theologians dominated philosophical thought. Historical scholars employ the "critical" term Dark Ages to refer to the dogmatism of the church during this era; a dogmatism that many of these scholars would argue limited knowledge production and distribution in many fields, including philosophy and the sciences. It is not my intent to disparage this era of Western history nor is it my intent to suggest that medieval philosophers had nothing to offer to the critical canon, though, for the most part, the leading philosophers were concerned with matters of the church and the Christian life. Early medieval philosophers such as Saint Augustine were interested in apologetics, or the defense of the emergent Christian church (Hakim, 2001). During the hegemony of the Catholic Church, which corresponds exactly to the Middle Ages, there were no real boundaries between religion, culture, and philosophy. During the millennia of the Middle Ages, the philosopher-theologians of the time concerned themselves with questions of God's existence, God's essence, and the relationship between humans and God.

The major historical and philosophical period that follows the medieval period in Europe is the Renaissance; and the Renaissance, which was really started as a re-engagement with the works of the classic Greek philosophers, lead into the age of Enlightenment. From the standpoint of critical literacy, its important to consider what precipitated the Renaissance after one thousand years of religious rule; it is also important to understand how the Renaissance points ahead to the oncoming Age of Reason and the rise of the Enlightenment philosophers. The growing discontent with the rising corruption in the Catholic Church is a leading cause of the Renaissance and the break with this hegemony. This is significant, because it shows that, even when power brokers dominate the means of knowledge production, there are still spaces for resistance, and possibilities for transformation.

The festering critique of the Catholic Church was greatly assisted by the second contributing cause of the Renaissance: the invention of the Gutenberg press (c. 1440) and the resulting free flow of information (significant to any conception of critical literacy is access to information). It is also significant that one of Martin Luther's (1483–1546) most scathing critiques of the Catholic Church concerned the inaccessibility of the scriptures to everyday people. Luther felt that the Catholics limited the interaction everyday Christians could have with the bible and with God in ways that inhibited their personal fulfillment and in ways that legitimized the patriarchal domination of the Catholic Church as a cultural institution. The cultural and societal transformations that led to the Renaissance had everything to do with literacy and the politics of knowledge production; the freedom from Catholic hegemony and the re-introduction to philosophical ideas of antiquity inspired intellectual and artistic environment that ultimately gave rise to artistic geniuses such as Da Vinci and Michelangelo, the scientific discoveries of Descartes, Bacon, and Hume, the foundations of the Enlightenment, and the rise of critical philosophy.

KANT, HEGEL AND THE FOUNDATIONS
OF CRITICAL PHILOSOPHY

The Enlightenment refers roughly to the century between the 1680s and the 1790s (the eighteenth century) and the intellectual movements that spawned across Europe. Its architects, who included philosophers, scientists, artists, and political theorists, aimed to "lift the darkness that fell with the Christian triumph over the virtues of classical antiquity" (Kramnick, 1995, ix). Some key moments include the operas of Mozart, who, in *The Magic Flute*, places the secular priests over the Temples of Wisdom, Reason, and Nature; the publication of the seventeen-volume *Encyclopedie*; and the Declaration of Independence, to name a few. The goals of the Enlightenment manifested themselves in the revolutionary fervor that swept through France, England, and America during the last quarter of the eighteenth century. They are also realized in the philosophical works of Kant and Hegel and the emergence of critical philosophy.

I have endeavored to situate Kant's work and the Enlightenment itself against the backdrop of what came before, namely a millennium of focus on the ideals of the Catholic Church and Christian religion. Too often we bypass this era and jump immediately to a critique of these Enlightenment values without acknowledging how revolutionary a break the Enlightenment period represented to all that came prior. Kant and other leading intellectuals used this newfound freedom to question the sources of knowledge; to really question what it means to know and how humans come to know what they know; how they come to form ideas of what is good, what is evil, what is just, and what makes a moral citizen. In philosophy, these questions are the domain of epistemology (the study of knowledge) and ethics. One important contribution of Kant to subsequent philosophy is his skepticism toward human knowledge, which has remained one of the cornerstones of critical thought. I hope to have shown that these ideas, though attributable to Kant, were present in the work of the classical Greek philosophers. That being said, I offer some background on the work of Kant and his contributions to subsequent schools of critical philosophy.

Questioning the source and nature of knowledge is central to each of Immanuel Kant's (1721–1804) three major critiques: *The Critique of Pure Reason* (1781), *The Critique of Practical Reason* (1788), and *The Critique of Judgment* (1790). Kant felt that the critical process was the only path to acquiring true knowledge that was not susceptible to dialectical illusions (Kant, 1788/1993). The critical process, for Kant, involved both self-examination (of what we have come to accept as reasonable and why we have come to accept these things) and challenges to current dogmas (which by their very nature suggest certain attitudes, actions, and judgments as reasonable). Only someone who had mastered the critical process would be able to separate true knowledge from the dogmatism and moral fanaticism of the day. Though the idea of the existence of any "true" knowledge would be questioned by poststructuralists of the twentieth and twenty-first centuries, Kant encourages a process that is remarkably similar to the one many of us continue to advocate. Becoming critically literate entails coming to understand ourselves separately from the discourses that surround us; becoming critically literate also entails having the skills and sensibilities to ask demanding questions of the ideas, concepts, and ideologies that are presented to us as fact. It is also important to understand that the process of becoming critically literate is about both the development of skills and the development of a process. I will talk more about this dual approach to critical literacy pedagogy (which precedes critical literacy praxis) throughout the book. Though Kant is not generally mentioned among the revolutionaries of the modern era, when one considers what came before and what has come since, his work must be regarded as revolutionary in its impact on philosophy and critical thought.

Georg Wilhelm Friedrich Hegel (1770–1831) is another Enlightenment philosopher interested in the construction of knowledge. Not satisfied with Kant's subjective explanations and the disunity of mind and body prevalent in the work of his immediate predecessors Kant and Descartes, Hegel set out to historicize and theorize a process of arriving at absolute knowledge or consciousness. The cornerstone of Hegel's system or worldview is the notion of freedom, conceived not as simple license to fulfill preferences but as the rare condition of living self-consciously in a fully rationally organized community or state (Blackburn, 1994). Hegel believed that history could be viewed as a progress toward this freedom. He embraced the spirit of the Age of Enlightenment in his beliefs about the inevitable progress of humanity.

Hegel believed that this progress would be propelled by a theory of knowledge. He admired the skeptics, but furthered these ideas in *Phenomenology of Spirit* (Hegel, 1979), where he charts the development of all the forms of consciousness. This idea of having a higher consciousness of self and moment has captured the imagination of philosophers from Marx to the Frankfurt School to Paulo Freire. *Phenomenology* runs through the states of mind necessary to progress from immediate sense consciousness to higher consciousness. Similarly to Kant, he was interested in how the people of his time came to know the world on their own terms when faced with so many competing dogmas. Hegel differed from Kant, however, who believed that absolute knowledge was unattainable.

Hegel encourages a skepticism toward knowledge and encourages a process for being able to filter through knowledge to arrive at the rational worldview needed for citizens of the Hegelian Utopia. For Hegel, the dialectic refers to the process of progress in human thought and in the world at large. The dialectic process, for Hegel, is one of overcoming the contradiction between thesis and antithesis, by means of synthesis. The synthesis is contradicted and the process is repeated until final perfection is reached. The Hegelian dialectic is notably referenced in the critical literacy theory of Paulo Freire, who argues that the dialectic process of reading the word and the world for members of marginalized or oppressed populations informs more sophisticated and empowering readings of both until a state of *conscientization* is reached (Freire, 1970). Another notable Freirian dialectic involves the tension between theory and action that results in praxis.

Although this dialectical process is commonly attributed to Hegel, it is important to acknowledge that the concept of the dialectic can be traced back to Heraclitus (fifth century B.C.E.), who was interested in processes of knowing and understanding the world. The work of Heraclitus precedes even that of the classical Greek philosophers, and his belief that the underlying source of unity consisted of laws of processes and oppositions influenced both Plato and Aristotle (Audi, 1999). This furthers the argument that the foundation of critical literacy is as old as the Western philosophical tradition. It also shows that being skeptical of knowledge and being able to understand the social construction of knowledge have been at the heart of literacy theory during this entire period.

MARX, ENGELS AND THE EMERGENCE OF THE REVOLUTIONARY PHILOSOPHER

The Enlightenment philosopher most connected with contemporary critical theory is undoubtedly Karl Marx. Karl Marx's (1818–1883) lifetime spanned the tumultuous nineteenth century: a century that witnessed urbanization, industrialization, and the globalization of capital on an unprecedented scale. Marx is probably the most significant social theorist of this period and his legacy over the twentieth century is unquestioned. At the peak of the Cold War in the mid-twentieth century, his ideas held sway through half of the world. Vilified in the West for his supposed contribution to the totalitarian regimes of Stalin in the Soviet Union and Mao Tse-Tung in the People's Republic of China, Marx has enjoyed a different treatment by Western intellectuals from the Frankfurt School to Althusser to the New Left, who saw in his ideas a struggle against the ideologies of capitalist oppression. Since the fall of the Berlin Wall and the coup that toppled Soviet Russia, there has been more tolerance of Marx. However, outside of "critical" circles the ideas of the philosopher remain much of a mystery. I will consider briefly what the ideas of this philosopher, economist, historian, journalist, and revolutionary have to offer to educators in the twenty-first century who are interested in enacting a critical literacy with urban youth.

The lifelong project of Marx involved the explanation of the historical and material conditions of capitalism, which, in his opinion, had led to the alienation and exploitation of the working class (proletariat) for the benefit and the accumulation of capital by the owner class (bourgeoisie). Marx theorized that these oppressive conditions would inevitably lead to the overthrow of the bourgeoisie in a proletarian revolution. One of Marx's enduring legacies to critical theory is his treatment (along with his colleague Friedrich Engels) of the concept of ideology. Marx and Engels defined ideology as false consciousness (Marx and Engels, 1988). Marx was extremely interested in how power was maintained by the bourgeois class over the proletariat majority, a population identified by Marx as the sleeping giant of capitalism. Marx, for instance, felt that it was in the interest of the ruling bourgeoisie in capitalism to portray the world as highly individualistic and competitive. Marx felt that the bourgeois ideology effectively concealed the social and collective life and, in effect, the proletarian revolutionary possibilities (Edgar, 1999). Although he is seen primarily as an economic philosopher, Marx developed the base–superstructure hypothesis that those who control the economic base also control the cultural superstructure (1983). Put another way, the ideas of the ruling class become the ruling ideas.

This concept was of extreme importance to Marx, who sought to explain how members of the proletariat accepted their oppressive conditions. He also sought to explain the relationship between the mode of production and the development of consciousness. Marx felt that the only strategy for overcoming the capitalist ideology (or false consciousness) included the development of a revolutionary "class" consciousness on the part of the proletariat. This idea of consciousness-raising as a strategy for contesting oppressive ideology has been a hallmark of critical thought up through present iterations of the discourse. Though these ideas have changed over time, it is important to understand how Marx envisioned the requisite consciousness and the relationship between a revolutionary class consciousness and the critical consumption and production of texts and language.

Although Althusser attempts to distinguish between the historical materialist Marx and the political economist Marx, a significant element of Marxism is the historical analysis of the material conditions of any society. As a critical literacy theorist and educator, I see the importance of urban youth having an historical understanding of the factors that have contributed to the present conditions in urban America. Without this understanding it becomes easier to accept "blame the victim" ideologies or to see individual cases as isolated and arbitrary rather than as part of a larger narrative. This historical method of social analysis implies a certain attitude toward texts and a certain form of textual consumption. Certainly Marx read other historians and philosophers of history, but he also consulted many original sources when outlining a theory of history of Western civilization. Our young people are required to take courses in history, but we know from eminent critical historians such as Howard Zinn (1995) and James Loewen (1995) that history textbooks can be just as ideologically oppressive as other state-sanctioned texts. In addition to reading history textbooks, critically literate citizens need to read original historical sources. I would further argue that critically literate citizens need to become themselves critical social historians. By social historians, I am invoking the sub-discipline of historical scholars who are explicitly critical of top-down research that ignores the local struggles of everyday actors. Social historians remind us that it is the everyday actors who are foundational to any understanding of radical social movements. In chapter 9 I will describe a project in which urban teens were apprenticed as critical social historians and amassed historical data about segregation and schooling in their own neighborhoods. Engendering a different relationship to history plays a role in facilitating the critical consciousness that Marx advocates.

Another major aspect of Marxist philosophy concerns an understanding of the contemporary political economy and the relationship between economic means of production and social relations. In this spirit, a Marxist-inspired critical literacy would encompass the social theory that correlates poverty, changes in employment opportunities, and increasing wage gaps between owners and workers with larger social ills such as schools and the criminal justice system (Anyon, 1997). Too often Marxism is regarded as a tool of communist, totalitarian propaganda rather than as a set of explanatory tools of an economic-political-social system that accumulates excessive resources in the hands of a few to the detriment of the many. A Marxist-inspired critical literacy implies the acquisition of a skill set and conceptual base to ask these larger questions about the workings of social institutions and economic forces without taking these institutions and forces for granted as either the best or the only alternative available to society.

Probably the most lasting aspect of the Marxist legacy concerns the theorizing of ideology and the articulation of a revolutionary praxis. From Marx, we learn that all information received via dominant institutions is interested information; normally information interested in perpetuating social inequities. This legacy has filtered through all subsequent critical discourses, many of which will be taken up throughout this chapter and the remainder of the book. Marx and his intellectual descendants would advocate that true literacy concerns an awareness of the effects of language; it understands the relationship between language and power and language and social institutions. This does not negate the importance of literacy as a set of technical competencies, but it does call for a literacy, especially among members of marginalized populations, that understands and counters the explicitly ideological orientation of language and texts. Marx predicts the ascendancy of popular media and schools in transmitting dominant ideals that his intellectual descendants (Adorno, 2002; Althusser, 2001; Gramsci, 1971) pursue and carry forward. Also, whereas others have equated literacy with freedom or emancipation (see section on the African-American tradition in the next chapter), Marx is credited with associating praxis with a revolution. Although Marx was only interested in the communist revolution, the idea of a revolution in ideals or values has taken hold.

THE FRANKFURT SCHOOL

The Frankfurt School is the term applied to a collaborative of social theorists, philosophers, economists, sociologists, and literary theorists associated with Frankfurt University's Institute for Social Research from the mid-1920s through the late 1960s. The key figures associated with the school include Max Horkheimer, who became director in 1931 and held that post until 1958, Ted Adorno, Herbert Marcuse, Erich Fromm, Walter Benjamin, and, in the second generation, Jürgen Habermas.

The Institute was founded through the endowment of a wealthy student and, from its inception until 1931, was run by a traditional Marxist. Production and visibility increased with the appointment of Horkheimer as director. The Institute remained at Frankfurt until the threat of Nazi ascendancy forced the scholars (all of them Jewish) into exile. Many migrated to New York, where the Institute remained active until the scholars were allowed to return to their native Germany in the mid-1950s (Piccone, 1998). The Institute continued under the leadership of Adorno and Horkheimer until their deaths in the late 1960s. Habermas, the intellectual descendant of the original members, played a major role in the countercultural movements of the 1960s and 1970s; though he represents the movement to this day, he is much more of a lone figure. The school died with the deaths of its prolific pioneers.

The Frankfurt scholars were all card-carrying Marxists, but they articulated a different form of Marxism from their Bolshevik contemporaries (a brand of Marxism later associated with the New Left). For starters, the Frankfurt School theorists did not believe in the inevitability of the proletariat revolution. Having witnessed the failed German strikes of the 1920s and the waning German proletariat, they were skeptical of this element of Marxist thought. Second, members of the Frankfurt School were explicitly critical of the Stalinist brand of Marxism that emerged in the Soviet Union. Finally, Frankfurt School theorists were influenced by Freud's psychoanalysis and were interested in studying more than economic production. These scholars turned their interests toward literature, love, sex, Enlightenment thinking, and the emergent culture industries. It was the school's Marxist-inspired cultural critique and social praxis that became known as critical theory.

In Horkheimer's inaugural address to the Institute he broadly defines critical theory as human activity that takes society as its object, and that attempts to transcend the tensions between individual spontaneity and the work-process relationship on which society is based (Macey, 2000, pp. 74–75). The Frankfurt critical theory is one that gives humans, as social agents, language and tools to challenge taken-for-granted assumptions. It is a model for praxis that promotes a free and self-determining individual and, therefore, a free and self-determining society. All of the theorists were aware of the role that ideology could play in over-determining social relations. Particularly they were wary of the ideology of modern industrial society based on exploitation and the construction of needs and desires that lead to alienation, unhappiness, and a culture of consumerism.

Along with Horkheimer (1895–1973), Theodore Adorno (1903–1969) emerged as a leading intellectual of the Frankfurt School. More than any of his colleagues, Adorno's work would influence later generations of cultural theorists, especially those interested in studying popular culture. In order to understand Adorno's work, it's important to understand his central hypothesis concerning popular culture; that is, that major culture industries utilized popular culture (film and radio primarily at that time) to promote dominant (capitalist, oppressive) ideologies. As a consequence, a great deal of Adorno's scholarship entails a dissecting and critiquing of the mechanisms that popular cultural artifacts employ to indoctrinate participants into a set of oppressive norms. Adorno's scholarship is important to the project of critical literacy for several reasons. First off, he more than any other helped make popular culture a legitimate site of study. Considering the inundation of popular media today, young people need to have the skills and language needed to deconstruct the messages sent to them via dominant media outlets, which are even more prevalent than they were in the era where Adorno was most prolific. Even though media can be used in the struggle for social justice, and media can be used to expose inequity and oppression, a primary purpose remains to promote dominant (and often dangerous) ideologies. That is, the media are frequently used to promote ideals and values that are harmful or dehumanizing to the primary consumers of these media. Further, given the relationships between media culture and the logic of consumerism, young people need critical literacies that enable them to perform counter-readings against this logic. I will say much more about the scope and possibilities of critical media pedagogies with urban youth in subsequent chapters; for now it's merely important to situate this work within the critical philosophical tradition where it belongs.

Herbert Marcuse's (1898–1979) work is important in his critique of industrialism's tendency toward repression and his argument for liberation and emancipation of human drives and desires. Marcuse argues that, although bourgeois society liberates individuals from the chains of the past, it does so on the condition that they keep themselves in check, and that the prohibition of pleasures is an important precondition for their illusory freedom. Culture and the arts are used to pacify rebellious desire and to inculcate a toleration of unfreedom of social existence. In *One Dimensional Man* (1964) Marcuse argues that in advanced industrial societies total administration of individuals is necessary. Even minor rebellions could be tolerated and then turned into a repressive force. Although most needs of citizens are catered to, there are false needs that are created to maintain a system of production.

Marcuse's work changes over time in his optimism that individuals could overcome this repression, but his work inspires different directions in what might be conceptualized for critical literacy. Marcuse forces a consideration of a critical literacy that liberates human desires and drives. This can be interpreted many ways. For example, the work of Marcuse was influential in the sexual liberation movements of the 1960s. Further, as with Adorno, Marcuse identifies the arts of the industrial age as a primary site of interrogation. Though I would argue against an overly negative and deterministic view of popular culture and other industrial (now postindustrial) art forms, it certainly makes sense to consider how media and the arts limit possibilities of human expression.

Jürgen Habermas' (b. 1929) contribution to critical theory lies in his explication of a process of idea exchange that is central to a critical democratic project. Habermas' discourse ethics are grounded upon a certain level of critical thought as well as a certain form of communicative action (Habermas, 1981, 1987), or speech act. According to Habermas, the ideal speech situation would be one in which free and informed individuals rationally discuss alternative possibilities without being coerced. Although Habermas holds out hope for a constitutional democracy to create such spaces, he also acknowledges the "democratic deficit" that results in the form of bureaucratic overkill and voluntary non-participation of citizens in electoral politics and in civil society (Macey, 2000).

Habermas' philosophy offers much fruitful ground for conceptualizing critical literacy. First of all, we must consider exactly what type of access to information, what processing skills, and what strategies citizens require in order to have contributions to make within these ideal speech situations. As with many other theorists, a Habermasian critical literacy focuses on the moment of dialogue: a type of interaction between individuals that is necessary for authentic knowledge to be produced. What are the ideal conditions for such a dialogue to occur? What are the shared understandings? What levels of respect for oneself and one's comrades are needed within these speech situations? How does knowledge become produced within these communicative actions?

Third, Habermas inspires a substantive focus for the pedagogy and curricula of critical literacy. Critical literacy educators can help students to learn and internalize what Habermas calls discourse ethics. That is, a great portion of the pedagogy of critical literacy must help students to learn how to speak, to write, and to listen as participants of larger discourse communities. This implies a mastery of the art of rhetoric, or composition skills in traditional and new media formats; but it also signals a tolerance of diversity and plurality, and a willingness to learn with and from others.

Also, substantively, a Habermasian critical literacy curriculum would deal with key issues within the public sphere and civil society. Along with conversations about philosophers, theorists, novelists, and poets, students must also discuss the goings-on in their schools, their communities, the nation, and the world at large. Another way to think about this is to foster approaches to philosophers, theorists, novelists, and poets centered upon real issues in the real world. This is not to discount formalist or aesthetic approaches to literary texts; but it is an argument for more critical literary approaches that would draw from Marxism, feminism, postcolonialism, queer theory, and African-American criticism.

Habermas is concerned with the sociopsychological oppression that can result from information transfer, either through bureaucratic channels or via mainstream sources. Therefore, these discussions about the public sphere must treat mediated information with a healthy skepticism and a consideration of the sources. All information, to a critical theorist, is interested (or biased) information; therefore it becomes important to triangulate sources of information when possible and to search for primary sources when available. In this vein, Habermasian critical literacy also points toward a certain set of research skills as well.

PHENOMENOLOGICAL EXISTENTIALISM

Whereas there have been some connections made between Marx, the Frankfurt School, and literacy education (particularly critical media literacy), very little attention has been paid to a series of parallel movements that emerged in France. Certainly, the existentialists (and most who will be identified would not sit so kindly next to this label) were not as tightly conceived a group as the Frankfurt School philosophers, but the primary architect, Jean-Paul Sartre (1905–1980), lived and operated in France from the late 1930s until his death in 1980. For most of this forty-year period he stood at the pinnacle of French intellectual thought; and it is important to contemplate the relationship between this significant intellectual moment, the evolution of critical theory, and, ultimately, the development of critical literacy education.

One of the core tenets of Sartre's existentialism is the concept of bad faith. Sartre felt that most people tend to eschew their true freedom and, instead, operate under the false pretense that they really have no control over their lives. The intentional attempts to fool the self led to this acting in "bad faith." The awareness of one's true freedom, however, often led to existential dread; ostensibly because most people would not be pleased with what they had chosen for themselves. Of course Sartre has been subsequently critiqued by the structuralist movements that succeeded him for not accounting for structural constraints on human actors, but, nevertheless the idea of existential freedom is an important one for critical literacy educators to consider. Primarily, I argue that we need to consider the relationship between uncritical readings of the world and a banking education (Freire, 1970) and the creation of dehumanizing conditions that foster a culture of bad faith. I believe that Sartre and the structuralists are not so far apart if we were to focus on dominant language and texts as the source of bad faith. Everyday citizens feeling as if they do not have power over their lives serves the interests of those who do not want anything to change. The primary institutions for transmitting social values remain schools and the corporate media. We cannot afford to lose sight of this reality. Further, we are challenged to identify the role of these institutions in proliferating a set of social and cultural norms that very much resonate with Sartre's conception of bad faith.

Existentialism, and particularly the idea of existential freedom, offer an important alternative consideration for the goals of critical literacy pedagogy. Certainly most of the neo-Marxist work of the Frankfurt School, and structuralism especially, point indirectly toward some kind of collective social movement against capitalism. The critique of capitalism and colonialism remain integral to existential thought, but the implied outcomes focus much more at the level of the individual. How does the individual learn to embrace her freedom? How does she act more fully within and upon the world? With what benefits and consequences for the individual and society? I will talk at length in the remaining chapters of the book about how this might play out in practice. For now, it is only important to roll out the idea of existential freedom as an important and legitimate outcome of critical literacy education.

FEMINISM AND POSTFEMINISM

Feminism, as a critical discourse, has served to simultaneously uncover the ideology of patriarchy in society and celebrate the intellectual and creative works of women. It represents another discourse rooted in the neo-Marxist tradition of uncovering and contending against the role of language and texts in proliferating dominant ideologies; in this case, patriarchy. Although there are many raging debates within feminism (or maybe more appropriately "feminisms"), all acknowledge the role of dominant texts and discourses in promoting the values and aesthetic of patriarchy.

When considering the importance of feminism to critical literacy, it's important to underscore that an understanding of this language of critique is not only important for women. Just as postcolonialism and other post-Marxist discourses are important for those implicated in the oppression, feminism supplies important links in the chain for all interested in contending against marginalizing discourses on all fronts. Feminism has made tremendous strides in bringing attention to the physical and linguistic oppression of women; one of its primary aims has been to make apparent the relationships between words and texts and our everyday reality, especially as it concerns the positioning (and repositioning) of women (Robbins, 1999). Scholars for whom the term has been applied range from literary critics to political advocates to French philosophers such as Simone de Beauvoir (1949/1989) and Julia Kristeva, who each point to "woman" as a socially constructed and contested term.

Drawing upon the spirit and the texts of feminism, literacy educators can help the girls and boys in their classes to deconstruct the dominant messages that are sent to them through new media outlets and classical texts that promote the values of patriarchy and through analyzing the outcomes associated with this value system. For example, we know that students derive their worldview largely from the corporate media outlets that they navigate on a daily basis. From a feminist perspective, students would learn to read these texts critically with an understanding of the multiple ways that dominant media reinforce a set of societal norms that inherently privilege men over women. Students will also become equipped to make connections between these sanctioned corporate discourses and the everyday popular cultural practices in more local contexts. This would include language, dress, and social interactions, to name a few.

A feminist critical literacy education in urban schools would also seek out texts written by authors who manifest a range of critical feminist perspectives. These texts could include novels, poems, plays, songs, films, essays, and philosophical texts. In addition to helping students to read (the word and the world) as feminists, a feminist-inspired critical literacy education would provide multiple spaces for students to write as feminists. Of course these textual products would include literary analysis and critiques of canonical texts, but they should also include opportunities for all students to produce original fiction and exposition written from a feminist (and Alice Walker would include Womanist) perspective (Walker, 1984). Allowing students to represent their multiple situatedness in the context of cultural (and countercultural) production is an important tenet of any critical literacy education. I will talk more in the second section of the book about how this might look in the classroom and other contexts where we might work with urban adolescents.

POSTMODERNISM AND POSTSTRUCTURALISM

Postmodernism and poststructuralism represent two of the more popular, yet esoteric and debated, fields of inquiry within the contemporary philosophical tradition. Leading architects of these movements have eschewed much of classical and modern philosophy and, in turn, many classically trained philosophers do not consider these fields as true philosophy or their practitioners as true philosophers. Nevertheless, the connections are so clear between the two that I feel comfortable situating each of these discourses squarely within the critical philosophical tradition. A compelling argument can be made about the connections between postmodernism, poststructuralism, and critical literacy. Each critiques the essential notions of the modern project such as rationality, progress, and the existence of ultimate truths, whether proponents are deconstructing the grand narratives that shape society's values (Lyotard, 1984) or showing how meanings are not fixed entities so much as they are created through ideological linguistic and semiotic systems (or discourses) situated within specific historical moments (Foucault, 1972). Postmodernism and poststructuralism also exist as suggestions for a method of inquiry, one that is always questioning the source of knowledge, the position of the creator of knowledge, and the particular values at work in shaping that particular moment. The nature of investigation associated with these two discourses as well as the explicit connections between knowledge and power are very connected to the project of critical literacy. With respect to the relationships between the post- discourses (particularly postmodernism and poststructuralism), although I do not mean to minimize the differences between them, I side with Best and Kellner (1991), who contend that postmodernism is a large enough conceptual terrain to encompass the other fields, such as poststructuralism.

Given that the locus of postmodernism consists of fundamental critiques of ideas of progress and grand narratives, or ultimate truths, it becomes difficult to nail down a single definition of the term. Many who are lumped under the umbrella of postmodernism would see very little in common with their peers who employ a similar term toward very different ends. Further, the term has come to acquire negative and nebulous connotations, conjuring up notions of cynical intellectuals in Parisian cafes talking in a language that only they can understand. Although there may be some truth to this incredibly simplistic stereotype, there are many important contributions that postmodernism has made to critical philosophy and, by association, to my conception of critical literacy. Here I touch briefly on the historical conditions that contribute to the moment known as postmodernity and the conceptual terrain known as postmodernism (Best and Kellner, 1991). I'll also briefly discuss two of the movement's intellectual heavyweights, Foucault and Baudrillard, and consider their possible contributions to our conversation about postmodernism, critical literacy and urban youth.

What is the postmodern?

In his landmark volume *The Postmodern Condition: A Report on Knowledge* Jean Lyotard defines the postmodern as an incredulity to all meta-narratives. For Lyotard and his contemporaries, there was a growing disillusionment with the meta-narrative of capitalism that had basically replaced the church as the meta-narrative of the modern era along with an increasing disillusionment with the competing meta-narrative of communism in the wake of the revelation of the Stalinist purges and the invasion of Afghanistan in 1956. The postmodernists represented a group of scholars who wanted to remain critical of these practices, but were unwilling to necessarily subvert themselves to any single ideology.

Some of the benefits of postmodern theories are that they complicate some of the simplistic elements of modern theories in ways that make those theories stronger. Postcolonialism, for instance, doesn't negate colonialism so much as it makes colonialism a stronger discourse. Along those same lines, postmodernism creates more reflexive and self-critical critical social theory. Postmodernism questions the notion of ultimate truth and, instead, opens up spaces to consider that knowledge is socially constructed. Finally, postmodernism allows for theorizing resistance, agency, counter-narratives, and multiplicity. One of the critiques of postmodern theories is that they sound wishy-washy (never really firm on anything). No one in postmodernism, according to its critics, is willing to say what they mean. For many progressives interested in action for social change, postmodernism sounds like weak and qualifying arguments in the face of a unified conservative front. Other critiques are that postmodernists may be premature in their prediction of the demise of grand narratives. Finally scholars have suggested that postmodernist thought leads to cynicism, apathy, and despair and that can be overly relativistic in a dangerous way. These arguments notwithstanding, postmodernism represents an important moment in critical thought that holds important implications for the future of critical literacy instruction. I would like to consider these implications through a more detailed look at two of its most articulate spokespersons, Foucault and Baudrillard.

Postmodern Philosophers and Critical Literacy: Foucault and Baudrillard

Foucault

Michel Foucault (1926–1984), a philosopher associated with the ideas of poststructuralism, ultimately eschewed the label of philosopher. He referred to himself as alternately an archaeologist or an historian of systems of thought. Foucault's intellectual project entailed uncovering genealogies of knowledge, particularly as this work relates to explaining how meanings become constructed within particular historical moments, and charting the ways that power operates within those societies given those historically constructed meanings. Important to the project of critical literacy are his methodological approach and his discussion of the nature of the relationship between power and knowledge. Methodologically Foucault joins a group of historian-philosophers that include the likes of Marx and Hegel. Foucault, however, breaks from these philosophers in his treatment of history. Rather than seeing some overarching trajectory toward progress or class conflict or a proletarian revolution, Foucault understood history as consisting of *epistemes* of knowledge, dominant modes of expression that rule particular periods of history. Rather than trying to articulate the progress of history, it is important to understand how power operates through discourse in particular periods of time. The work of the philosopher-historian, then, is to understand how the subject is variously constructed through discourse. Foucault's histories help us to understand the various sociohistorical constructions of madness, discipline and punishment, scientific knowledge, and sexuality.

Foucault's poststructural philosophy is important to the project of critical literacy in at least three respects. First and foremost is the treatment of history. Any historical analysis of any particular term or concept will reveal how it changes and shifts in different historical periods or cultural contexts. This is important because it reveals that meanings aren't fixed, that they change and are constructed within existing relations of power. Foucault's work moves forward from traditional notions of Marxist history because he doesn't simply talk about the narrative of history as the history of ruling ideas. There is no absolute working of power or totalizing narrative to Foucault's history of Western civilization, which shares many of the critiques of dominant discourses without Marx's sense of inevitability. Human actors shape history even as they are shaped by the order of discourse within which they themselves are shaped.

Foucault offers a unique methodological approach for the critical literacy theorist. Foucault's work implies a different method of reading "upon" texts or even reading texts in that he promotes an approach that understands texts as series of statements that are situated historically, socially, and culturally; a set of constructed statements whose meaning is valid only within this context. Foucault-inspired work entails developing capacity for these sorts of readings of the world and the word. Critical literacy praxis, however, goes beyond (or awry from) the work of Foucault in using these readings to advocate for social change. It is possible, I argue, to use the tools of Foucauldian discourse analysis to understand and intervene in contemporary discourses; knowing about the order of discourse makes one a better consumer (and producer) of discourse. Foucault goes to great lengths to show that the future is not inevitable, but he stops short of empowering the reader to use analyses of history and of the living present to intervene in the trajectory toward the future.

Finally, Foucault's work inspires critical literacy in its complex treatment of power. Whereas many Marxist and neo-Marxist theories treat power as unidirectional (what is enacted by the oppressors on the oppressed) Foucault understands power as always existing within a context of resistance to that power. Rather than offering a theory of history or of society that is overly deterministic, Foucault's work shows us that even the most seemingly ingrained ideas (concepts of discipline, morality, the treatment of homosexuals) change over time, possibly in ways that grant more power to those who had been historically oppressed. Such a reading of the past (and the present) is infinitely more optimistic for those populations (such as urban teachers and students) who find themselves on the other (and "Othered") side of history.

Baudrillard

The postmodern media philosopher Jean Baudrillard (1929–2007) warns of how emergent communications technologies have created a virtual, simulated existence (Baudrillard, 2003). He explains how all of the world is a screen and information is mediated. The consequences of *virtuality* are myriad, including the alienation of ourselves from ourselves. Leading contemporary society toward the end of history and of faith in any reality, the virtual is also the viral and leads to proliferation of AIDS, cancer, and computer viruses to name a few. The undifferentiated virtual existence necessitates the arbitrary creation of the other; the end of the real leads to disembodied violence of hatred, psychedelic violence of drug use; the fear of sex and sexuality and the mistrust of information. Baudrillard's influences are Marx (though he critiques the Hegelian notion of history as progress of ideas), Saussure,

Barthes (structuralism, semiology—the sign is an important component of Baudrillard's conception of the virtual with the interplay between the sign and the disappearing referent), Nietzsche, and the media philosopher Marshall McLuhan.

Baudrillard's theorizing moves from Foucault's discourse (linguistic) to virtuality, to simulation, to media and the screen; a shift towards a post-text discourse or a philosophy after the linguistic turn of the twentieth century. It is a twenty-first-century philosophy of the image or the screen instead of the language or the text. Nietzsche also influences Baudrillard when he examines our powerlessness and impotence at the hands of the virtual. Rather than champion the intellectual progress inherent in virtual technology, Baudrillard holds the mirror to our faces to show us what we have lost in our separation from the 'real' and who we have 'virtually' become. Baudrillard is also an exemplar of postmodern cultural studies; he uses everyday popular cultural events as the topics of his philosophical analysis reminiscent of Sartre and Barthes. His work is important to critical literacy education specifically in its process and in its choice of subject matter. Any meaningful literacy education in the twenty-first century must pay explicit attention to the virtual and to the role of media culture in shaping everyday life for better and for worst.

THE FREIRIAN TRADITION

No conversation about critical literacy pedagogy would be complete without a treatment of Paulo Freire's (1921–1997) life and work. I feel comfortable placing him at the end of this chapter, because it allows me to situate Freire's work in the context of his antecedents such as Marx, Engels, Gramsci, the Frankfurt School, and the existentialists, all of whom influenced him greatly. There were also other influences, particularly from the anti-colonial tradition, that I will take up in the next chapter. Finally, I do not want to imply that by placing Freire last that I am situating him after the postmodern moment, a moment that is still with us even though Freire, unfortunately, is not. Freire's work has existed alongside, within, and frequently implicitly against some of the tenets of postmodern theory. Freire's work comes last primarily because it serves as the most appropriate launching pad into my own work in critical literacy education.

Paulo Freire's work begins with the concept of humanization, and the reality of dehumanization. In neocolonial and late capitalist societies, many "oppressed" peoples experience the tragedy of dehumanization. For Freire, the educational system plays a major role in this process of dehumanization. Through a banking education that promotes rote learning and the transmission of passivity and acceptance of dominant belief systems, schools play a major role in the reproduction of oppressive norms. What is most revolutionary about Freire's work, however, is that he also envisioned a form of education that would be about the development of *conscientization* (roughly translated as critical consciousness). This radical, problem-posing education would form the foundation of a movement, as participants in the process of radical education would be more prepared to engage in revolutionary praxis, the combination of careful reflection and transformative action. For Paulo Freire, the pedagogy of the oppressed was, in reality, a pedagogy of individual and social transformation.

Literacy and literacy education were important components of Freirian pedagogy. Freire believed that the achievement of conscientization involves a continual reading and rereading of the word and the world. Freire borrowed from the Hegelian dialectic in believing that the informed reading of the word and world would lead toward the development of a consciousness that would in turn lead to transformative action. At the heart of this, however, remained a critical reading of the word. Especially, one could argue, a critical reading of the social world as manifested in sanctioned texts.

Toward these ends Freire developed a literacy campaign in his native Brazil that worked with illiterate adults. Freire believed that the adults would be able to ultimately acquire dominant literacies if they were first taught by drawing upon the language and experiences that were most meaningful to them. Once these students were granted permission to engage in authentic dialogue about the injustices in their own world, they would have a grounded context within which they could learn the dominant literacies that they could then use to interrogate, deconstruct, and ultimately subvert the implicit logic contained in these words.

At the risk of too simplistic a summation of the relationship between Freire's work and critical literacy (which is really the project of the entire book), there are a few central tenets that stand out. First of all, Freire implicates literacy education in the problem of dehumanization and the project of humanization. There's no denying, from a Freirian perspective, the politics associated with literacy education. Though we may not be explicit, all literacy educators make political choices that carry with them significant social, economic, cultural, political, and psychological consequences. Second, Freire properly identifies the starting point of critical literacy education as the lived experiences of everyday people. In my own work, I have drawn upon Freirian principles of critical literacy education to justify the use of popular culture in literacy education with urban adolescents (Morrell, 2004b). Third, Freire implies a process of critical literacy education; one that involves problem posing and the positioning of students as teachers and intellectuals involved in intense dialogic exchanges and a continual interrogation of the world around them. Finally, Freire identifies outcomes for critical literacy education that include acknowledging one's own humanity as well as being informed and engaged participants in the process of social change. Although we would be remiss if we didn't place some value on improved academic literacy achievement, we would be negligent if the achievement were our only goal. In other contexts I have talked about a pedagogy of access and dissent (Morrell, 2005), in which we have as our simultaneous goals academic (and professional) access and social justice. A Freirian model of literacy education allows us to think about how we might accomplish these dual ends. In that vein, I situate my larger work, and the work of this book, within the Freirian tradition.

Of course there are many post-Freirian and contemporary scholars who are engaging in "critical literacy work" all over the world. Scholars such as Barbara Comber, Jeff Duncan-Andrade, James Gee, Norman Fairclough, Glynda Hull, Doug Kellner, Michele Knobel, Colin Lankshear, Allen Luke, Carmen Luke, Jabari Mahiri, Sonia Nieto, and Vivian Vasquez, scholars that I consider as friends and colleagues, are pushing the envelope of what counts as literacy and what should be considered as the goals of literacy education. These wonderful scholars have expanded the fields of multicultural education, sociocultural theory, critical pedagogy, new literacy studies, teacher education, and media cultural studies, to name a few. From their collective effort we have moved to include media literacies in conversations of critical literacy, we have included analyses of culture and gender alongside class-based explanations of inequality, we have considered the implications and applications of this work for the training and development of teachers, and we have developed critical action-oriented research methodologies that help us to understand and intervene in the project of developing better, more empowering curricula and pedagogies.

It is not my intention to give short shrift to the most recent generation of critical literacy scholarship. There are, however, several current publications that do this very well. I intend to connect the Western philosophical and anti-colonial traditions to a body of coherent research projects in urban classrooms in attempts to develop a grounded theory of critical literacy practice. For this reason I do not focus on contemporary scholars as much as I lay out the trajectory that has led us to this moment. My hope is that we may, through this process, both broaden and clarify how we view critical literacy education, its manifestations, and its possibilities for twenty-first century, postindustrial urban education.

CRITICAL PHILOSOPHY, CRITICAL
THEORY, CRITICAL LITERACY

To the extent that critical literacy is tied to critical philosophy and the Western philosophical tradition, it must be primarily concerned with an understanding of the socially constructed nature of knowledge, the uses of socially constructed realities (and belief systems) to maintain systems of oppression and control, and the linguistic and textual processes involved in unpacking and subverting the ideologies contained within these socially constructed "truths."

It should be apparent, though, that the intent of critical literacy as I have laid it out in this chapter is not to replace problematical dogmas with other dogmas. Indeed the various authors and schools presented do not share similar ideas about the nature or project of critical literacy, even as all are valuable informants to any discussion of critical literacy praxis in urban education. Future discussions should concern themselves primarily with the processes (and their corresponding pedagogies) that empower individuals and collectives over the texts that simultaneously circumscribe and constrain social thought and dominant cultural practices. My pragmatic approach draws from these predecessors as they help to illuminate and sharpen my focus as a scholar and practitioner; my conceptual task is to document this approach and the new theories that emerge from an examination of my own efforts. In the following chapter I address a different, though no less important, set of mentors who have resided on the outskirts of this critical tradition.

3

"Othered" Critical Traditions

Though the term "critical" certainly emerges from and is indebted to the Western philosophical tradition, I want to acknowledge a separate, distinct, and sometimes parallel tradition that informs my theorizing of this term. These traditions I designate as "Othered" critical traditions. Though some (especially postcolonial studies) borrow heavily from Western philosophical movements such as postmodernism and poststructuralism, and others (such as the African-American tradition or hip-hop) emerge from Western imperialist nations, these traditions are "Othered" because of the status of the practitioners within them. Said (1979) theorizes the "Other" as a central antithesis to the European ideal, tied in an inextricable yet imbalanced power relationship. That description perfectly fits these scholars who, because of race, class, color, or ideology, are akin to, but not a central part of, the mainstream tradition of critical thought.

I argue in this chapter that "Othered" scholars have a great deal to offer to the traditions of intellectual thought and activism that have heretofore claimed or been associated with the modifier "critical." However, for various reasons many of these scholars are not anthologized alongside Marx, Althusser, Gramsci, and Foucault. When I look at anthologies on critical theory or journals devoted to contemporary applications of critical theory, I rarely see any of the following thinkers mentioned in them. Nevertheless, the writers, artists, activists, and revolutionaries mentioned in this chapter are central to my conceptual framing of critical literacy and they predict and illuminate many of the practices I will describe in subsequent sections of the book. Max Horkheimer asserts that critical theory must always offer space to critique itself. Herein lies my cultural critique of mainstream critical theory; I consider it as a critique by inclusion.

Particularly, in this chapter I will highlight the work and ideas of writers and scholars operating within critical colonial discourses, leading proponents within the African-American intellectual tradition, and philosophers and practitioners operating in the new media of film and contemporary music. I also include a section on writers and intellectuals from the Latin American and Caribbean traditions to complement the postcolonial discourses, which heavily featured voices from Asia and, to a lesser extent, Africa. I find this unfortunate, as Latin America and the Caribbean have offered some of the best examples of the relationships between literacy praxis and social revolution. Since Toussaint L'Ouverture and the revolution of Saint-Domingue in the 1790s, Latin America and the Caribbean have been regions where marginalized populations have continually fought for liberation and self-determination; their numerous social revolutions offer a great deal for scholars in the Western tradition who are interested in developing a grounded theory of literacy praxis for individual and social transformations.

This chapter will contain separate sections dealing with anti-colonial discourses and postcolonial discourses. The anti-colonial discourses will feature the work of scholars who predate Said's 1979 publication of *Orientalism*, the first major work in the area of postcolonial studies. Though many other writers implicated by colonialism had written critiques of the problematic system of relations, I do not feel comfortable ascribing that term after the fact. Also, given the nature of postcolonialism primarily as a literary field, I have categorized these other intellectuals under the banner of anti-colonial discourses. Some of these anti-colonial scholars include Frantz Fanon and C. L. R. James, who chronicle and theorize the African and Haitian revolutions respectively. I will also represent the intersections between the Negritude movement, the Commonwealth Literature movement and my emergent theory of critical literacy.

The postcolonial discourses section will be heavily focused on the work of Edward Said, Gayatri Spivak, and Homi Bhabha and their intellectual descendants. I will also draw from anthologies and metatexts that attempt to historicize and codify this nascent yet powerful avant-garde literary tradition. Specifically I pay attention to how these scholars employ the methodologies of critical theory to interpret the multiple ways that mainstream Western discourses have articulated the culturally marginalized other. I also explore the implications of postcolonial theory for considering the texts that are worthy of literary study.

The African-American tradition will draw from a century and a half of intellectual discourse that includes the work of Frederick Douglass, W. E. B. DuBois, Zora Neale Hurston, Marcus Garvey, Carter G. Woodson, Huey

Newton, Angela Davis, bell hooks, Cornel West, Henry Louis Gates, Geneva Smitherman, and Molefi Asante. I will discuss how these authors have conceived of the role of literacy and literacy education in the development of a revolutionary consciousness and the various models of critical literacy praxis that have been offered through their work.

The Latin American and Caribbean tradition will draw upon scholars and activists as diverse as Pablo Neruda, Aime Cesaire, and Bob Marley. I look at the role of committed poetry, Negritude literature, and the roots reggae movement as examples of critical literacy or as movements that inform a theory of critical literacy education. The final section of this chapter will focus on new media philosophers and the architects of contemporary youth subcultures such as hip-hop in order to demonstrate how participants in youth popular cultures are, in reality, the new social philosophers. I will examine the strategies employed by these new media philosophers as I attempt to theorize literacy as social praxis. I will pay particular attention to the role that documentary filmmakers and hip-hop and reggae artist-activists, the purveyors of rebel music, have played in this regard.

ANTI-COLONIAL DISCOURSES

The rise of the work of Edward Said, Gayatri Spivak, and Homi Bhabha in the 1980s popularized the academic use of the terms "colonialism" and "postcolonialism." It is important to understand, though, that as long as Western colonialism has existed there have been anti-colonial voices chronicling the ways that colonial regimes use language and literacy to maintain colonial hegemony. This process takes multiple forms ranging from the prohibition of literacy instruction to totalizing and dehumanizing education to absolute control of mechanisms of information production and exchange. Throughout this process intellectuals revealed and contested these practices in the struggle for freedom, equity, or social justice.

In *The Black Jacobins* (1963) C. L. R. James chronicles the Saint-Domingue–Haitian revolution led by the former slave Toussaint L'Ouverture. One does not need formal training in critical theory to understand the horror of the treatment of African slaves by their French masters. In describing this treatment, James writes:

> Their masters poured burning wax on their arms and hands and shoulders, emp-tied the boiling cane sugar over their heads, burned them alive, roasted them on slow fires, filled them with gunpowder and blew them up with a match; buried them up to the neck and smeared their heads with sugar that the flies might devour them; fastened them near to nests of ants or wasps; made them eat their excrement,

drink their urine, and lick the saliva of other slaves. One colonist was known in moments of anger to throw himself on his slaves and stick his teeth into their flesh ... The blowing up of a slave had its own name—'to burn a little powder in the arse of a nigger': obviously this was no freak but a recognized practice. (pp. 12–13)

The survival of such an institution depends greatly on fostering fear, distrust, self-doubt, and a climate absent of any public critique. Language and literacy play a vital role in achieving all of these ends. Towards the former, slave owners instituted rigid Negro codes that prescribed the relationships between blacks and whites on the island of Saint-Domingue. They also tapped heavily into the language and ideology of race and racialization to legitimize the cruel treatment of blacks and to ensure separation between the white colonists, the growing Creole population, and the black slaves. Colonists (and the colonizing nations) borrowed from religion and science to justify the social order. They used the dominant texts of their time to put forward pseudo-intellectual arguments about the depraved character and inferior intellectual capabilities of the populations that were being enslaved. Toward the latter end the French prohibited their slaves from becoming literate or having any communication with the outside world. The less slaves were able to engage the world of letters or enter into critical dialogues that exposed them to alternate realities, the more likely they would be to tolerate the despicable conditions they were subjected to on a daily basis.

Even under these conditions anti-colonial discourses were able to proliferate among oppressed slaves and French sympathizers, creating spaces for critique, organizing, insurgency, and, ultimately, freedom. Toussaint L'Ouverture, who is generally recognized as the leader of the first revolution of black slaves in the Western hemisphere, understood the importance of critical literacy to fomenting rebellion against colonial imperialism of his French masters. Toussaint would comment that it was his reading of anti-colonial texts written by French intellectuals that gave language to his emergent thoughts. It was the reading of Abbé Raynal's revolutionary anti-slavery text *Philosophical and Political History of the Establishments and Commerce of the Europeans in the Two Indies* that set him on the pathway to becoming a revolutionary leader.

Toussaint became a powerful general who was able to use numerical force to overrun the French colonists, but he also used the power of rhetoric to persuade disenchanted slaves to follow him. It was the critical language that Toussaint employed, helping his fellow slaves to understand the inhumanity of their treatment and the human rights to which they were entitled that led them to risk their lives to follow him. Toussaint and other slave leaders were also able to translate the ideals of the French Revolution to the slave armies while also translating the plight of the slave rebels to a growing sympathetic voice in France.

For many in colonized lands of the Americas, the Saint-Domingue (or Haitian) uprising became a symbol of revolution and an inspiration of the possibilities that lay ahead for those intellectuals who were able to capture the imaginations of oppressed colonized populations. Within the next two decades (1804–1824) enslaved and indigenous populations would expel European colonists from much of the Americas, including revolutions in South America led by Simón Bolívar and Manuela Sáenz, and upheavals in Mexico, which led to the expulsion of the Spanish. It is important to understand the use of language of political and critical philosophies of the Enlightenment along with calculated action to change the destiny of an entire continent and instilling a revolutionary aesthetic that continues to capture the imagination of the oppressed to this day! It is no coincidence that Hugo Chávez, leader of present-day Venezuela, has termed his movement the Bolivarian revolution.

The ideas promoted by leading Enlightenment intellectuals such as Rousseau and Locke and the evidence of the revolutions of Haiti and Latin and South America contributed to a praxis and idealism that manifested itself throughout the nineteenth and twentieth centuries through the words and deeds of actors such as José Martí in Cuba and Pancho Villa and Emiliano Zapata in Mexico. Of course we know that the colonial era did not vanish quietly into the night; there would be another two centuries of conflict between forces of Western imperialism and voices of indigenous resistance. With these examples, though, the rise of intellectualized anti-colonial discourses that were used to organize a powerful model of revolutionary resistance were firmly entrenched in the public imagination.

In the mid-twentieth century, a map of the continent of Africa revealed a patchwork of colonial territories held by European nations, who relied on raw materials and labor to fuel their high-powered industrial economies. Only twenty years later, however, this same map would show that a majority of the colonial territories had won their independence from their colonial masters. How did this happen? How were five hundred years of systematic rule overturned in only a quarter of a century? Any answer to this question has to examine the case of Algiers and the work of the Diaspora psychiatrist-intellectual-activist Frantz Fanon.

A product of the French-Caribbean island Martinique and Parisian university training, Frantz Fanon (1925–1961) would emerge as the voice of African revolution and a galvanizing voice (along with Fidel Castro) for what could be the most vibrant decade of international indigenous resistance in human history. A trained psychiatrist, Fanon began his work analyzing through his clinical practice the psychology of oppression or the impact of colonialism on the mental health of colonized populations in Africa and the Americas. His work with the Algerian resistance, through such texts as

A Dying Colonialism, *Wretched of the Earth*, and *Black Skin, White Masks*, also shows how a population can shake off the cloak of mental and physical oppression and transform into a collective of revolutionary resistance.

In each of these texts Fanon clearly articulates the systematic practices of colonial powers to use language and texts to promote colonial ideologies. Whether these ideas promote the superiority of Western science and religions or they promote the inferiority of non-Western languages, customs, or even darker skin tones, the domination is total. In the words of Fanon, the result of this domination is that the oppressed want to become like the oppressor; whether it is the colonized who wants to be like the colonizer, or the African who wants to be white, the doctrine of self-hatred and worshipping of Western ideals is a central element of social control. Fanon is also clear on the role of language to transform these dominant ideologies. In *A Dying Colonialism*, for example, he chronicles the ascendance of an indigenous radio station and the changing ideologies of indigenous Algerians, who began to turn off French radio stations even as they were turning away from French customs and traditions and reclaiming their own. Even though violence and active resistance were an important component to the Algerian revolution, Fanon traces the antecedents of these activities in the changing ideologies of the people represented by a change in language and a change in the tools that they employed to deconstruct dominant language and texts. Appropriately so, Fanon locates the genesis of the African revolutions in the ideological and linguistic changes of the African peoples.

Fanon's works had an immediate impact on revolutionaries throughout the world from Fidel Castro in Cuba to Paulo Freire in Brazil, to the Black Panthers in the United States. Fanon's work is so central to the project of revolution and to critical literacy because he understands the psychological importance of renaming and reclaiming individual and collective identities. Fanon's work is also an important complement to the Marxist, neo-Marxist, and structural discourses of his contemporaries that focus on social class and economic oppression. Fanon's work does not discount these discourses; rather he adds important linguistic, cultural, religious, and racial components of oppression that are crucial to understanding the sheer totality of Western imperialism.

Looking at these authors and works is evidence of the vibrant history of anti-colonial discourse that runs counter to the colonial tradition of the eighteenth, nineteenth, and twentieth centuries. Such a study reveals that leading intellectuals understood the role of language and texts in promoting or eschewing dominant modes of thought. These intellectuals were also able to push forward critical thought, bringing to bear a certain praxis that had not existed even in the works of authors such as Marx or Socrates. They were also able to complement structural and economic critiques with conversations about race, culture, religion, and color. For all of these reasons they stand as important contributors to any corpus of critical thought; especially as we consider the multiple challenges that we face in urban education, where we must account for issues of race, culture, and nation in the promotion of dominant ideals and where we must have a revolutionary praxis tied to any intellectualizing of ideals.

When one fully grasps the persistence and pervasiveness of colonial oppression it is easy to become disheartened. However, this history is also filled with amazing examples of the power of revolutionary discourse to change the trajectories of people and nations. If, for example, the Haitians, the indigenous peoples of Latin and South America, and the Algerians and African nations were able to overcome dominant imperial systems of oppression, it is not unimaginable that, with a modicum of vision and inspiration, we would be able to organize collectives and create learning spaces that would fundamentally alter the way that literacy education is conceived and practiced in urban classrooms across the country. I may be simple minded or a narrow reader of history, but the study of the past always leaves me saddened by the sheer evil enacted against humanity, but more optimistic about the sheer magnitude of the human spirit and the ability to endure and overcome.

POSTCOLONIAL STUDIES

As the world becomes increasingly interconnected and people find themselves implicated in one another's lives on an unprecedented scale, educators need to find ways to help their students understand the consequences of this globalization while also understanding the myriad of experiences of variously situated peoples in the "new global village," especially those people who have been subjugated during the era of European colonial expansion. Many have acknowledged the role that literature has historically played in defining or articulating cultural values. As the writer and cultural critic Toni Morrison has stated, "National literatures reflect what is on the national mind." Given this reality, activists, writers, and literary scholars have begun to champion the literatures of once-colonized populations; as well, they have developed approaches to literature that explore and critique the representations of ethnically marginalized groups in colonial/postcolonial contexts.

Postcolonialism represents a major conceptual umbrella for these literatures and approaches to literary texts. My use of the term "postcolonialism" includes a number of post-World War II literary movements that include postcolonialist studies narrowly defined, but also includes the Negritude movement, the Commonwealth Literature movement, and other anti-colonialist discourses that exist outside of the framework for literary studies articulated by key postcolonial theorists. As chronological markers, though, it is important to identify Said's *Orientalism* as a key moment in postcolonial theory, as well as the decades of the 1980s and 1990s, which witnessed a proliferation in studies that referred to themselves as postcolonial (Macey, 2000). Two major (and highly contestable) intellectual questions form the focus of this brief representation of postcolonial theory and its theorists: when did postcolonial studies begin and what are postcolonial studies? To these questions, I add a third, which concerns the relationship between postcolonial theory and the project of critical literacy education in urban schools.

Although it happened differently in different parts of the world, all colonial interchanges involved the settlement of European people in new lands, generally inhabited by indigenous peoples, for the cultivation of lands and development of products that would be of service to the mother (European) nation. Additionally Loomba (1998) comments:

> The process of 'forming a community' in the new land necessarily meant unforming or reforming the communities that existed there already, and involved a wide range of practices including trade, plunder, negotiation, warfare, genocide, enslavement, and rebellions. (p. 2)

Throughout the centuries, colonialism has been maintained by force, including torture, maiming, and even death (James, 1963); but it is also maintained largely by the domination of ideas, particularly in the industrial age after most of the formal structures of oppression, such as slavery, have been officially disbanded. The Italian sociologist and philosopher Antonio Gramsci (1971) talks about how industrial capitalist societies use hegemony instead of force to maintain inequitable power relations; manufacturing the consent of the oppressed toward their oppressive conditions. According to Gramsci, schools existed as the primary site of cultural education, for better or worse. Gramsci's educational project targeted schools and teachers in the development of a revolutionary proletarian culture that he hoped would counter the dominant culture of his time (Gramsci, 1991). Edward Said (1979) made connections between the work of Gramsci and Foucault (1972) and the emergent field of colonial studies by examining how Western powers had used dominant discourses of schooling and the media to maintain oppressive narratives of the colonized subject.

It is important to acknowledge, however, that the indigenous peoples who found themselves bombarded with European imperialism did not take to their colonization easily. As soon as colonialism became an economic, cultural, and political reality, anti-colonial and postcolonial ruptures in thought and action occurred among "colonized" peoples. To underscore this point I quote at length from Ashcroft, Griffiths, and Tiffin (1995):

> European imperialism took various forms in different times and places and proceeded through conscious planning and contingent occurrences. As a result of this complex development something occurred for which the plan of imperial expansion had not bargained: the immensely prestigious and powerful imperial culture found itself appropriated in projects and counter-colonial resistance which drew upon the many indigenous local and hybrid processes of self determination to defy, erode, and sometimes supplant the prodigious power of imperial cultural knowledge. Postcolonial literatures are a result of this interaction between imperial culture and the complex of indigenous cultural practices. As a consequence, postcolonial theory has existed for a long time before that particular name was used to describe it. Once colonized peoples had cause to reflect on and express the tension that ensued from this problematic and contested, but eventually vibrant and powerful mixture of imperial language and local experience, postcolonial "theory" came into being. (p. 1)

In methodological terms, postcolonial theory tends to be dominated by theoretical discourses associated with postmodernity or, in other words, the deconstruction of Derrida, the psychoanalysis of Lacan, or the discourse analysis of Michel Foucault (Macey, 2000). The big names associated with postcolonialism are Said, Spivak, and Bhabha, although Loomba (1998) warns against name-brand theory. Said (1979), for example, draws upon Foucault (1972) and Gramsci (1971) to illuminate the "Othering" of the oriental in Western discourses. Spivak (1999) focuses on subaltern voices of resistance, and Bhabha's (2004) work emphasizes the hybridity and interconnectedness of colonial and marginalized discourses.

Macey (2000) contends that the best work in postcolonial theory has followed the original thesis put forward by Said: that colonial conquests resulted in an attempt to administer colonial subjects through a process of othering, which included the generating of pervasive images of effeminate Indians, savage Africans, and inscrutably sinister Orientals that are so common in the literature of Empire. Mills (1997), however, would contend that postcolonial theory also looks for indigenous resistance to these dominant texts and motifs and, in its best moments, stands as a counternarrative to the dominant positioning of "the Oriental."

There are many important applications of postcolonial theory to the project of critical literacy education with urban youth. Postcolonial theory merges many of the methodological tools of critical postmodern and poststructural theories with the question of culture, making it the most decisively "cultural" of the literary theories. This is ideal for humanities courses, in which students are often forced to encounter dominant texts, many of which reinforce the stereotypical images of the Other that are chronicled in the writings of key postcolonial theorists. Rather than avoid these texts, which is generally impossible but also not advisable in my opinion, teachers and students can employ the tools of postcolonial theory to make sense of these texts as being representative of a larger discourse of marginalization and exclusion.

The work of Said, Spivak, and Bhabha, in particular, is important in that it expands the scope of what counts as literature for the postcolonial theorist. In addition to the classical literary texts, these authors study television, the news media, and all other communications outlets that Western society uses to disseminate information about itself and those that it implicitly classifies as different, alien, foreign, or other.

Postcolonial theory also holds implications for the selection of texts to study in the humanities courses at the secondary level. In addition to the classics of Western civilization such as the texts of Homer, Shakespeare, and Hemingway, there are a host of literary texts, written by subaltern authors, which chronicle the conditions of colonized peoples over the last five hundred years. As part of a critical literacy education, I argue, urban youth should be exposed to the work of intellectuals and theorists such as Fanon, Spivak, Said, and Bhabha. They should also be exposed to novels, poems, and plays of authors such as Salman Rushdie (*Midnight's Children*), Aimé Césaire (*And the Dogs Were Silent*), Jessica Haggerdorn (*Dogeaters*), Isabel Allende (*House of the Spirits*), Pablo Neruda (*Canto General*), and Chinua Achebe (*Things Fall Apart*).

THE AFRICAN-AMERICAN TRADITION

The contemporary educational scholar Theresa Perry comments that, throughout the history of Africans in the Americas, there has been an emphasis on literacy for freedom and freedom for literacy. In an essay that appears in her 2003 text *Young, Gifted, and Black*, Perry traces the biographies of several prominent African-American figures from Frederick Douglass and Harriet Jacobs to Malcolm X and Barbara Jordan, all of whom comment on the role that a critical literacy played in their development as intellectuals and activists. This message is corroborated by the educational historian James Anderson, whose work *The Education of Blacks in the South: 1860–1935* chronicles the extremes to which African-Americans would go during and immediately after slavery in order to receive a literacy education.

The work of Perry and Anderson is important in at least two key respects. First, their work does an excellent job of refuting popular beliefs that African-Americans are not interested in public education. To the contrary, these scholars demonstrate how African-Americans have repeatedly risked their lives and livelihoods in order to gain access to literacies of power. It is not insignificant that the most important decision in the history of the United States Supreme Court, *Brown v. Board of Education*, dealt with the historical educational injustices levied against the African-American community and the right of this population to receive a fair and equitable, integrated literacy education.

The work of Perry and Anderson is also important in that it shows that, for African-Americans, literacy has always been tied to social critique, to uncovering systems of oppression, to access to previously denied discourses, and to power and social change. Its disturbing, then, that African-American scholars are so seldom associated with the critical literacy tradition in the United States when critical literacy has been so central to becoming and being African-American in the United States. In developing my model of critical literacy I would like to consider how African-Americans have discussed the relationships between language, literacy, race, and power in the United States context.

It makes sense to begin with a discussion of the classic slave narratives of the nineteenth century, most notably the writings of Frederick Douglas and Harriet Jacobs. I'll talk more about these texts as important genres of critical writing in chapter 8, but, as part of the African-American tradition, these texts are important in that they demonstrate the cognizant relationship between literacy and freedom from the ideologies of race and slavery. In Douglass' autobiography, he equates his true freedom with his acquisition of literacy. Jacobs' acquisition of literacies of power also made it impossible for her to live under (and against) the dehumanizing conditions of slavery. Without privileging dominant literacies over the local and cultural literacies that the slaves already possessed in abundance, it's important to understand the significance of acquiring dominant literacies to an emancipated worldview. In fact, this is a point on which there is agreement between slave and master. The masters understood the power of literacy; that's why they forbade their slaves to become literate. The slaves understood the power of literacy, and that's why many risked life and limb to acquire it.

During the early twentieth century, the Fisk and Harvard-educated sociologist W. E. B. DuBois emerged as the dominant voice for African-American literacy education. In his 1903 classic *Souls of Black Folk*, DuBois shows his prescience and his understanding of the American psyche when he predicts that the problem of the twentieth century will be the problem of the color line. DuBois begins his text by discussing the problem of double consciousness, which he defines as the African-American self-gaze, the seeing of one's self through the eyes of someone who hates you; being at once African and American; feeling a two-ness and a host of irreconcilable strivings in one tormented soul. DuBois understood implicitly, and made explicit, the relationship between dominant language and the ideology of race embraced by both blacks and whites at the time. He also understood that a critical education could prove revolutionary for African-Americans, not least in the transformation of the consciousness of African-Americans and their relation to the dominant discourses and dominant texts of the time.

During the 1920s large numbers of African-Americans found themselves congregating in northern centers such as New York City, where they had slightly more access to literacy education and the mechanisms of information distribution. This combination of literacy and textual distribution played a major role in ushering in the Harlem Renaissance. Basically the writers and musicians of the period confirmed the fears of the slave owners and the hopes of intellectuals such as Jacobs, Douglas, and DuBois. Once the newly freed slaves acquired dominant literacies, they used these literacies to create texts that were highly critical of the condition of African-Americans. Whether it was the poetry of Langston Hughes or Claude McKay, the novels of Zora Neale Hurston or Jean Toomer, the academic writings of Alaine Locke, or the philosophical and journalistic tracts of Marcus Garvey, it is difficult if not impossible to separate the "critical" literature of the Harlem Renaissance from the project of critical literacy.

In 1933, Carter G. Woodson would write what is probably the most famous treatise on African-American education even some seven decades later. His *Miseducation of the Negro* predates the critical pedagogy of Freire, Henry Giroux, and Peter McLaren by forty years, but it is no less important than these other revolutionary works. The text begins with Woodson's now famous assertion:

> When you control a man's [sic] thinking you do not have to worry about his actions. You do not have to tell him to stand here or go yonder. He will find his "proper place" and stay in it. You do not need to send him to the back door. He will go without being told. In fact, if there is no back door, he will cut one for his own special benefit. His education makes it necessary. (1933/1990, p. xiii)

Woodson's text shows all the ways that "classical" education has removed African-Americans and African peoples from the narratives of science and history. Left without models of intellectualism, miseducated African-

Americans are left to associate intellect and advancement with their white counterparts. The education of African-Americans (even in historically black colleges and universities) becomes a process of de-Africanization and, subsequently, dehumanization. Woodson equates the revised history and racial inferiority that are at the heart of "classical" education with a host of psychological, social, and economic outcomes for the African-American community in the United States at that time.

The intersections between Woodson's scholarship and the project of critical literacy are twofold. First, Woodson joins a long list of scholars who called for a critical reading of the knowledge of the day. Woodson challenges African-Americans to bring a critical reading to the Eurocentric narratives of science and history to which they were exposed. He also calls for a critical self-analysis of the conditions of African-Americans, featuring a linguistic analysis of the language of deficit and dysfunction that prescribes action.

Additionally, though, Woodson outlines a radical program of re-education for African-Americans in which he challenges scholars, educators, and professionals to utilize their critical literacies to re-insert the African-American story into dominant narratives. This project requires African-Americans, for instance, to become astute historians and intellectuals of the highest order. Woodson's message is clear: critique is important, but, by itself, critique is not enough to fundamentally transform the education of African-Americans. What is needed is a praxis of textual and linguistic production that provides future generations of African Americans with counter-texts that they can employ to combat the continued miseducation that proliferates in social institutions such as the media and public schools. For these reasons, many see Woodson as one of the primary architects of African-American history and African-American studies; two disciplines that draw upon critical literacies to fundamentally reconstitute knowledge in the Diaspora and to fundamentally reconstitute the African-American subject as an intellectual, as a product of an intellectual and culturally rich tradition, and as an historical actor and potential agent of change.

Douglass, Jacobs, Hughes, Hurston, Garvey, and Woodson have influenced African-American scholars, artists, and activists, to the present day. In the 1960s Malcolm X exhorted African-Americans to read the dictionary, to understand the connotations of whiteness and blackness that were imbedded in the English language. He also encouraged African-Americans to become students of history in his highly intellectualized portrait of the African-American revolutionary. Along similar lines Black Panthers interpreted Fanon's *Wretched of the Earth* to develop a plan of action for African-Americans in industrial urban centers. One of the primary emphases of their ten-point program included a critical literacy education for urban African-Americans. Angela Davis provided a model of the African-American intellectual activist combining race, gender, and philosophy to articulate an aesthetic for the African-American woman revolutionary. Part of Davis' project consists of un-naming and re-naming, but it's also about producing text, even becoming text as part of a revolutionary movement.

Literary figures such as James Baldwin, Nikki Giovanni, LeRoi Jones, and the Lost Poets ensured that the ethos of African-American literature would continue to be poignant and critical. Musicians such as James Brown used that popular genre to share critical messages with a growing discontented public providing a soundtrack to the Black Power Movement. Today these traditions are upheld and promoted by philosophers such as Cornel West and Henry Louis Gates Jr.; educational scholars such as Theresa Perry, Lisa Delpit, and Gloria Ladson-Billings; and literary figures such as the Nobel Laureate Toni Morrison. These scholars are joined by intellectuals from television, film, and hip-hop music; I will discuss their contributions to critical literacy later in this chapter. Common to all of these writers, thinkers, and activists is an understanding of the power of language and texts, not only as determinants of social reality, but also as the substance of revolutionary transformation.

THE LATIN AMERICAN AND CARIBBEAN TRADITION

There are tremendous overlaps between the work of Latin American and Caribbean scholars and the other movements that I have described (and will describe in this chapter). It is important to note the Caribbean genesis of much anti-colonial scholarship, particularly in the writings of Frantz Fanon and C. L. R. James. It is also important to acknowledge the contributions of Latin American and Caribbean scholars to the postcolonial literary canon. Further, the most widely recognized writer associated with the critical literacy tradition is the Latin American Paulo Freire, who appears in numerous places throughout this text. In addition to the works and words of these scholars, who appear elsewhere in this text, it seems necessary to devote a section to talking about other scholars, particularly the committed poetry of Pablo Neruda, those who have contributed to the Negritude literary movement, and those musicians and artists associated with the roots reggae movement.

Pablo Neruda's Poetry for the People

Gabriel García Márquez proclaimed Pablo Neruda (1904–1973) as the greatest poet of the twentieth century in any language. There is no question that he is the most published poet of the century and the one most quoted. His works have been translated into every major language on the globe and, in his native Latin America, he is nothing short of a literary icon. The notable Argentinean-Cuban revolutionary Ernesto "Che" Guevara cited Neruda's poetry during his now famous trek across the South American continent in the early 1950s and he carried Neruda's poetry with him during the siege in the Sierra Madre Mountains that became the Cuban revolution. Guevara is not the only revolutionary to take a book of Neruda's poetry into the heart of battle.

Certainly for all these reasons and more (including the quality and sheer volume of fifty years of published poetry) Neruda has to be considered as one of the most important poets, not only of the twentieth century, but of all time. Neruda is known for his powerful love poems, and for his amazing use of seemingly simple language to communicate the profound and the sublime; he is also known as one who was unwilling to separate his art from political activism—a decision that would win him fame among the masses of people around the world and also the scorn of the leaders of nations, including his own.

Neruda (born Neftali Reyes) was born in 1904 and raised as a child in Temuco, a small town in southern Chile. In 1921, at the age of seventeen, he fled his home to study and write in the national capital of Santiago. At a young age he achieved fame throughout his homeland as a poetic talent for his love ballads. Neruda used his fame to earn a position as a Chilean consul. Though the position didn't pay much, it was one that allowed him to see a good portion of the world at a young age. It was a position that would take him to the continents of Asia and Europe during key moments of the twentieth century. Through his travels around the globe, Neruda came into direct contact with the suffering of everyday people along with the extravagance and insensitivity of the ruling elite in many of these nations. He also came into contact with the other leading artists of the day who were using their creative talents for political and subversive purposes. He witnessed the struggles of the Spanish Republicans against Franco in the Spanish Civil War, where he ultimately participated with other writers and artists (such as Lorca and Picasso) in using their creative energies to support Spanish resistance to Fascism. Neruda's *España en el Corazón* (Spain in My Heart) is a tribute to the victims of the Spanish Civil War and, in his own words, his first proletarian poetry. Through these experiences, Neruda grew to understand the power of his poetry to move people, to alert them to injustice, and to point toward greater possibilities for the human family.

As Neruda's political involvement began to grow, his writing began to change. He eschewed the esoteric surrealist-inspired writing of some of his early work and learned to write in a way that would impact real people, whom he increasingly began to see as his primary audience. This abrupt and noticeable shift for an already established poet opened Neruda up to criticism from high culture literary types who saw his changing style as simplistic or overly political. Neruda (1977) takes up the subject of the role of the poet and of poetry in his posthumously published *Memoirs*, in which he writes:

> This one thing, where poets publish for other poets, doesn't tempt me, doesn't lure me, only drives me to bury myself deep in nature's woods, before a rock or a wave, far from the publishing houses, from the printed page . . . Poetry has lost its ties with the reader, he's out of reach . . . It has to get him back . . . It has to walk in the darkness and encounter the heart of man, the eyes of woman, the strangers in the streets, those who at twilight or in the middle of the starry night feel the need for at least one line of poetry . . . This visit to the unexpected is worth all the distance covered, everything read, everything learned . . . we have to disappear in the midst of those we don't know, so they will suddenly pick up something of ours from the street, from the sand, from the leaves that have fallen for a thousand years in the same forest . . . and will take up gently the objects we made . . . Only then will we truly be poets . . . In that object poetry will live. (p. 260)

Nowhere is Neruda's attitude toward poetry and the role of the poet more clearly articulated than in his most important, wide-ranging, and overtly political work, *Canto General*. In this epic poem, translated as a General Song, Neruda celebrates the creative forces of nature, his native Chile, indigenous heroes, and the working-class peoples around the world. He also critiques capitalist and Fascist regimes of his time and proclaims the victory of the international Communist revolution. It is significant to mention that Neruda wrote large sections of *Canto General* while in hiding and in exile from his own government, who wanted to persecute him for his political views and for the political tone of his poems (Feinstein, 2004). It is also significant to note that a poet could have this sort of impact on the world of letters and on the lives of everyday people who were struggling in Chile and around the globe.

Neruda's example is an important one to acknowledge in critical literacy education. Generally, when we point to seminal texts for students, we point to the prose of modern or contemporary philosophers. Rarely do we think about the words of the poets. Neruda shows us the power of art, and specifically poetry, an intentionally emotive written genre, to move people to question oppression and to organize for change. For those involved in popular movements, this makes perfect sense, but, in academic circles, the connections are not frequently made. This is unfortunate as Neruda's poetry for the people provides us with texts to add to the critical literacy bibliography while he also provides a model for critical literacy production. I will revisit this theme of production and genre throughout the book, because it is so important to challenge the existing ideologies concerning textual production in literacy education. My own views will be quite clear; I see a need for increased attention to fiction and new media texts both in what counts as a worthy text to study and in what counts as appropriate texts to create in the context of a literacy classroom.

Negritude Movement

The Negritude movement's foundations are in the work of the French Afro-Caribbean writer Aimé Césaire, who demanded that the existing establishment of European intellectuals accommodate him and the other emergent African-Diaspora literary talents of the time. The movement also served as a clarion call to other African peoples around the world to view themselves and their cultural productions with pride. Negritude's progenitors directly challenged Eurocentric notions of intellectual and Eurocentric aesthetic ideals that predominated at the time. The Negritude movement intended to celebrate a black culture that had been dismissed by many as primitive and barbaric (Macey, 2000). Frantz Fanon commented that it was only with the appearance of Césaire that negritude or blackness became a condition that would be assumed with pride by a French West Indian.

Though African-American writers of the Harlem Renaissance influenced the Negritude movement, its true origins lie with surrealist-inspired African and West Indian students who were active in Paris in the 1930s. Its influence grew in the 1940s and 1950s with the beginnings of French decolonization and the sanction of a leading intellectual, Jean-Paul Sartre, who hailed Negritude poetry as the only true revolutionary poetry of the day.

Negritude offers important contributions to a conception of critical literacy in that its rhetorical moves are intellectual, but they are emotive. Critical literacy demands that its practitioners take a sophisticated and complex view of the world and of knowledge. It is also important, though, that students, teachers, and researchers understand the importance of pride and of cultural celebration, particularly as it concerns members of ethnically marginalized groups. Literatures should be critiqued using a variety of historical, social, and cultural lenses, but oppressed literatures need to be excavated and promoted with a sense of pride and purpose as well. Further, students and teachers need to envision themselves as authors of these culturally and ethnically affirming texts, and intellectuals need to understand that this production is itself a form of critical praxis.

Reggae Music and Culture

> slaves were uprooted, detribalized, denamed, dehumanized . . . Through it
> all music was the one means through which the slave held onto the past and
> endured the present. Any discussion of the blues, the calypso, the reggae must
> begin at this point . . . Of them all, reggae is the most explicitly revolutionary.
> It is commentary; satirical at times; often cruel; but its troubadours are not
> afraid to speak of love, of hope, of ideals, of justice, of new things and new
> forms. It is this assertion of revolutionary possibility that sets reggae apart.
> (Manley, 2004, pp. 218–219)

As with hip-hop music and culture, reggae music is a worldwide phenomenon
with tremendous influence in the Caribbean and the United States. The roots
of Jamaica's modern music are in rebellion and independence (Bradley, 2001).
Reggae music specifically is a genre born, in part, out of a combination of
the rising influence of the Rastafarian religion, the economic and civil unrest
in the post-independence period, and the intense pride in separation from a
colonial power (Britain). It is, therefore, a (chronologically) postcolonial and
(ideologically) anti-colonial musical form. It is also an explicitly pedagogical
musical form whose artists know how to combine lyrical mastery and satirical
social commentary with a brilliant defiance that is both entertaining and
pedagogical (Cooper, 2004).

Within the reggae tradition, I focus on the specific tradition of roots
reggae, which took hold of the genre in the late 1960s and early 1970s. The
radical social climate of the 1960s internationally and the election in Jamaica
of the leftist People's National Party created a climate for the production of
a more explicitly spiritual and political reggae music (Bradley, 2001) most
notably spread through the lyrics of the international spokesperson and
reggae ambassador Bob Marley, hailed by Jacobson (2004) as:

> one of the most eloquent artists of social unrest in the second half of the twentieth
> century. Marley became an icon in what used to be called the Third World through
> his exhortation to "Get up, stand up" and his across-the-board condemnation of
> "de downpressers." (p. 209)

Other important artists of the initial "Roots and Culture" phase include
Burning Spear, The Mighty Diamonds, and the DJ Lee Perry.

The twenty-first century has witnessed a return to roots reggae in Jamaica
through contemporary artists such as Buju Banton, Cappleton, Cocoa Tea,
and Luciano. There are at least five tenets of roots reggae past and present
that lead me to classify it as a rebel music: reggae's roots are in rebellion and

independence; roots reggae music is both a postcolonial and an anti-colonial musical form; roots reggae music is explicitly pedagogical; roots reggae music is explicitly spiritual; and roots reggae music is explicitly political.

An in-depth analysis of roots reggae discourse reveals a number of salient critical themes including the Black Holocaust (also known as slavery); the Rastafarian religion; African heritage; colonization/de-colonization of the mind; emancipation; economic injustice; revolution; black heroes and heroines; African/Diaspora history and culture; cultural pride; urban decay; and the revolutionary potential of roots reggae music. Many of these themes are exemplified in this passage from a popular roots reggae text:

> The whole of the nation/Living in these tenements,/Crying and applying to their council/For assistance every day/Now that their tribulation so sad/Now that their environment so bad/High rise concrete/No back yard for their children to play/ African children/I wonder do they know where you're coming from,/African chil-dren/In a concrete situation (Aswad, "African-Children")

What stands out immediately is that the artists refer to Jamaican urban residents as African children; a population that ostensibly has been relocated in the Americas for four centuries. Time, for these artists, does not diminish the spiritual and cultural connections to an African homeland that are fostered through the Rastafarian religion and reggae music. Next, the penultimate phrase poses a question to the listeners in the African Diaspora: do you know where you're coming from? The critique is clearly one of separation on many levels. Most obviously, there is a geographical separation of several thousand miles and a chronological separation of four hundred years. More significantly, though, the artists are identifying an ideological separation as they link the lack of knowledge about African histories and cultures to current conditions on the island (and indeed the region). The remainder of the passage entails a sociological critique of contemporary conditions of urban decay that define the "situations" of many urban Jamaicans; situations caused by the physical, historical, and ideological separation from cultural roots. The remedy is clear: learn about the history and reestablish these vital links for the future of African Diaspora peoples. The musical text is poignant, yet a pedagogical and inspirational one, in which reggae artists are positioned as intellectuals,

Roots reggae is informative to the critical philosophy project in that it presents a model of street intellectualism rooted in a critical reading of an oppressive society and active resistance against that oppression. Further, roots reggae encourages its listeners to become engaged activists and cultural historians who educate themselves about disregarded values and histories. The reggae songs themselves exist as critical texts to be devoured and studied by popular audiences en route to higher consciousness. Given that its core listeners and producers have always been impoverished members of the African Diaspora, roots reggae serves as an important link between Diaspora popular culture and critical theory. The reggae texts themselves, I argue, should be considered as part of the critical canon along with other powerful literatures such as the poetry of Neruda and Nikki Giovanni, the corpus of the Harlem Renaissance, or the songs of the Civil Rights movement. I would go further to suggest that no contemporary critical theory is complete without acknowledging the contributions of new media philosophers who have emerged from youth subcultures. It is to these philosophers that I will now turn.

NEW MEDIA PHILOSOPHERS AND ARCHITECTS OF CONTEMPORARY YOUTH SUBCULTURES

Several years ago—not so long ago really—when enrolled as a graduate student at the University of California at Berkeley, I was charged with putting together a list of texts that I thought were central to the critical tradition as part of my qualifying examination for doctoral candidacy. In addition to many of the scholars that I have already mentioned, I included a few exemplars from youth popular culture. For instance, I included alongside Marx and Horkheimer hip-hop artists such as Public Enemy's Chuck D or Lauryn Hill of the Refugee Camp. Needless to say, my usually progressive dissertation committee was not sold on the worthiness of these artists to be included among the intellectual giants that were also on the list. Fortunately, I was able to win the day, earning the right to include popular artists alongside the traditional intellectuals for my comprehensive exam list. Here I am doing it again.

And I am doing it for a reason. The rationale that I gave to my committee (and I still agree with) is simple: I told them that the hip-hop artists and filmmakers that I included on my list were the most viable social theorists of urban America. Whereas a well-written book by a notable intellectual would sell several thousand copies, an album from the Refugee Camp might sell several million copies in addition to receiving constant airplay on video shows of MTV and VH-1. Along the same lines, a documentary film by Michael Moore or Morgan Spurlock (director of *Super Size Me*) might be watched by tens of millions of viewers. When we look for today's critical social philosophers, in addition to the literary and university ranks, we need to look at the creative forces behind contemporary music, television, and film. This group would include musical artists such as Bono of U2 and Lauryn Hill of the Refugee Camp and filmmakers such as Spike Lee and Michael Moore who use lyrics and moving images to provide substantive commentary on the human condition, particularly as it relates to the social, material, economic, and political conditions of urban America. No contemporary survey of critical philosophical is complete without including the work of new media philosophers and architects of contemporary youth subcultures within this "Othered" critical tradition.

Well, what are the new media philosophers and musicians and filmmakers who are the architects of urban popular subcultures telling us about the social, cultural, political, and economic conditions of urban America? I have argued that these postindustrial urban intellectuals are using hip-hop lyrics, websites, and digital film to articulate the inequities of contemporary society, to increase public consciousness, and to advocate for resistance against the status quo. These philosophers are explaining urban culture making links between socioeconomic conditions, the state apparatuses of the criminal justice system and schools that promote cultures of oppression, and inequitable outcomes for young people today. Consider the impact of the recent slate of critical documentaries that have taken on the United States Government and major corporations. Michael Moore's controversial documentary *Fahrenheit 9/11* critiques the 2000 presidential election and the subsequent involvement of the United States in Afghanistan and Iraq. The 2004 selection of *Fahrenheit 9/11* for the Palme d'Or prize at the Cannes Film Festival legitimized the politico-philosophical filmmaking style of Michael Moore, who employs humor and the techniques of documentary filmmaking along with meticulous research and a critical lens to say something powerful about the workings of power in contemporary American society. Michael Moore's documentaries give language to the rage and frustration that many Americans feel. They are inspirational even as they are pedagogical for contemporary intellectuals and activists. They are also intensely entertaining to consumers of popular media and examples of the new media "edutainment," entertaining even as they educate a new generation of activists and organizers.

An important lesson of the history of philosophy is that you may not always find the elite philosophers in academic philosophy departments; at no time has this been as true as it is today. When analyzing texts such as *Roger and Me*, *Bowling for Columbine*, *The Naked Truth*, and *Fahrenheit 9/11*, one can only claim Michael Moore as a legitimate and important contemporary philosopher. In these times of new media communications, it is as likely these days to find critical philosophers operating behind a camera or a microphone as it is to find them behind a lectern or an oak desk in a university office. This is not meant as to disrespect academicians so much as it is to acknowledge the intellectual work that goes into critical film and music-making today.

Along these same lines, the 2004 documentary film *Super Size Me* takes on the major food corporations as the protagonist-filmmaker invites the audience into his personal world as he undertakes a thirty-day binge of McDonald's fast food that sends him to the hospital and almost to his death. No one will question the power of these two films or the impact they have had on informing public opinion of the war in Iraq or the fast food industry. Few, though, would associate these critical film texts with the 2500-year Western philosophical tradition, a connection I believe needs to be made if we are going to accurately locate our philosophers of the present and the future.

Hip-hop culture is also a site of urban, postindustrial philosophy. Most adults view hip-hop as a problematic genre of music filled with images of violence, misogyny, and conspicuous consumption rather than as a complex culture of resistance, celebration, and social critique. However, most marginal or non-participants in the culture are only exposed to the music of Top Forty hits played on the radio or seen through MTV and the only news they hear about hip-hop is negative, pathologizing, and regulated by conservative, mainstream news media. This huge misconception on the part of the larger public is attributable to the co-optation of rap music by the corporate executives of the culture industries to the exclusion of hip-hop's other elements. Those who experience hip-hop via MTV and the evening news miss out on the sophisticated, sometimes contradictory, and multifaceted nature of the culture. Hip-hop, first and foremost, is a culture of urban youth production that emerged in urban America only a generation ago, yet has become an international force that is ascendant among musical genres (Farley, 1999). Hip-hop is also a vibrant culture practiced in many activities that extend beyond rap music. Before we go any further, it is important to re-theorize and reclaim this term and explicate the culture that produces and exists alongside the music

Hip-hop is a worldwide phenomenon with extensive influence over youth in the United States and the Caribbean, particularly urban and Africa Diaspora youth. The old-school artist and founder of the Temple of Hiphop KRS One asserts:

> Hip-hop is a collective consciousness. It is generally expressed through the unique elements of Breakin, Emceeing, Graffiti Art, Deejayin, Beatboxin, Street Fashion, Street Language, Street Knowledge, and Street Entrepreneurialism (Hip-hop's nine elements). . . . Hip-hop is practiced as an alternative behavior capable of transforming subjects and objects in an attempt to manifest a collective consciousness. Hip-hop is a state of mind. (www.templeofhiphop.org)

There is no question that the proliferation of hip-hop music and culture is a mixed bag. While more people than ever are attracted to the music and culture, they have also been co-opted and marketed by mainstream corporate interests that have highlighted the gangsta image, the objectification of women, and, of course, the ideals of capitalist consumption. It is also important to note, however, that this critique is levied as strongly from artists on the inside as it is from adults and conservatives on the outside of the culture. These artists, along with prominent hip-hop historians (Dagbovie, 2005; George, 1998; Light, 1999) insist that, at its core, hip-hop is a social commentary, a call to action, and a celebration of urban youth language and culture (Alim, 2006; Spady *et al.*, 2006): what I have termed critical hip-hop. From these histories and counter-critiques emerge important components that qualify critical hip-hop as a rebel music.

First, hip-hop originated, at least in part, as a critique of postindustrialism; its producers chronicling and lamenting the economic and structural conditions that had strained life and limited financial opportunities for those who hail from inner city ghettos. Hip-hop culture has also existed as a righteous voice of resistance against poverty, injustice, racism, police brutality, and an inequitable educational system, to name a few (George, 1998). Those who see themselves as producers of critical hip-hop also view their charge as a pedagogical one. KRS One's 1990 album entitled *Edutainment* serves as a model for critical hip-hop artists who view themselves as public entertainers and as public pedagogues. Classic artists such as X-Clan (*To the East, Blackwards*) and contemporary artists such as Lauryn Hill send messages pertaining to closer ties with an African homeland or positive messages about young black girls learning to love and re-educate themselves (*Miseducation of Lauryn Hill*).

There is also an element of critical hip-hop that is concerned with social activism. Throughout its thirty-year history, hip-hop artists have been using lyrics to promote political messages and even political action. Public Enemy's role in the late 1980s of consciousness-raising transformed rap into a political tour de force. KRS One's "Free Mumia" and Lauryn Hill's "Rebel" are good examples of how hip-hop artists and songs have fostered social activism; encouraging listeners to see themselves as agents of change who can fight against injustice and oppression in the world.

A close analysis of hip-hop discourses reveals a number of salient themes including violence and crime in urban ghettos; urban poverty; Black Power movements; corruption and greed in American government; racism in American society; connections with an African "motherland"; the importance of acquiring a critical consciousness; indoctrination via school and the media;

youth resistance; the history of hip-hop; and the continual struggle for the heart and soul of hip-hop culture. Many of these themes, for example, are found in the following verse from a popular hip-hop track:

> The subconscious psychology that you use against me,/If I lose control will send me to the penitentiary./Such as Alcatraz, or shot up like al Hajj Malik Shabazz./High class get bypassed while my ass gets harassed./And the fuzz treat bruh's like they manhood never was./And if you too powerful, you get bugged like Peter Tosh and Marley was./And my word does nothing against the feds,/so my eyes stay red as I chase crazy baldheads,/WORD UP. (Refugee Camp, "The Beast")

The analysis offered by the artists is consistent with a Gramscian analysis of dominant hegemony, what the artists refer to here as "subconscious psychology" proliferated via media and educational discourses. The artists also make an explicit link between these dominant discourses and the actions of contemporary urban residents, many of whom (over a million in the United States alone) find themselves incarcerated. Explanations for the actors and the system of incarceration are subjects of complex sociological analysis; making connections between structural inequalities, dominant discourses, and the everyday actions of marginalized populations, many of whom have voluntarily committed criminal acts. Gramsci asks how majority populations in Western democracies submit to conditions that disserve their self-interests without resorting to revolution; the Refugee Camp takes a similar line in asking how a million African-Americans have submitted to a set of conditions that have led to their incarceration.

Next, the artists link the struggles and violence of their contemporaries with those of the Black Power movement, specifically the (government-sponsored) assassination of Malcolm X (an Afro-American with Caribbean roots). They then transition to the inequitable treatment of the urban poor while staying with the theme of the United States as a repressive police state. Here, their work provides a critique of the social theory of Gramsci, who contended that hegemony had replaced forced coercion of the police state. From history and the actions of CIA and FBI we know these activities happen in tandem; Refugee Camp's urban sociological analyses are more accurate than Gramsci's. The verse concludes with a more explicit critique of the way that the American intelligence community handles those who have become "too powerful" (read too critical). It is interesting that these hip-hop artists cite two roots reggae artists, Peter Tosh and Bob Marley, as primary targets of United States' surveillance. In one succinct, hard-hitting verse, these young artists have demonstrated the complex and poignant social critiques that are frequently disseminated through critical hip-hop, yet rarely acknowledged or valued by larger publics who consistently and categorically denigrate the entire genre and its practitioners.

It is also important to note that this is not a genre focused on deterministic analysis or the denigration of urban culture. Hip-hop artists also reveal urban culture as a site of struggle and resistance and their lyrics are frequently celebratory of an ethos of independence of social norms. Critical artists within the culture have helped to theorize contemporary postindustrial urban subculture while pushing forward on neo-Marxist analyses of alienation and other outcomes associated with capitalist mode of production. I will talk at more length about these philosophers in chapters on popular culture, media literacy, and cyberactivism; but it is important for now to position these artist-activists as philosophers in the tradition of Socrates, who ranted through the streets of Athens 2500 years ago with many of the same observations of the people of his time.

OTHERED NARRATIVES OF CRITICAL LITERACY AND THEIR IMPORTANCE TO LITERACY EDUCATION

There are many similarities between the "Othered" scholars featured in this chapters and the architects of critical theory that I covered in chapter 2; both groups bring a skepticism toward knowledge, an understanding of the relationships between knowledge and power, and an understanding of the workings of dominant knowledge systems to oppress the many for the benefit of the few. Scholars from both traditions also understand the nature of ideology and the power of critical consciousness; that is, when everyday people come to a knowledge or understanding of their conditions, they are more likely to be able to confront and transform those conditions. Critical scholars from the Western tradition and these "Othered" traditions have each theorized the transformative agent as someone who understands the workings of power at an intellectual level and is able to translate that intellectual energy into action for change.

There are important contributions that scholars from these "Othered" traditions can offer to the corpus of critical thought with implications for the field of inquiry and more specifically for our theorizing of critical literacy education in urban American contexts. First and foremost these scholars make central the reality of race and racism. It is possible to infer a racial critique of society from reading critical scholars such as Karl Marx or Antonio Gramsci, but the centrality of the issue to understanding the workings of Western societies is largely missing from their class-centered analyses of society. It is only from reading the likes of Fanon or Spivak that one begins to understand the social, psychological, and economic impacts of five hundred years of racialization on Western society.

A critical analysis of race in American society is important to any empowering literacy project in America's urban schools which are, for the most part, largely non-white. The Council of Great City Schools reports that twenty-two of the nation's largest twenty-five school districts are majority non-white. Numerous research reports also reveal the continued significance of race to understanding academic achievement in America. According to recent reports put out by the National Center for Educational Statistics, white students continue to out-perform their African-American, Latino, and Native-American counterparts, even when class is held as a constant (USDE, 2005). The only way to fully come to terms with the racial achievement gap in literacy education is to understand the historical and contemporary significance of race to the construction of knowledge and the subject in Western society.

These scholars are also important in the models of praxis that they provide, either in their scholarship or in their lives. The anti-colonialists, the postcolonial theorists, the African-American and Caribbean scholars, and the intellectuals from contemporary media and youth subcultures offer an energy and urgency that resonate with educational scholars and other parties interested in transforming urban literacy education. Whether they are fleeing the shackles of slavery, reconfiguring approaches to the literary canon, introducing the world to new genres of music, or contemplating the revolution of a continent, these scholars are all doing something proactive as they are also thinking and engaging in intellectual activity. And so must we, as literacy educators and scholars, do something as we engage in important intellectualizing and reflection of our critical literacy practice. The students and their families and communities deserve no less; and nothing less will work to confront the considerable challenges that we face in the process.

I hope that I have shown these two chapters to be not detours from, but foundations for what is to follow in this book. To say one is committed to "critical" work in literacy education is not to say something simple, but something profound. For critical literacy educators in urban America have placed themselves within a longstanding global tradition of intellectualizing and action of the highest order. In what follows I will play out several examples of how these critical foundations might translate into literacy practice with urban adolescents in classrooms, in communities, in special programs, and via critical media consumption and production.

4

Teaching Popular Culture in an Urban Secondary English Classroom

THE CURRENT TERRAIN OF ENGLISH EDUCATION IN SECONDARY SCHOOLS

The dominant practice in secondary English classrooms remains the teaching of classical literature via a New Critical approach in which the text is seen as preeminent and the literature teacher serves as the diviner of meaning, judging how well students are able to arrive at the correct interpretation of a literary text (Appleman, 2000, p. 4). It is important to historicize the New Critical approach to literature if we are to understand its ascendance and its almost doctrinaire sway on the imagination of secondary literacy teachers in the English language arts. Almost by chance, the rise of New Critical approaches to textual analysis proliferated just as the discipline of "English" as we know it emerged as a mainstay on college campuses in the early portion of the twentieth century (Scholes, 1998). One can only consider the rapid and complete ascendancy of New Critical approaches to literature and the primary use of literature itself as a revolution in language study, quickly displacing philology and rhetoric, which had been dominant for centuries in the Western tradition. This rapid ascendancy becomes important as we begin to consider, for many historically and socially valid reasons, multiple logics for the secondary literacy classroom that supplant the hegemony of traditional literature instruction.

This is not to advocate for the end of literature pedagogy in English classrooms. Many thoughtful scholars before me have advocated for literature instruction on philosophical and humanistic terms as an integral part of a curriculum aimed at the development of complete and tolerant human beings (Langer, 1995; Scholes, 1998). Though I would argue for a broader adolescent literacy curriculum that included new media texts (Alvermann, 2001; Buckingham, 2003; Mahiri, 1998), and a broader definition of what counts as literature (Eagleton, 1983), I would not want to eliminate novels, poetry, and plays from the English language arts curriculum; it is not a question of whether to teach literature but what literature and how. The need then becomes to find methods of approaching literature that are more consonant with the goals of a critical literacy education. One approach to a critical English language arts instruction would include the use of critical literary theories to unpack canonical and contemporary literary texts.

Critical literary theories are analyses of canonical and contemporary works that extend beyond common sense interpretations to reveal the multiple ways that texts create meaning and shape human identities (Culler, 2000). Critical literary theories are subversive, because they call authority (of the author or the text) into question (Bonnycastle, 1996). Critical literary theories position the reader in a different relation to texts, not as a subordinated passive reader trying to divine an ultimate meaning, rather as an agent empowered to read upon and against the text (Scholes, 1986). Critical literary theories not only help develop readers who are able to critique social structures and cultural practices; they can also help students to know themselves better and participate as more actualized tolerant beings in the human family. Critical literary theories are related to critical literacies in that they also enable students to discuss relations between literature texts and ideals and values in the dominant society (Eagleton, 1983) while coming to a better understanding of their own humanity. Finally, it is important to understand that the process of using critical literary theories to deconstruct texts is an act of critical textual production in and of itself (Barthes, 1975a).

Writing exists as a second dominant component of the English language arts curriculum. Although it does not share the pedestal with reading and responding to literature, the teaching of writing plays a prominent role in the conceptualization of the discipline. In addition to creating independent readers, English teachers are also charged with preparing writers who are able to create expository texts in grammatically correct standard language. Writing is an essential literacy skill for personal and interpersonal communication, for professional membership and for civic life; those who cannot write must operate within the same social, economic, and political constraints as non-readers. For these reasons, writing is a central component of language arts instruction at the K-12 level, and writing courses are even mandatory at the university level for all students regardless of major or future career interests.

For most of the past generation, writing instruction has been dominated by the process approach that builds upon the cognitive tradition in psychology (Villanueva, 2003). Within the process approach, students begin by brainstorming ideas and move to rough drafts that are continually revised after receiving feedback from peers and teachers in individual and small group conferences (Atwell, 1998; Elbow, 1973; Murray, 1972/2003; Villanueva, 2003). Donald Murray represents a cohort of scholars in the early 1970s that challenged teachers to consider the teaching of writing as a process and not a product. Murray (2003, p. 4) divides process into three phases: pre-writing, writing, and rewriting. Pre-writing, which takes eighty-five percent of the writer's time, is everything that happens before the writing of the first draft. This could include everything from washing the dishes to making an outline of the desired piece. Writing is the act of producing the first draft. Rewriting involves the reconsideration of the draft in terms of content and substance. In the 1980s, Nancie Atwell's *In the Middle* served to popularize the practice of the writer's workshop with secondary classroom teachers. In Atwell's writer's workshop, which draws upon many of Murray's ideas about the writing process, students brainstorm together, read drafts of each other's work, and have individual and small group conferences with the writing teacher.

In the field of composition studies, however, the hegemony of the writing process is increasingly challenged by post-process theories that are more centered upon sociocultural approaches to writing instruction (Kastman Breuch, 2003; Kent, 1999). These theorists and educators imagine writing as much more fluid and dynamic than the straightforward cognitive model of the writing process as articulated by Murray and Atwell. In this vein, Kastman Breuch writes:

> Many post-process scholars, largely influenced by postmodernists and anti-foun-dationalist perspectives, suggest that the process paradigm has reduced the writing act to a series of codified phases that can be taught. These critics suggest that process pedagogy simply offers us another foundational explanation of writing. (p. 97)

These critiques of the writing process are important for a number of reasons. First, they help us to move beyond the idea of a single sequentially ordered set of activities that lead one to become a writer. Additionally they open up spaces for sociocultural theories of writing that treat the process of becoming a writer as a cultural practice in which beginners are apprenticed through interactions with experts and texts produced serve some authentic purpose. The yielding of process approaches to writing also opens up space to consider the act of writing (and the teaching of writing) through critical lenses.

Critical scholars have only recently entered into these discussions concerning the purpose and "processes" of writing instruction. These scholars have been contending for changes in the purpose of writing from producing grammatically correct texts, or writing to make an arbitrary argument, to writing as an act of social justice (Benson, 2002). I consider myself as very much influenced by these post-process and critical approaches to writing praxis in secondary schools. Though we cannot abandon the essentials of the writing process as laid out by Murray, it is important to push on the ideal of a single process, it is important to consider the multiple ways that students can apprentice as writers, and, most importantly, writing needs to be further theorized as an empowering literacy practice. I will say more throughout the book about writing as an act of freedom. I will also talk at length about a critical literacy education that is first and foremost concerned with critical textual production. In this chapter and in later chapters, I will attempt to show how this critical textual production manifests in classroom and non-traditional school settings like a critical research seminar for urban teens. I should say, though, that even with the changes at the avant-garde of writing instruction, in practice, the words of Applebee ring true: even though these changes are lurking on the horizon, much of English instruction has not changed, most classrooms focus on literature much more than they do on writing, and most students do not receive even the process approach to writing instruction. In the critical literacy framework that I advocate, all of that would change.

What is the relationship between writing instruction and critical literacy? In any empowering theory of writing instruction, students still need to understand the mechanics and use of language, so there is a relation between academic literacies and critical literacies. However, academic writing is promoted through participation in meaningful communities of practice. Further, within a critical theory of writing instruction, even those texts that emerge from the classroom have a purpose and audience much larger than the teacher or the classroom: students produce texts that can change the world. Critical textual production also pushes the genres of representation to include popular, poetic, and multimedia texts as valuable texts in the literacy classroom. I argue that secondary literacy classrooms need to consider critical literacy on all of these fronts. We need to reconsider the reasons that students write in our classrooms, the ways that they learn how to produce these texts, the nature (genres) of the texts produced, and what happens to these texts once they are produced.

There are certainly other components of critical English instruction in addition to the teaching of reading and writing, though these "language arts" seem to garner the most attention within the discipline. In other places

(Morrell, 2005) I have argued for a critical English education that also pays close attention to the disciplines of critical linguistics, new literacy studies, ethnic and cultural studies, women's studies, and new media studies. As the world becomes an increasingly smaller, heteroglossic, and intercultural "global village"; as technological transformations impact communicative competencies; and as questions of culture, gender, and power anchor conversations about humanity and core democratic values—any discipline that deals, at heart, with language and texts must encompass a conversation of these seminal issues. In what follows, I briefly outline how a critical literacy framework in a secondary English classroom might encompass the most recent work in these respective fields.

CRITICAL LANGUAGE STUDIES

A critical English education demands that we offer our secondary students a historical and conceptual overview of language studies and language education that includes classical and contemporary rhetorical and philological approaches. There is a need to examine how twentieth-century philosophers of language such as Wittgenstein (2001a) and Bakhtin have theorized the uses of language in the modern world. In our courses, we need to look to work of sociolinguists such as Labov (1972), Smitherman (1999), Hymes (1974) and Gee (1996), who have investigated how language is practiced in social and cultural contexts. A critical English education should also turn to linguists and poststructural philosophers such as Foucault (1972), Althusser, Pecheux, and Fairclough (1995), who have examined the role of language and discourse in the creation of the subject and the maintenance of dominant ideologies. I encourage teacher educators to consider how rhetoric and philology can form the central corpus of language education at the secondary level, giving adolescents access to these same discourses. Gee (1999) suggested that a powerful strategy for literacy education would be to make students social theorists of social languages. I agree that allowing students the language to make sense of the ideological nature of language in the United States could go a long way to promoting navigational strategies and cross-cultural understanding while also increasing language and literacy skills.

Similarly, Fairclough (1995) argues that there is an intimate relationship between people's critical language awareness and the development of their own language capabilities and practices. Given that a key component of critical pedagogy is the raising of consciousness (Freire, 1970), a critical English education that forefronts inquiry into the relationships between language, literacy, culture, and power can make students and teachers conscious of the various uses of language and literacy in society while also developing skills needed to facilitate academic achievement (Morrell, 2005).

New Literacy Studies

The past twenty years have witnessed the revolution of the sociocultural framework of the New Literacy Studies (NLS), a sub-field which seeks to expand and challenge the prevailing concepts of literacy that underlie much classroom instruction. Key theorists such as Street (1995) and Barton and Hamilton (2000) critique autonomous models of literacy and argue instead for the existence of multiple culturally informed, socially situated literacies. Their fellow literacy theorists de Castell and Luke (1983) further argue that literacies are also tied to existing power relations. I advocate that English educators borrow from NLS to argue for the practice of ethnographies of literacy; that is, investigative work to determine how adolescents are literate as members of various out-of-school cultural communities. Moll (2000) and Barton (2000) have each provided examples in which ethnographies of literacy have played a prominent role in the preparation of English educators. NLS opens up spaces for consideration of multiple literacy practices outside of schools as points for connection with academic instruction. In my own work (Morrell, 2004b), for example, I draw heavily from NLS to make the case that teachers can draw upon urban youth's literacy practices related to popular culture to promote academic and critical literacies. There is also space in a critical English education for secondary students to function as ethnographers of language and literacy. I have engaged in classroom practice and conducted research that shows the empowering literacies associated with apprenticing youth as researchers of languages, communities, and cultures (Morrell, 2004a).

TESOL

With the growing number of English language learners entering America's classrooms, English educators need to be proactive in the area of Teaching English to Speakers of Other Languages (TESOL) as well. A critical English education should confront the politics of language learning, for speakers of non-standard dialects as well as speakers of other languages. It should also strongly advocate for students' right to communicate in their primary language (see Conference on College Composition and Communication, 1974). Critical English educators should also help teachers and students to develop language to understand the cultural and political ramifications of learning Standard English. Ideally the English education community would be out in front of the next Ebonics issue and would be mobilized to prevent passage of "Unz-like" initiatives that seek to end bilingual education.[1] A critical English education would see these issues as relevant, if not central to the discipline.

Cultural, Ethnic, and Gender Studies

Though cultural studies, ethnic studies, and gender studies are not normally associated with English education, I would argue that they are foundational to my conception of a critical English education. For, if we acknowledge the centrality of language to our development as raced, gendered, classed beings, then we must also consider the possibilities for English education to create spaces for the development of resistant and empowered identities. In the electives that we require for preservice English teachers, in our methods courses, in professional development, and in our recommendations for secondary English content, I contend that we need to ensure greater dialogue with these discourses. Part of the conception of a critical English education is considering who should be invited to the party. I have endeavored, in research and practice, to include scholars from these fields.

A major issue in English education concerns what "counts" as literature. The concept, one that is central to English education, is also one that is implicitly understood, but rarely defined. As a former English major and graduate student in English education, I can never remember the word being defined. In my own studies, I have come to understand that the term has changed in definition over time, particularly with the rise of the study of fiction at the secondary and postsecondary levels. Literature used to mean anything written; so conceivably one could study the literature on stem cell research or social movements. Over time, however, literature has come to be associated with fiction, and with fiction that has been sanctioned as meritorious.

This is extremely problematic when it comes to text selection and expanding the parameters of the discipline to include topics such as ethnic, racial, and gender studies. It is difficult, even, for teachers to make the case for the addition of new fictional texts in their curricula. Looking back upon

---

[1] In 1998 Ron Unz sponsored Proposition 227 (also known as the Unz Initiative), which sought to eliminate bilingual instruction in California schools. California voters passed the initiative. Arizona voters passed a similar initiative, Proposition 203 (English for the Children), in 2000.

Arthur Applebee's (1974) extensive surveying of English teachers reveals that the practices of English classrooms changed very little over the decades of the 1960s to the 1990s. When one considers how the world changed in those intervening decades, including the social upheavals and the accompanying literature, I find that quite shocking.

I should contextualize these comments by stating that I do not advocate for the elimination of classic literary texts from secondary English education. I do think, however, that there needs to be space in these classrooms for students to study diverse anti-colonial and postcolonial fictional texts, and students should be exposed to non-fictional literatures that deal with race, class, gender, oppression, freedom, and revolution. In chapter 5 I will show how students transformed their reading of critical social theory into sophisticated critical research projects on race, class, and educational inequality in urban America. Without expanding the scope of what counts as literature, such projects would not have been possible.

Media Studies

A critical English education also demands an examination of changing literacies in the new media age (Gee, 2003; Kress, 2003; Lankshear and Knobel, 2003). As new media predominate and transform the nature of our communication and our lives, there must be an explicit focus on media studies and media pedagogy in English education (Durham and Kellner, 2000; Kellner, 1995). We need to prepare our preservice teachers by examining the emergent discourse of media and cultural studies, noting how scholars from Adorno (2002) to Hall *et al.* (1996) have analyzed film, television, music, and the electronic media. We also need to prepare them by opening up spaces to consider media literacy pedagogy as media production, analyzing, for example, how scholars and pedagogues have worked with high school students with desktop video production and uses of digital rhetoric.

This chapter examines the critical teaching of English in secondary education through the analysis of data collected through six years of instruction in an urban classroom in northern California. I begin with an introduction to North High, the site of these interventions, which took place between 1993 and 1999, the years I worked at the school as an English teacher. I then explain the relationship that formed in my pedagogy and research between critical literacy and popular culture. In the majority of the chapter, I look at classroom units that explore the connections between popular culture and critical literacy. These units include the study of youth violence, critical poetry and hip-hop culture, popular film, violence in society, attitudes toward

AIDS, and the ills of urban education. In an examination of these units, I try to demonstrate where students acquire the critical reading, writing, and language skills needed for successful navigation of academic discourses and the literacy skills required of an engaged citizenship in a multimodal multicultural democracy.

LITERACY AND POPULAR CULTURE

As a secondary English teacher, I was initially appalled by the disconnect that existed between the students' out of school literacies and the world of the literacy classroom. For example, the students' literate practices that were part of their everyday participation in home, community, and popular cultures were not reflected in their performance in academic contexts. The same students who read magazines cover to cover, memorized song lyrics, played video games, wrote e-mails and web logs, and text-messaged friends on cell phones were also completely disengaged from the literacies of school. Of course I did not enter into the classrooms at North High with a well-formulated research question about critical literacy education and popular culture; nor did I possess as strong a sense of the problem statement as I just articulated. I was twenty-three years old and I merely had a strong belief that students possessed brilliance and passion that were being neither acknowledged nor accessed inside of literacy classrooms. The results of the failure to connect were academic failure and complete disinvestment from academic life. It was this strong belief and frustration at the academic failure and consequences of that failure that led me to study language, literacy, and culture in graduate school while I continued to teach at North High. I knew that I needed more information and more tools for understanding the disconnect if I was going to create any transformative practice for my students. I hadn't yet imagined that I would create studies and texts that would reach out to other teachers in other classrooms; my initial foray into classroom research was purely personal and pragmatic; I had to find a way to achieve success with my English students or something inside of me was going to die.

I argue that the six years I spent as a simultaneous doctoral student and high school teacher enabled me to make many of the bridges between theory and practice that the field claims to encourage. It was in graduate school, for instance, that I became familiar with the work of Carol Lee, Brian Street, David Barton, Mary Hamilton, Alan Luke, James Gee, and a host of other scholars associated with the New Literacy studies (see New London Group, 1996; Street, 1984). It was the work of these researchers that allowed me to fully grasp what was happening to my students, and their words led me down the conceptual path that I still travel in literacy research and education.

It was from the NLS scholars that I learned that there were multiple forms of literacy, that literacies were socially situated and tied to cultural practice, and that literacies were always to be contextualized within existing power relations (de Castell and Luke, 1983). Once I was able to grasp the critique of autonomous notions of literacy (which assumed one transcendent culture-free and value-free literacy) and acquire the ethnographic spirit of the New Literacy Studies, I was able to ask the question that would begin my voyage as a critical teacher research and ultimately launch my career as an academician: how are these adolescents literate and how can I make connections between these literacies and the literacies of the classroom?

Almost immediately in the micro-ethnographies of literacy that I conducted on the literacy practices of urban adolescents in and around North High, I began to notice that the students manifested multiple literacies via their participation in popular culture. I noticed many parallels, for instance, between the kinds of literacy practices associated with youth participation in popular culture and the academic literacies that English teachers (such as myself and my colleagues) wanted students to manifest (Morrell, 2002). As an example, students read widely across books, magazines, and Internet sites to keep themselves abreast of the latest trends in fashion or sports or video games (Morrell, 2004a). These students also watched films and television, listened to popular music, and employed the tools of rhetoric to engage in critical and substantive conversations with each other about texts in these genres. They wrote notes (and later e-mails) to friends. They wrote poems and lyrics for hip-hop songs in their personal notebooks. Their non-school lives were saturated with sophisticated literacy practices; and this was true for even the most underperforming students. To label these pupils as illiterate bordered on irresponsible; to say that their literacies were not valued placed the onus squarely on the dominant institution responsible for the devaluing as it also pointed toward a viable plan of action for my curriculum and pedagogy.

As I read more from the Birmingham Centre for Contemporary Cultural studies (CCCS), I also began to understand that the students didn't just consume popular culture; they also produced popular culture as participants in the everyday culture of the central cities. Popular culture did not just consist of films and music videos; it was also a set of cultural practices employed by urban youth as they both navigated and resisted the dominant world around them (Docker, 1994; Lipsitz, 1994). This cultural production was evidenced in street art and fashion, street language, and resistant, youth-inspired subcultures and genres of music such as punk, hip-hop, and grunge rock.

From this conceptual frame and within this vibrant context for learning and practice, I was able to design a yearlong English curriculum that tapped into all of these forms of popular culture to make connections between youth literacies and academic ones. Initially, this work was, for me, conceived as a one-way bridge from the local to the academic. As an English teacher I strongly believed in my obligation to help my students gain access to the literacies of power that had often eluded them. Although I never lost sight of the importance of academic literacy development, I became increasingly interested in the connections between a critical pedagogy of popular culture and the development of critical literacies. Given that context, in the following units I describe the nature of the instruction and explicate the ways that students are developing and manifesting academic competencies, but I also focus on how the students acquired literacies that allow them to deconstruct dominant narratives and to prepare texts that advocate for individual freedom and social transformation. I discuss five units that formed the core of the course of a year of "regular" senior English class. The first unit covers a six-week period when students watched the *Godfather* trilogy while also reading Homer's *Odyssey*. The second unit also covers a six-week period when students analyzed hip-hop music as a postindustrial urban poetry form while also learning about how poets have functioned historically as social commentators. The third unit covers Richard Wright's *Native Son* and focuses on the culminating activity, which is a reenactment of the Bigger Thomas trial. The fourth unit covers "In the Killing Fields of America," a 1995 CBS documentary on violence in American society, and the final unit covers research that students conducted after reading excerpts of Jonathan Kozol's 1991 book *Savage Inequalities*.

THE ODYSSEY/GODFATHER UNIT

I first started teaching the *Odyssey/Godfather* unit with several important goals. First and foremost I wanted to help students to navigate the formidable canonical text of *The Odyssey*. The first time I attempted to teach this text at North High, the books were so ragged we had to use staplers and tape to hold them together. The class set dated back to 1964, seven years before I was born! When I inquired with the book clerk about the outdated texts, she informed me that no new texts had been ordered since no one figured that the students would read them. I then shared this with my students and we took the text as a collective challenge. I called a local independent bookstore who basically sold the book to the students at cost. Buying *The Odyssey* and owning such a seemingly formidable and esoteric academic text served as an amazing statement that the students were making to peers, to teachers, and to the school administration, who often conceived of the student body as unmotivated and lacking core literacy skills. Making a symbolic statement, however, was not my primary goal. Once we had decided on the text and purchased copies, I needed to figure a way to make the unit as accessible and interesting as possible for the students while also building academic and critical literacy skills.

At the same time as I began teaching *The Odyssey*, I had also been working with a close colleague investigating the possibilities of making connections with popular cultural literacies and academic concepts. We both became interested in thinking about the intersections between film and epic poetry. Both of us were amateur film buffs and huge fans of Francis Ford Coppola's *Godfather* trilogy. We decided to have the students watch and critique the *Godfather* trilogy while they were reading *The Odyssey*. The result of this brainstorm became one of the more popular units of the year that culminated with major presentations and a debate on the role and positioning of the hero in contemporary American society.

Both *The Odyssey* and *The Godfather* are examples of epics; they also cover an epoch. By epic, I mean those pieces of literature that are larger than life; that portray the deeds of warriors and heroes; that reflect the ideals and values of a culture; and that have national significance (Cuddon, 1999). By epoch, I mean that they covered important eras in the Western historical tradition. I wanted the students to analyze this classic Western epic (*The Odyssey*) given that so many of our values and philosophies are derived from the Greek or classical tradition. I wanted students to form a critical perspective of these values as they transitioned into citizenship in the society that adhered to them. For example, I wanted students to theorize the role of the hero in the epic. What characteristics are associated with heroism? What is the role of religion? What is the treatment of women? How is violence justified or glorified? Along the same lines, the *Godfather* trilogy stands as an epic of the twentieth century American narrative of an immigrant family. It is, in short, the story of Vito Corleone and his son Michael; a cinematic chronicling of their rags to riches story and the contradictions that accompany the rise to power in America.

For the first few weeks, students read *The Odyssey* at home while watching *The Godfather* in class. Once every few days we would check in with *The Odyssey* to make certain that students were following the plot, etc. Most of our time, however, was devoted to the study of *The Godfather*. I should be explicit in describing exactly how we viewed the film in class. First of all, the students watched the film with the lights on and with notebooks out. Any student had the power to request that the film be paused to capture a shot or to catch up on note-writing. We would average twenty minutes of film a day. We would stop fifteen minutes early so that the students could discuss the segment. I have talked about this critical film watching elsewhere (Morrell, 2002, 2004b). The students were participating in a social activity, watching the film, while developing academic competencies and honing note-taking and analytic skills. We would occasionally stop and have the students compare notes to see whether they were taking down an appropriate amount of notes. One student assignment (and form of data collection) consisted of them handing in their notes periodically. I was generally pleased with the level of detail, organization, and critical thought expressed in these notes that students took during class. Mostly, though, these viewings provided an opportunity for students to draw upon their expertise in "reading" film to develop sophisticated close analysis of the film text. Even the positioning of a camera or a prop in the background was subject to intense debate during the debriefing periods.

In my analysis as a teacher-researcher, I found multiple ways that students were able to demonstrate critical literacies through their work on this unit. The unit serves as an example of critical literacy instruction in that it is using literature to explore complicated themes in the larger world. I would like to turn toward examples of students' writing to demonstrate how the unit developed critical literary skills and critical literacies. I collected and coded the final unit examinations of an untracked class at North High that consisted of students who, from pre-unit interviews, indicated that most had not read complete novels or been asked to write interpretive essays. As I also collected achievement data for this class, I know that none of the students had ever enrolled in Honors English and that the average GPA for this class was very much the same as the larger student body. Similarly, the demographics of the class were very similar to those of the larger student body at North High. For these reasons, I think that the data are all the more compelling as they demonstrate what the "average" students at this "underperforming" school are capable of with respect to the development of academic competencies and with respect to the understanding and advocacy for social change. I looked for examples of students being able to make core arguments; students being able to support arguments with evidence from the text; students demonstrating substantive understanding of the text; students being able to read their world onto and into the text; and students relating issues in the film and epic texts into larger sociopolitical issues.

The Odyssey/Godfather Exam. I modeled my unit exams after the types of exams that I took as an undergraduate English major in college. Rather than have multiple-choice tests or fill-in-the-blank answers (which were largely the norm at North High), I devised a test in two parts. The first portion of the exam (worth 50 points) asked the students to identify characters and places from the epic and the film trilogy. Students would receive complete credit for identifying the character or place, how it functioned in the story, and why it was significant. Out of a list of fifteen, students were to select ten. The second portion of the examination (worth 100 points) asked the students to respond to two essay prompts. The first prompt asked the students to choose one of two arguments to make regarding the status of Odysseus and Michael Corleone as epic heroes or as critiques of the epic hero. The second essays asks students to use specific textual and film references to make the argument that women

---

Odyssey/Godfather Final Examination

Part I—50 points

Pick ten of the following fifteen characters from *The Odyssey* and *The Godfather* to identify explaining who they are, what they do, and how they are significant to the epic. At least five IDs must be from each work (5 pts each).

Calypso	*Connie (Corleone)*	*Antinous*
Poseidon	*Orestes*	*Cardinal Lumberto*
Polyphemus	*Mentor*	*Don Lucchesi*
Nausicaa	*Grace Hamilton*	*Mary Corleone*
Eumaeus	*Vincent Mancini*	*Mosca*

Part II—100 points

11. (50 points): Pick *one* of the following sides to argue making specific references to the text and film when appropriate:

The Odyssey and *The Godfather* are classic epic tales where Odysseus and Michael Corleone are characterized as epic heroes.

Or *The Odyssey* and *The Godfather*, although classic epics, provide ample critiques of Odysseus and Michael Corleone as epic heroes.

12. (50 points): Make the following argument using specific textual and film references:

Although females during the periods when *The Odyssey* and *The Godfather* were written were subordinated to the men, the major females (& goddesses) in these two epics are able to manipulate the power dynamics to achieve the results they desired.

in the two works who were structurally subordinated were able to manipulate power dynamics to achieve the results they desired.

I now present an analysis of the essay data from the examination as examples of the relationships between critical literary theories and critical literacies in this untracked urban secondary English classroom. I begin with short identifications that demonstrate how the students were able to demonstrate critical comprehension; both an understanding of the text, but also context and significance. Witness the examples from four students whose grades and prior experiences in English classes would characterize them as marginal student. In the following they make arguments concerning Odysseus and Michael Corleone's status as epic heroes and the role and treatment of women in the two epics.

> **London:** The Odyssey and Godfather, although classic epics, provide ample critiques of Odysseus and Michael Corleone as epic heroes. If you really think about what Michael and Odysseus did, they were not heroes. Michael lied to everyone, he killed his own brother, and he was even alone at the end of the Godfather III because no one wanted to be around him. He lied to Kay (his wife) telling her that he loves her, but he only wanted to use her for having kids and to watch them. He lied to a lot of people. Instead of killing his brother Fredo, he could have had him sent away instead of having him killed. Fredo didn't have any power anyway, what could he have did to Michael? He wouldn't have been able to come near Michael. Odysseus had to get help from Athena lots of times, he should not even be considered as being a hero. Heroes don't cry or show weakness. A hero is strong who really doesn't need anyone's help. Penelope is at her home with tons of suitors, and she doesn't sleep with anyone, but after every woman that Odysseus sleeps with he would go cry somewhere, a hero is supposed to be strong. And the example with Penelope and the suitors just goes to show you that she is stronger than Odysseus in will power.

> **John:** Odysseus is also a hero because he had went to a war to help his friend's wife. He had come back alive when all of his men were dead. When you went to save somebody when they are in trouble that will make you a hero. Odysseus is also a hero when he came back to his palace and see all of the suitors there and he had killed some of them including the leader. He was a good warrior by winning and taking his palace back.

> **Van:** The females in *The Odyssey* were able to manipulate the men in the epics. For example, Athena was able to get what she wanted from Telemachus and Odysseus. Although she got permission from her father (Zeus) she knew exactly what she had to do and how to do it. Athena transformed herself into different people in order for her to manipulate them easier. Athena wanted Telemachus to be strong and have courage and in order for her to do that she became a man because she knew that Telemachus would not listen to a woman. The only way Athena knew that Telemachus would listen to her is by becoming a father figure for him since that is what he never had. Athena got Telemachus to be stronger and have courage after

she talked to him and guided him. Athena got what she wanted when she saw that Telemachus was becoming a man.

Hong: In the *Godfather*, Connie was a weak woman at first. She was afraid of everything. When her husband beats her, she is afraid to tell Sonny (her brother). . . . But later, she comes back to the family and living with Michael (Corleone, also her brother) and taking care of his children to make her stronger. [In *The Godfather: Part III*] she orders the death of Joey Zasa and Don Altobello. She makes Vincent (Corleone, the new Godfather) kiss her hand. She helps Vincent become the third generation of the Don Corleone family. She is the one who keeps the family together.

What is most important to me here is the level of textual authority demonstrated by these students. When provided spaces for authentic conversation and when asked real questions about these texts they demonstrate a willingness and ability not only to decode these texts, but to interrogate these texts and present well-formed arguments about these texts. These four students demonstrate their willingness to critique authors, motives of actors in texts, and the larger values of the society in which the texts were produced. I argue that this form of agency, even textual agency, is important in facilitating the individual and collective emancipatory projects. Texts that achieve the status of literary are usually inculcated with values that legitimize the very oppressive material conditions that lead to the existence of North High and the high levels of poverty and unemployment in the city. Developing the skills to decode and to interrogate these texts can transfer to decoding and interrogation of all texts. Additionally, a critical reading of these texts is also a critical reading of the conditions promoted in the texts, building what Freire calls a reading of the word which informs a reading of the world (Freire, 1997).

THE "POET IN SOCIETY" UNIT

As mandated by the district standards, English teachers at North High were required to teach several distinct periods of English and American poetry. By the time students reached their senior year, they were to have been exposed to Elizabethan literature, Romantic literature, and the literature of key American movements such as the Harlem Renaissance, to name a few. This made sense to me. Even though I have argued for expanding the range of texts included in an English curriculum, I believe that poetry is a powerful form of cultural expression and that poets have played a historically significant role in providing radical social commentary and in making readers aware of the beauty and tragedy that are a part of the human condition.

I was surprised and disappointed to find out that my high school seniors had not read any of this poetry. Most of their English classes had focused on the development of basic literacy skills to the exclusion of any substantive discussions of meaningful literature. If the students did read poems, the poems were usually anthologized in the literature textbooks and the students were usually asked to respond to questions at the end and move on to the next text. I also learned that my students did not have a particularly high view of poetry, and they did not see any relevance between poetry and their everyday lives. At the same time, their lives were completely immersed in the emergent urban hip-hop culture; a culture whose primary form of expression was poetic. Some even contend that "rap" is an acronym for rhythm and poetry.

I knew that I needed to design a unit that exposed my students to the powerful role that poets have played historically, while also making connections to the powerful poetry that played a major role in shaping their own worldview and their popular cultural practices. Toward these ends a colleague and I designed the "Poet in Society" unit to provide a historical analysis of poets as social commentators. We studied the major historical periods of poetry, attempting to understand the various messages that poets were conveying to their contemporaries. To these historical periods, we also added hip-hop as a contemporary poetic form existing largely as a youth-led response to urban postindustrialism.

The unit carried three major assignments. For the first, students worked in groups to compare and contrast a classic poem with a contemporary hip-hop poem. After a week of study and preparation, they presented their analysis to the class in the form of a one-hour lesson complete with Q&A from the audience. As an example, one group compared T. S. Eliot's "Love Song of J. Alfred Prufrock" with Grand Master Flash's "The Message." For the second assignment, students selected a song about which they would write a five- to seven-page critical essay in which they examined, among other things, structure, content, form, and social significance. The final assignment consisted of an anthology of poems that the students wrote. We studied varying forms ranging from sonnets to ballads and poems written about topics ranging from nature to war. The students wrote ten original poems for their anthology and presented five to their classmates in a staged reading.

The unit served to develop critical consumption of classic and contemporary poetic texts. Here, I would like to focus on a sample of the critical production associated with the unit; that is, I would like to explore how a particular student used his knowledge of contemporary urban poetry to develop his critical analysis and writing skills. Consider this introduction to an essay that analyzes Richie Rich's "Do G's Get to Go to Heaven":

In the song "Do G's Get to Go To Heaven," Richie Rich discusses the justification of the righteousness of the actions of sinners. Throughout the song, Richie engages in many critiques of social and political issues. He addresses some of the issues like sexism, scapegoating, and poverty. These issues are present in his everyday life, and it is the way society is. In the very beginning, Rich is already questioning who's really at fault when there is crime and poverty. Is it the criminal or is it society? "Who holds jurisdiction over my twisted thoughts? Am I to blame for what happens off in this game?" He's saying that people's actions are results of the conditions handed down to them by society.

In this analysis of a contemporary hip-hop song, the student combines close reading, sociological analysis, and personal experience to come to a deep understanding of the poem. The student implicitly recognizes the popular cultural text as a piece of social critique and credits the author/rapper with being able to point to the social causes of cultural practice. What's more, the student also demonstrates a knowledge of the genre of literary essay writing in that he states a clear hypothesis, provides evidence, and then proceeds to analyze that evidence. The essay continues for seven pages where the student continues to provide evidence that the song indicts society for playing a major role in causing many of the urban problems that the song addresses. I argue that this complex reading is facilitated by the students' knowledge of hip-hop music and culture and the conditions that are described in the song. The student is then able to use his knowledge to construct an academic argument and to develop his academic essay writing skills.

THE BIGGER THOMAS TRIAL

Richard Wright's *Native Son* stood isolated on the North High bookroom's shelves as one of the most dense and formidable texts on the department's reading list. At four hundred pages of perma-bound text, the book existed as a mammoth for students, many of whom had not read any novel cover to cover during their tenures at the school. Also, given that the novel dealt with such taboo issues as rape, murder, racism, and economic injustice, the book was often passed over by teachers, and rarely ended up being taught in the school.

I had a feeling, however, that the Bigger Thomas story could be compelling for urban adolescents, who would undoubtedly relate to his rage, frustration, and social isolation. Even though the story was, by then, sixty years old, there were so many parallels between his life and theirs. Bigger Thomas was a teenage black boy growing up in poverty with a single-parent household; he and those around him often manifested poor performance in school and faced limited prospects for a fulfilling and high-wage earning job on the other side of their education. Bigger was forced to watch his mother struggle to make ends meet for her children; he saw the shame that she endured on a daily basis in her work. At the same time, living in a big city he was exposed to the incredible wealth that some American citizens enjoyed. Usually it was citizens who did not look like him or his friends. It is not surprising that these experiences take their toll on Bigger and thousands of youth like him; while his explosive actions are unforgivable, they are understandable and worthy of explanation if we want to prevent the continued creation of Bigger Thomases in the future. I would venture to say that each of my students could point to a Bigger Thomas in their family or in the neighborhood. Every year that I taught at North High, a young black male student had killed or been killed; all the more reason to read the book and examine the relationships between social structures and cultural practices.

The students became enthralled with Bigger and his story from my reading of the opening scene in Bigger's apartment with the rat. We read silently and collectively throughout the book and I posed critical questions for each section, all dealing with issues of justice and an analysis of oppressive structural conditions. As a class, we never necessarily sought to justify Bigger Thomas' actions, but we wanted to make sense of his actions in a way that situated the individual within and against an oppressive society. In many ways, our analyses of Bigger and his life were parallel to the work of social scientists such as Pierre Bourdieu and William Julius Wilson who attempt to show how cultural practices are situated within oppressive institutional structures.

Bourdieu's (1990) analysis centers around his idea of *habitus*, which really concerns how unconscious actions are historicized in structured oppressive practices. Wilson (1996), on the other hand, identifies what he calls ghetto-related behavior, which is an outcome of life in jobless ghettos. It is no coincidence that Wilson's study was conducted in the very neighborhoods that Bigger traverses in the Wright novel. This haunting yet beautifully written story provides a context for urban adolescent students to develop their sociological imaginations in C. Wright Mills' (1959) sense of the term while also gaining the tools of literary and textual analysis.

The anchoring activity of the *Native Son* unit involved a reenactment of the Bigger Thomas trial. At the end of the reading, I divided the class into two equally sized groups to form the prosecution and defense in the trial. Each group was responsible for choosing its own witnesses, lawyers, and lawyer's assistants. It worked out so that each person in the group would have to take on some meaningful role in order to help the group. As a major goal of the activity, I wanted students to visit fundamental issues surrounding race and justice even as they inhabited a familiar schemata such as the court trial to develop skills of critical reading, critical writing, and critical oral rhetoric. I will say more about each of these as exemplars of the critical literacies that students learned via their participation in the Bigger Thomas court trial.

Critical Reading

Reading instruction in secondary English classrooms needs to move students beyond decoding and comprehension of texts to helping them become critical consumers of texts; literate agents who are able to understand texts of all genres as interested historical and ideological creations. As educators, we strive to help students to read literary texts for aesthetic appreciation, but we also want them to understand how language is used to persuade, to inform, to evoke, to represent "truths" and cultural ideals. One of the goals of literary reading, I think, is to help our young to reveal the human condition in all of its complexity while engaging in a meta-analysis of how authors and texts make these internal and external conversations possible. These ways of reading texts and the world, what I will call critical reading strategies, need to exist in addition to the New Critical approaches to literary reading that are often promoted in secondary English classrooms.

In the context of this unit and court trial, students engaged in critical readings of the text as they examined the commentary that the authors and the characters made on race, gender, poverty, and justice. Students critically analyzed the discourse of protagonists in the film *A Time to Kill* who represented victims and victimizers as they developed larger analyses of the themes of the text. For example, the students deconstructed the statements of characters like Mr. Dalton who, on the surface, appear very friendly but who are very much implicated in the reproduction of social inequality that manifests itself in the lived conditions of Bigger Thomas and his family. When preparing for their trial, they also engaged in critical readings of the text in search of evidence that might shed light on the structural causes of Bigger's actions.

Critical Writing

There were multiple forms of writing attached to the preparation for the trial. For example, students created reading notes on the text, they developed opening arguments, they wrote scripts for witnesses, they brainstormed questions for direct examination and cross-examination, and they anticipated questions that would be asked of their witnesses. Finally, students mined the text, transcribing data that could be used as "evidence" in the case.

I also used the court trial to teach students critical essay writing skills; particularly as they relate to making an argument through writing. The structure of legal writing closely parallels those forms of essay writing that are aligned with academic literacy; how to generate a thesis; how to search for evidence that will prove or disprove a point; how to present that evidence in rhetorically powerful ways; how to call in witnesses to support an argument; how to refute, via cross-examination, the arguments made by opposing witnesses; and how to prepare and pre-empt cross-examination of one's own witnesses and evidence. The various written genres associated with litigation found themselves as the anchor pieces of the casebooks that I required of all students. The casebooks were completed part individually and part as a team/group. These books contained:

- all the questions prepared for the witnesses of each team and scripted responses;
- all of the anticipated questions to be asked of each team's witnesses in cross-examination;
- all of the questions prepared in advance for opposing witnesses in cross-examination;
- the opening arguments;
- all notes taken during the trial (trial notes are mandatory);
- a five- to seven-page summation/analysis of the trial.

The casebooks became quite a production, averaging over fifty pages per student. As a teacher and researcher, I analyzed these casebooks for instantiations of academic and critical literacies. In their zeal to demonstrate the merits of their particular case, students became meticulous and thorough in the arguments that they constructed. Following is an example taken from the closing arguments made by the defense in the case of *The State of Illinois v. Bigger Thomas*:

> Let us begin with the background and home life of my client Bigger Thomas. He was raised in a fatherless, one-room flat with two younger siblings by his mother. Although he had his faults, as all children do, he was looked upon as the father figure to his family. He provided safety and comfort and was relied upon by his family. Bigger was not a raving criminal as the prosecution would have you to believe, but a frustrated young man with hopes and dreams and a deep frustration because he knew that the elements around him would limit his success.

This statement provides an excellent example of a complex and compelling argument that ties together the facts of the novel along with a sociological analysis of race and class in Bigger Thomas' society. Obviously the student-lawyer is having fun with the genre of the court trial, but her argument is well made and she is meticulous in her use of facts to make her case. She also possesses an in-depth (and first-hand) understanding of the impact of race on the psyche of young African-Americans. She feels it important enough to frame her argument around the contexts in which Bigger Thomas lived in order to explain the action of the novel.

Critical Oral Rhetoric

For most of its 2500-year tradition, Western language instruction has been dominated by rhetorical training. The most literate citizens were those who were able to deliver thoughtful oratorical arguments in public venues. Facility with oral language was an important academic and civic skill. Teachers created spaces for students to deliver arguments orally as part of their academic training. At the dawn of the twentieth century all of this began to change as newly sprouting English departments took up the study of literature as their primary activity rather than the practice of oral rhetoric. A little more than a century later, the study and practice of rhetoric have practically vanished from most secondary and tertiary curricula. With the New Critical literature study paradigm, reading has taken the primary role, writing has a much smaller secondary role in literacy education, and the art of public speaking has virtually vanished. From a personal standpoint I can say that I have received a Bachelor's degree in English, an English teaching credential and Master's and doctoral degrees in language and literacy without ever haven taken a course that deals explicitly with public speaking!

All of this occurs within a context in which oral rhetorical skills are as important to critical engaged citizenship as they have ever been; the lack of official spaces for students to acquire these skills in literacy courses is a real tragedy. As a literacy teacher I was acutely aware of this absence in my department's curriculum and recognized in the court trial the opportunity to develop oral rhetorical skills among my students. This makes sense when one considers that, in the move toward literature study in the discipline of English, legal studies have remained the one academic field that values the importance of the study and practice of oral rhetoric. Unfortunately, it is much more likely that an attorney will have formal training in rhetoric than a literacy educator.

Within the frame of the court trial, there were multiple opportunities for students to develop these oral/rhetorical skills. By default, most of the students took on at least one speaking role either as a witness or as an attorney. These roles forced the students to consider and develop their ability to make orally compelling arguments. Students were challenged to pay attention to all of the rhetorical devices that are outlined in Aristotle's classic tract. They needed to know how to inspire contempt or pity; when to appear scholarly or when to connect with a witness. They also needed to think through the best way to make opening and closing arguments, and how to use language to make a witness' testimony seem believable or incredulous. And, within the schema of the court trial, there existed a space for the meta-level conversation about the uses of oral language for these multiple purposes. Such a context, I would argue, is prime for continuing discussions of rhetoric and its role in critical citizenship. It is possible to go much further than the trial; to have students study the history of the practice of rhetoric in developing their own awareness of themselves inhabiting a rich tradition of citizens and scholars who have operated as skillful, intentioned manipulators of oral language. It is even possible to bring in examples of powerful rhetoric from film and popular culture to have the students examine while they are developing their own abilities.

After the trial, it became necessary for me to refine my classroom assessment to include at least a third of students' grading on orally based assignments. I realized that no rubrics existed to evaluate these classroom literacy practices because they were so rare. The literacy development in the Bigger Thomas trial demonstrates the relationship between academic and critical literacy learning in secondary English education. I believe that the classroom praxis in this unit underscores the centrality of academic literacy to critical literacy. All of the critical literacy practices have some relationship to or draw upon in meaningful ways, the literacies of power that are traditionally taught in the academy. Critical reading requires basic decoding and comprehension skills, critical writing requires an understanding of grammar, syntax, vocabulary, and a facility with the techniques of word and letter formation. Even critical rhetoric is built upon an ability to process information via traditional academic literacies.

This unit also reveals the numerous spaces for critical literacy education in academic contexts. It may be important at this point to say more about what makes these classroom practices "critical" and not just academic. First, it is important to acknowledge that the reading, writing, and speaking practices in the Bigger Thomas trial occur within a context that encouraged urban adolescents to question the practices of their criminal justice system; it forced them to contemplate how a sanctioned text could have multiple meanings as well as ideological foundations that could be oppressive; it also forced them to understand how their own reading, writing, and speaking could be potentially empowering; it challenged them to consider that meanings are always contestable and that the power to effectively convey meaning orally and through writing are important professional, civic and academic skills.

THE KILLING FIELDS: VIOLENCE IN AMERICA

In 1995 CBS produced "In the Killing Fields of America," an award-winning documentary that chronicled violent crime in the country. During the two-hour documentary, Ed Bradley, Holly Fine, Paul Fine, Dan Rather and Mike Wallace, and the CBS News crew swept through the cities of New Orleans, East Palo Alto, Brooklyn, Atlanta, and Minneapolis, covering various forms of criminal activities ranging from hold-ups to drug related crime to child abuse. As I watched it from my home the documentary struck me on a personal level, but it also struck me as something that would be extremely relevant for my students. Every year that I taught at North High, at least one student was murdered. Additionally, students' family members were often implicated in violence, which was all too prevalent in the city and in the schools. I wanted to use "Killing Fields" to promote discussions about youth violence, but I also wanted to generate reflective and proactive writing on the topic. With these goals in mind I designed a unit that incorporated viewing the video documentary as a class, engaging a series of documentary prompts for discussion, and researching and writing a final research-policy paper that would be presented to the class. The prompts for discussion solicited student opinions about prison conditions, sentencing laws, welfare laws, and the responsibility of the government, of parents and community institutions in preventing violence. Some of the prompts included:

- What can the government do to deter crime that it is not already doing?
- How much should a juvenile criminal's upbringing come into consideration when sentencing?
- What is the parent's responsibility for ensuring that their children are respectable law abiding citizens? What is their responsibility in keeping their children away from activities they know to be inherently dangerous or life-threatening?
- What are some things (name at least three) you can do in your everyday lives to help eliminate the problem of violence in America? How and when will you do these things?

The final assignments were negotiated with students and forced them to learn skills of secondary research (though if I did it again I would allow for more of the independent critical research in the tradition of the summer seminars) while also reflecting on their own experiences with violence in school and in the community. The students were encouraged to write policy papers based on their research where they either highlighted or created successful programs to deal with important social issues within communities that mattered to them.

In what follows I examine some of the students' written responses to these discussion prompts and excerpts from one student's final paper. My goals here are to provide a sense of how students understood the causes of youth violence and how they experienced violence in their everyday lives. I also want to analyze student writing to understand how the topic of youth violence allowed for the demonstration and development of critical literacies among the students in my classes. This first passage is from a short writing assignment in which this young woman is talking about what to do about violence in her school.

> **Alicia:** When a person is found guilty of committing a violent act against someone I feel that the school should deal with both parties. At North High, if a person has a fight usually the person that started the fight is put on suspension. Suspension is a way to punish a young adult if there is a parent to get on the person and explain that suspension isn't good, but many times parents work and leave their children at home by themselves. I was suspended before and I stayed home. On my "day off" I visited most of my friends, got my hair done and went to the movies. I don't think I learned anything on my punishment.

Alicia provides interesting critiques of the school's current disciplinary problems and is able to integrate her personal experiences and those of her peers with social analysis to problematize a fairly standard practice at most schools. What is important is that Alicia feels the freedom to say something critical about the practice of suspending students who fight and that she also feels that her own experiences are significant enough to bring to bear in an academic discussion. Elsewhere I have talked about students not feeling that they have anything of value to offer from personal experience to the substantive academic discussions of the classroom. Schools themselves, who paint urban youth as pathologies to be fixed or cleansed and re-educated, initiate many of these feelings of alienation. Freire (1970) refers to this process as "banking education" because students are perceived as empty receptacles that need to be "deposited" with information that only the teachers possess. My sense of American classrooms is even worse than what Freire proposes. I believe that students in urban schools are seen as adulterated receptacles that must first be emptied out before being re-filled with socially valued information.

The alternative to the banking education is what Freire termed "problem-posing education," in which teachers and students engage in authentic dialogue centered upon real problems or concerns in the community. I believe that the discussion prompts that followed the documentary led to examples of this dialogue, and the spirit of those discussions is captured in the response by Alicia to violent conditions in her school. These second and third passages are excerpted from the conclusion of Samantha's final paper. She assesses reasons that schools, media, and the larger society do not work to change patterns of violence and offers real strategies along with a heavy dose of inspiration for such work:

> **Samantha:** Since we started schooling, we have been faced with problem solving and the steps we need in order to attain the solution. The forms of violence I just brought up have solutions; some of them having more than one. It is our duty to figure them out. Do we really want the violence to decrease or are we in fact lazy and neglectful? So far, this nation has proven generations of neglect on problem solving, therefore becoming an accomplice to violence. To better understand this statement, it takes two to tango. Such examples can corroborate the picture of the teenage girl who goes to the doctor every six months to get a new fetus removed (hmmm . . . I wonder if there are sex education seminar classes and workshops at her school. I doubt it). The murderer (have the state jails got over-crowded again?). Police who beat us (when will people ever learn that we can prove them wrong?). Don't write on walls write in books. Turn the stereotype over.

Samantha's response contains a nice balance of structural critique while acknowledging the power of human agency. For example, she equates major social problems (teen pregnancy and urban violence) with major dysfunctions in social institutions such as schools or the criminal justice system. At the same time, she holds individuals in the public accountable for devising solutions to stem the violent tide in the city. In other words, whereas the structures are the targets of critique, the everyday citizens are the agents of change. Finally, Samantha associates critical literacy practices with the elimination of urban violence. She admonishes (presumably her peers) to write proactively with the sense that writing (in books) might actually transform mindsets and end problematic assumptions about segments of the population.

The agency and sense of efficacy are underscored in this final excerpt from her paper:

> **Samantha:** The end to violence has to start with us. It hits every home worldwide. If we neglect and give excuses to these violent acts we will only be empowering the wrong people. It can be a cycle in which everyone is at fault and committing their own suicide. It is up to you.

The use of the term suicide (a metaphor that runs throughout the piece) is extremely powerful in articulating Samantha's views on human freedom in the existential sense. She has shown an acute understanding of the role of oppressive social structures in creating oppressive social and material conditions, yet she believes ultimately in the freedom of humans to overcome these circumstances. Jean Paul Sartre and Simone de Beauvoir would be proud. Even though she doesn't follow the neo-Marxist structuralism that is at the heart of much critical theory, this is an inherently critical text in its skepticism of institutions as ideological and in its belief in the power of the conscious agent to transform her surrounding. Again as with Alicia's paper, this work reveals the existence of curricular spaces that ask students to pose and attack real problems in the world; it demands an efficacious identity on the part of the students and it positions texts as potentially transformative in substance.

This final passage is written as part of a short prompt that addresses government responsibility in addressing social ills that befall urban communities:

> **Kimberly:** The government can sponsor organizations that work with youths in urban areas to show them how to stop the cycle of poverty and violence that they are so used to. Government officials like the state attorney general should spend time living in these sections of urban cities. They could commit themselves to a particular city for a weekend each month, learning the names of the kids and trying to understand their problems.

Kimberly's comments are both constructive and critical. While she addresses a concern about the disconnect between policymakers and the communities of need, she is also developing a project or at least a process whereby these senior level administrators and officials might learn a great deal more about the schools and the children for which they make public policy. Kimberly's comments point to the importance of dialogic spaces in a problem-posing pedagogy. Her text identifies a critical process that might lead to the desired changes: more humanized state officials and less violent schools and communities.

This unit was important in that it encouraged students to think systematically and structurally about violence in their communities. In other words, the discussion prompts and writing assignments forced students to make connections between urban violence, education, the media, and the political economy. Students were motivated to talk and write about an issue that, though they confronted it daily, they had few opportunities to discuss in sanctioned spaces such as academic classrooms. As they developed as social theorists and sociologists of urban violence, they were also able to demonstrate critical literacies of understanding the connections between state actions, student consciousness, and violent acts. Students like Samantha spoke of the role that critical literacy could play in preventing this type of violence in the community. Others like Alicia took a balanced approach to social analysis; one that simultaneously held students and parents accountable for violence while also challenging institutions such as schools and the criminal justice system.

If I had the project to do again, I would have finished with some school- or community-based action project that encouraged the students to channel this passion into positive action in the community. Clearly, the students' responses show their willingness and the level of thought they devoted says something about their commitment to anti-violence in the schools and communities. Additionally, these students have formed well informed, sophisticated statements about urban youth violence that need to be heard by people with decision-making power. Leaving these words in the hands of a teacher to grade and file them away, even as part of a research project, is criminal. These words should have become the blueprint for some form of collaborative action.

CLASSROOM RESEARCH ON SAVAGE INEQUALITIES

Every year we started class with a research project that involved reading Jonathan Kozol's *Savage Inequalities*. I knew that juniors and seniors came into my class having personally experienced more than a decade of inequitable schooling conditions. This latent knowledge affected them individually and collectively. For example, I knew that students would often feel inferior when the time came to apply for colleges or to take standardized assessments such as the SAT or ACT. Students would also panic when they received work that they perceived as too difficult for them. Some students had developed individual defense mechanisms, but saw no hope for the school or their counterparts. Most students, however, wanted desperately to do something to change the realities they had dealt with so that others would have a different path.

A colleague and I designed the "Savage Inequalities in Urban Schools" unit for all of these students. We wanted to tackle head-on the feelings of academic inferiority and the "Stereotype Threat" (Steele and Aronson, 1995) that would inhibit students' performances on class work and the college admissions process. We wanted to develop a sociological language to understand structural inequality in schools that would allow students to separate the conditions of the schools from their own sense of self; many of them had embraced the inequity as something unchangeable or else something that was their fault. Finally we wanted a classroom unit that would make students aware of their own agency; that they could do something about the problems that they and their peers and the school faced. With this in mind, we designed an action component to the research project. It was our goal that students finish the first unit armed with confidence in their abilities, but also excited about engaging in work that was socially meaningful. We also wanted to balance between gaining skills and attitudes that would help students individually to navigate the class and college admissions and gaining a sense of collective energy and responsibility to work toward solutions to problems that they encountered on a daily basis. Many of the top students, for example, could easily have focused on their own "escape" from the conditions at North High rather than envisioning themselves as implicated in the future of a school and community that they may have been preparing to leave.

The design and implementation of this unit gets at the heart of the project of critical literacy instruction for urban adolescents. As teachers, it is impossible to have an either/or mentality. It is not fair to the students to promote collective action at the expense of individual skill development and individual achievement. By the same token, it is socially irresponsible to only focus on achievement without situating the history and culture of underachievement in some sociological context for the students. Additionally, we continually found that students were more motivated to engage in work that was socially valuable and the socially valuable work provided the entire context that we needed to develop the individual literacy skills that the students needed in order to succeed academically and to contribute as engaged and thoughtful citizens.

In the "Savage Inequalities" unit, students developed these skills by reading complex sociological texts that ranged from the Kozol piece to Bourdieu, Marx, and Paulo Freire. They also consulted educational databases to gather statistics on funding and academic achievement at their school and at similar schools around the district and the state. Students learned how to conduct basic research; they conducted interviews with administrators, politicians, and peers, they visited other school sites to collect data. One research group visited a nearby high school in an affluent district that was in the process of completing a 4.75 million-dollar renovation of their athletic facilities while the students at North High had to share chemistry books in class and copy down the problems to complete at home, since the books could not come with them.

CONCLUSION

I have attempted to present myriad data sources to provide an in-depth picture of life and work in these secondary literacy classrooms and how the project of critical literacy, how it has been conceived, can take shape within restrictive structural spaces like a high school English classroom. First and foremost, I want to show that it is possible to design and carry out critical literacy units within the restrictive frameworks of schools. Several of the units here touch upon key classical texts in English studies such as Shakespeare or *The Odyssey*, or twentieth century African-American literature. Those that do not clearly involve the students in projects that develop the basic academic literacies of reading, researching, and expository writing.

As both a classroom teacher and university researcher I attempted to collect student work to show the possible productions that accompany this type of committed classroom work. Space considerations limit what I am able to show at any given time, but the quality and quantity of the work speak for themselves as authentic literacy products, by anyone's definitions. The students at North High have written essays, case analyses, investigative reports, and Shakespearean sonnets. They have compared and contrasted poems, presented their work orally to peers, and engaged in mock trials; work that is usually reserved for the most elite prep schools in the country or even work that is completed at the elite postsecondary institutions where I have had the privilege to work.

In conclusion it is important to point out that the critical literacy project is not insignificant to the academic literacy development. Two of the key challenges that urban secondary literacy educators face are disengagement from the work and inability to access the content. The critical focus is essential when dealing with both. On the one hand the students are motivated and engaged because the work deals with relevant individual and social issues. It becomes about more than getting a grade; the students envision the project, and rightly so, as something larger than themselves, or the classroom or even the school. On the other hand, the work also allows students to make connections with their literate lives outside of the classroom and the work allows them to access all of their intelligence, wit, and spirit in the process.

The remaining chapters in this section all deal with hybrid learning spaces: those that are related to, but not completely contained in the public school classroom. I hope that they are not seen as irrelevant to the real work that needs to be done in schools and classrooms. I do believe that a decade of work in these unique spaces has allowed me to expand my own horizons for what is possible inside of traditional literacy classrooms. With that in mind, I explore literacy development in community-based research, critical media production, and cyberactivism with urban adolescents.

5

Conducting Community-Based Research with Urban Youth

WRITING THE WORD AND THE WORLD

Those of us who study and teach writing as a tool of resistance and social change for urban adolescents are indebted to the work of critical pedagogists who have provided a language to describe and deconstruct structures of oppression in the cause of social justice. McLaren (1989) asserts that:

> Critical pedagogy challenges the assumption that schools function as major sites of social and economic mobility. Proponents of this pedagogical theory suggest that schooling must be analyzed as a cultural and historical process, in which select groups are positioned within asymmetrical relations of power on the basis of specific race, class, and gender groupings. (p. 166)

According to McLaren, critical scholars reject the claim that schooling constitutes an apolitical and value-neutral process. Critical pedagogy is intended to provide teachers and researchers with a better means of understanding the role that schools actually play within a race-, class-, and gender-divided society. In this effort, theorists have generated categories or concepts for questioning student experiences, texts, teacher ideologies, and aspects of school policy that conservative and liberal analyses too often leave unexplored.

Aronowitz and Giroux (1991) argue that the challenge of postmodernism is important for critical educators because it raises crucial questions regarding certain hegemonic aspects of modernism and, by implication, how these have affected the meaning and dynamics of present-day schooling. Postmodernist criticism is also important because it offers the promise of deterritorializing modernism and redrawing its political, social, and cultural boundaries, while

113

simultaneously affirming a politics of racial, gender, and ethnic difference. Moreover, postmodern criticism does not merely challenge dominant Western cultural models with their attendant notion of universally valid knowledge; it also resituates us within a world that bears little resemblance to the one that inspired the grand narratives of Marx and Freud. In effect, postmodern criticism calls attention to the shifting boundaries related to the increasing influence of the electronic mass media and information technology, the changing nature of class and social formations in postindustrialized capitalist societies, and the growing transgression of boundaries between life and art, high and popular culture, and image and reality. Aronowitz and Giroux ultimately argue for a critical postmodernism that develops forms of pedagogy that incorporate difference, plurality, and the language of the everyday as central to the production and legitimization of learning (p. 187).

In a similar vein, McLaren (1997) advocates the construction of a politics of difference, derived from the framework of resistance postmodernism, which creates narratives of liberation and freedom that critique master narratives, yet doesn't disintegrate into chaos and fragmentation. He concludes by encouraging educators to take up the issue of difference in ways that don't reinforce notions of monocultural essentialism and to create politics of alliance that move beyond race awareness week. He also advocates a resistance postmodernism that takes multiculturalism seriously calling attention to the dominant meaning systems readily available to students, most of which are ideologically stitched into the fabric of Western imperialism. Finally, he calls for a critical pedagogy that provides both the conditions for interrogating the institutionalization of formal equality based on the imperatives of a white, Anglo male world and for creating spaces to facilitate an investigation of the way in which dominant institutions can be transformed so they no longer reinforce indifference to victimization and asymmetrical relations of power and privilege.

This critical postmodern pedagogy opens up ample spaces for critical educators who are interested in literacy instruction for social change. Critical pedagogy is, of course, fundamentally and intimately linked with critical literacy. There can be no liberation of self or other without tools or language to perform counter-readings of dominant texts that serve the interests of power. Freire (1970) remarks that acceptance of dehumanizing conditions is promoted via a banking model of education in which teachers are charged to disseminate knowledge to passive and empty receptacles of students who then embrace problematic and subordinating logics that are passed on as neutral and natural maxims for life. Reading, in this model, means simply decoding messages that are sent by power brokers through hegemonic curricula and media narratives. Freire and Macedo, by contrast, promote a framework for critical reading as a part of radical pedagogy that

> has as its goal to enable students to become critical of the hegemonic practices that have shaped their experiences and perceptions in hopes of freeing themselves from the bonds of these dominating ideologies. (1987, p. 55)

Freire and Macedo's work has, for some time, been a cornerstone for critical literacy; it provides a framework for teaching literacy and interacting with dominant texts in empowering ways. Reading, for these scholars, is a counterhegemonic activity. It is active in the sense that it is also a freeing of one's self from the seemingly unyielding grasp of dominant narratives.

Critical literacy educators, however indebted to the work of Freire and Macedo, cannot be satisfied with instruction that develops students who are able to read the word and the world, so to speak. Critical literacy instruction needs to fundamentally be concerned with the consumption, production, and distribution of texts; counter-texts that not only name the workings of power, but critical texts that serve as the manifestation of an alternate reality or a not-yet-realized present that only enters into the imagination through the interaction with new and authentically liberating words that are created by writers as cultural workers. Critical pedagogists have necessarily focused on the critical consumption of dominant texts, but this chapter argues for a change in focus from consumption to production—what I call *Critical Textual Production* (CTP). Moving from a model of consumption to production in critical literacy instruction necessarily requires a synthesis or at least a meaningful dialogue between the discourses of critical pedagogy and of rhetoric and composition as critical educators and writing instructors consider how it is that we teach students to construct texts that serve as counter-narratives to these dominant texts that they have gained the ability to deconstruct.

Compositionists and rhetoricians are perfectly poised to help emergent writers to gain understanding of the power of language through the production of critical texts. I argue that the consumptive aspect of critical literacy will not be lost; rather it will be subsumed in the process of producing alternate texts such as websites, brochures, editorials, research reports, essays, and fictional works like novels, poems, plays, and short stories. I urge urban secondary literacy educators to heed the necessary call of critical composition pedagogy; to help students prepare for writing lives as engaged citizens and not just university students or future professionals. Certainly we want students to master the discourses of the university, but we should also want them to perceive writing as something that begets more than superior grades in courses or entrance into rewarding careers. Writing can be about re-making and re-articulating reality. As many classical and modern rhetoricians have held, those who have the power to manipulate language have the power to rule the world.

Ultimately, as literacy educators, we must consider the genres of texts that students will need to produce in their lives as engaged citizens and forefront these in composition programs and English and language arts classrooms as we strive to develop a generation of critical composers whose texts challenge us to reconsider our world. This will necessarily entail the creation of courses and curricula that foreground critical community-based research and writing for social justice; selections that blur textual genres and cross the fictional divide in having students use stories, poems, even film to portray alternate realities; and texts that infuse new media into the critical composition process. Literacy educators inhabiting these new pedagogical spaces will be required to devise strategies to meaningfully distribute student-generated critical texts, giving them a utility that is larger than the actual class. The resulting critical textual production can become a way to get students excited about writing for social change, not just learning to navigate the various discourses of a university or a profession. It is a composing process centered within the existential experiences of people. It is for people. It is personal and political all in one.

It is important, then, for critical literacy pedagogists to theorize, through critical examinations of their practice, the elements of praxis that will lead to the production of critical texts that contribute to the struggles for individual liberation and collective social change. Drawing from the work of Freire and Macedo, I propose several core tenets of critical composition pedagogies that aspire to these lofty goals: 1. *Historicity*. Critical composition pedagogy must begin with students' experiences as citizens of the word. 2. *Problem-posing*. A critical composition pedagogy must embrace, as its curriculum, the real world problems and struggles of marginalized people in the world. 3. *Dialogic*. A critical composition pedagogy must entail authentic humanizing interactions with people in the world. 4. *Emancipatory*. A critical composition pedagogy must confront individual alienation and social injustice and have as its project liberation from oppressive realities. 5. *Praxis*. A critical composition pedagogy must be about action and reflection upon that action.

Other important considerations for critical composition pedagogies concern the nature of relationships between participants: who has voice and authority to speak and write, and what counts as legitimate work. In their chapter on "Rethinking Critical Theory and Qualitative Research," Kincheloe and

McLaren (1998) identify new "standards" for critical scholarship. The authors promote humility as opposed to arrogance or assuredness, trustworthiness in lieu of validity, collective participation instead of individual authorship, and lived experience rather than predetermined methodological or theoretical approaches. These tenets are so central to the transformational writing associated with critical composition pedagogy that they were highlighted in our summer seminar, a university-level literacy course we offered to inner city high school teens for college credit during a summer session. Though I provide a lengthy introduction to the summer seminar program in chapter 1, I will reiterate that for six consecutive summers (1999–2004) I worked in a research institute that offered a summer program for teens attending underperforming urban schools in the greater metropolitan area. For five weeks each summer, twenty-five to thirty students from various neighborhoods around the city convened to learn about and participate in critical research projects. Students worked in small groups led by local K-12 teachers where they designed and carried out their own projects, usually investigating issues related to educational equity and youth empowerment. In the following sections, I will discuss the role of critical composition in the work of the seminar.

THE CRITICAL RESEARCH SEMINAR

How, specifically, does the seminar promote critical textual production and to what ends? First off, writing is not an isolated task from the seminar; writing is absolutely necessary to the work of the seminar, which is to design and carry out critical research projects in the city's neighborhoods and schools. Critical textual production is, at once, the means and the end of the seminar. During their five-week involvement in the seminar, students compose continually in the form of journals, lecture and discussion notes, literature summaries, field notes, interview protocols, analytic memos, research reports and PowerPoint presentations. To support their writing, students are armed with laptop computers and composition notebooks that they use when "in the field."

On the first day, we begin with an introduction by having students talk about either something they like about their school or something they would like to see changed. Inevitably, students who attend some of the poorest schools in the nation are quick to take advantage of the opportunity to share the deplorable conditions of their schooling. Many, who have already completed twelve years of public schooling, admit that it is the first time anyone has asked them such a question. Responses are candid and often emotional as students gain affinity through the sharing of personal and often painful narratives of schooling. Freire (1970) encourages critical educators to use people's historicity as a starting point in any liberatory dialogue:

> Dialogue is the encounter between humans, mediated by the world, in order to name the world. Those who have been denied their primordial right to speak their word must first reclaim this right and prevent the continuation of dehumanizing aggression. If it is in speaking their word that people, by naming the world, transform it, dialogue imposes itself as the way by which they achieve significance as human beings. (p. 69)

By situating that initial critical dialogue simultaneously in the personal and social worlds of urban teens, and by making explicit and immediate connections between dialogue and writing, the seminar's two composing trajectories are initiated: writing for personal understanding and writing for social change.

Over the course of the seminar, students write to learn more about their own experiences as youth attempting to navigate an often troubled world. Later during the first day of class, students are given their laptops, shown how to plug in, and asked to spend thirty minutes responding to the following prompt:

> Recall an experience you've had with a teacher that you remember vividly. The memory can be vivid either because it is especially positive, painful, or unique. In as much detail as possible re-tell this narrative and explain what makes it so emotional for you.

Students, who are all plugged into the Ethernet and given e-mail accounts if they don't already have one, e-mail their responses daily to their literacy teachers, generally practicing K-12 teachers in the Los Angeles area or graduate students at the university. The students then receive daily feedback on their responses via e-mail comments and dialogue with fellow students and teachers in the seminar. These writing prompts culminate in the creation of an individual critical text that reflects upon the processes of critical literacy and critical research. In our most recent seminar, students had these four options to choose between:

1. *A Critical Memoir:* Write a critical memoir that recounts a portion of your educational experience. Explain the event in as much detail as possible. Use theory to make sense of the event. Use your knowledge of critical research to discuss what could have been done differently.

2. *On Being a Critical Researcher:* Talk about your journey as a critical researcher. What have you learned? What advice would you offer to others (students, teachers, parents, community activists) who may be considering such an enterprise?

3. *A Personal Letter:* Write a personal letter to an author, an artist, ancestor, or other activist who has influenced your journey as a critical researcher. Explain to this person how they have shaped your image of yourself as a critical researcher.

4. *An Issue Piece:* Write a brief essay to a policymaker or an elected official, in which you combine experience and theory to discuss an issue related to equity and access. This topic doesn't have to relate to your group's research project.

These individual essays are critical texts in that they allow students a different, more enabling language to make sense of their own experiences. They also generate different relationships, not only to those experiences, but to the structures in which they occurred. They are also critical texts because they are shared with others, either others in similar situations such as students and parents, or others, such as teachers, researchers, and policymakers, who are in a position to transform these realities. For example, student texts were published in an online journal that receives thousands of hits and are also being considered as mini chapters in a *Handbook on Critical Research* to be published and distributed to local and national audiences. Several students have submitted their work to other outlets including school newspapers and non-mainstream publications; portions of two narratives are incorporated into a peer-reviewed research journal article.

The second writing trajectory pertains to writing for social transformation. After beginning with students' personal experiences in urban schools and communities, the seminar then moves toward reading, research, and writing activities designed to provide explanations for the current inequities in urban schools and communities that are not rooted in deficit logic. These problem-posing sessions transition into the development of research questions: questions that the students initiate as they work in teams of four or five under the guidance of a practicing teacher in Los Angeles area schools. In past seminars, students have studied the media's portrayal of urban youth, the potential role of hip-hop music and culture in school curricula, teens' access to a livable wage, teacher quality, school safety, and the digital divide, to name a few.

A significant portion of the seminar is spent "in the field," or in the streets, neighborhoods, and schools of Los Angeles. One year, we situated the seminar within the Democratic National Convention. Students attended rallies, protest marches, and community forums; in addition, they circulated among delegates, media personnel, and candidates for political office. During other years, students have visited school sites to dialogue with students and teachers about the material conditions of urban schooling and about their personal experiences in urban schools and classrooms. Research teams have also visited community centers and surveyed neighborhoods in search of learning resources and access to technology. One group used Geographic Information Systems (GIS) software to map the distribution of liquor stores to libraries in a densely populated low-income census tract within the city. They located fifty-eight active liquor stores and one semi-functional library in a neighborhood with 77,000 residents squeezed into a two-mile radius.

Composing is a key activity while conducting research in the field. Students transport their laptops or composition notebooks wherever they go and they will be seen scribbling field notes on a city bus en route to a march, transcribing interviews with journalists and candidates, writing analytical memos, or performing preliminary analyses of a media survey. Some have even been inspired to produce an editorial or cross the fictional divide to compose poetry or song lyrics that help to make sense of what they are seeing and learning.

Seminar participants also have access to digital video cameras and audio recorders, which they utilize to capture and incorporate sounds and images into their final group texts, which are PowerPoint presentations, traditional research reports, and short documentary films. In a recent seminar a group of students assembled digital video footage taken from a school site into a video montage that they then accompanied with a hip-hop soundtrack as evidence of the social and physical ecology of the school. Other groups have used digital photographs to augment their reports on neighborhood conditions or on youth popular culture. Over the course of the six summers that the seminar was offered, we became more systematic and intentional in infusing new media and digital rhetorics into the working of the seminar. We contracted a guerilla filmmaking crew and Internet activists to help us challenge and expand our notions of critical textual production.

Once out of the field, students return to the university to engage in data analysis and to assemble the final group reports and presentations. Guidelines for the final paper evolved over the years to include the following:

1. **Introduction**
   a. **The Problem (Justification for the Research)**—This should be the initial portion of the introduction where you explain the relevance of the research you are conducting.
   b. **The Research Question**—Given the need for the research, what specific question is your study attempting to answer? Why is your question significant or important?
2. **Literature Review**
   a. Upon what theories or prior studies are you basing your research? What are the terms or concepts that need defining?
   b. How does your study build on these theories and concepts?
3. **Methods**
   a. Describe in detail the schools, classrooms, students, politicians, activists, community members, etc. that you encountered in your study. To ensure anonymity, choose pseudonyms for the schools and all people you include in the study.
   b. Explain the process or method your paper will employ to explore the question that you have asked. Will you conduct interviews, surveys, perform ethnographic research, or design an experiment? What is the rationale behind your methodology?
4. **Reporting of Findings**
   This is the body or meat of your paper where you introduce, cite, synthesize, and critique the data that you collect.
5. **Conclusion**
   a. What significance do these findings hold for educational policy and research? What do these findings suggest about the broader issue of youth access? What further research would you suggest? How would you like to pursue these issues in the upcoming school year?
   b. Based on your expert status, you need to take some leadership and exert some authority to help solve the problems you mention in your introduction.
6. **References**
   a. You are required to have a minimum of 3 references to readings.
   b. All papers will cite references using the APA style.

Although the guidelines for the final papers may seem overly regimented, there is a definite goal to help the students to have confidence in writing traditional research reports. One of our charges was to "demonstrate" to the university that students who were not gaining entry into the university could indeed perform the literacy tasks associated with university coursework.

During this final week of the seminar, a great deal of attention is paid to composition. Students meet in the mornings to discuss their individual essays and in the afternoons they work as research teams to compose their research.

Each year, students presented their work at a conference-like event that involved university faculty, parents, community leaders, policymakers, and other students. Papers, films and presentations were witnessed and commented upon by faculty at the university as an assessment of the quality of the student work. In other outlets, students subsequently delivered lectures and presentations to graduate seminars in departments of education and sociology; their papers have been presented to the California Writing Project (CWP), the National Coalition of Educational Activists (NCEA), and the American Educational Research Association (AERA). Further, the student-initiated, student-generated research has influenced state legislation, most notably through the Educational Bill of Rights in the State of California, which was sponsored by Representative Judy Chu. Finally, and most importantly, this research has helped the student participants to acquire much needed skills for academic advancement, professional membership, and civic engagement.

The critical research and writing seminar is not without problems or challenges. As co-director, I struggled with issues of control versus freedom in determining how much of the seminar needs to be pre-planned to ensure efficiency and how much needs to be responsive to the emergent dialogue among the students. I was frequently aware of the contradictions of my heavy-handedness when selecting readings and class assignments, but I also worried about offering a seminar that was haphazard and chaotic or asked too much of students too soon. I also struggled with trying to find a balance between experiences in the field and serious time devoted to the craft of composition. Without the field experiences, students would lose access to writing material and they would lose opportunities to engage in socially meaningful activity. However, without sufficient time devoted to writing, students would end up with brilliant but incomplete thoughts and they would lose the opportunity to develop great material into great writing.

On the whole, however, there is ample evidence to suggest that students enjoy and are enriched by their seminar experience. In follow-up interviews and surveys, students comment that they learned a great deal and were inspired to continued work for social justice. Students keep in touch via e-mail communication and contributions to the university-sponsored website. Faculty members from across the university have consistently testified to the quality of student research and writing and have invited student researchers to guest lecture in their university seminars. Approximately ninety-five percent of the seminar participants either have been accepted to or are attending two- and four-year colleges and universities. Many continue to work with the seminar either as researchers or as mentors to a future generation of critical scholars and there is always more interest on the part of recent alumni than there is space to accommodate them.

The work of the students in the seminar also has a large impact on the populations that they interact with for their study. For instance, in our most recent seminar, the students visited an inner city middle school to explore the facilities and conduct focus group interviews. After the focus group interviews, we stayed on the campus for lunch. Once word had passed about the nature of the interviews, the seminar students were swamped by literally hundreds of the middle schoolers demanding that their stories be heard. Several of the middle school students were interested in knowing how they could become part of the seminar movement. There was a similar occurrence at one of the poorest high schools in the county where the seminar students also visited. After conducting focus group interviews, which were in reality more like dialogues, a growing number of the school's population followed our seminar students around the school attempting to learn more about the nature of the research and sharing more about their experiences at the school. Again, the seminar students were barraged with comments such as "What can we do?" and "How can I join?" For these "research subjects" simply having the opportunity to have their stories shared and to publicly utter their narratives of schooling was an enabling experience. In what follows, I take a closer look at the various forms of textual production that accompanied the students' voyage through the world of critical research.

STUDENT CRITICAL RESEARCH AND
TEXTUAL PRODUCTION

The Uses of the Composition Notebooks

There were multiple uses for the composition notebooks issued to the students at the beginning of the seminars. During the general class sessions, students took notes on lectures and small breakout group discussions. Early during the seminar, teachers checked the notes to see that students were learning what level of detail was appropriate in note-taking. Students were also encouraged to look at the notebooks of their peers to see how they had annotated similar conversations.

In small group sessions, students were also asked to annotate the conversations, but there were other uses of the notebooks during these segments. For example, students were assigned texts to read and produced reading notes, summaries, or short answer essays for group discussion. Later, during the seminar when groups were preparing the literature review portion of their research reports, the students would often refer back to their reading notes.

Students also used notebooks to produce research instruments such as surveys and interview protocols. Prior to entering the field the students would need to generate interview questions for various research subjects as well as survey questions. For example, in a recent seminar a group investigating urban schools' technological learning resources needed to produce interview questions for students, teachers, and administrators in addition to an observation protocol to be used on school-site visits.

When in the field, students were encouraged to take ample field notes. They would record their observations and perceptions of the various locales in the composition notebooks. For example, during the summer of 2000, students took public transportation to downtown Los Angeles where the Democratic National Convention was being held. While downtown, students had the opportunity to walk around through impoverished neighborhoods, through the official headquarters, and through the headquarters where activists groups were centered. Even though students were equipped with cameras, seminar teachers foregrounded the necessity of capturing the environment with field notes while helping students to develop this capacity.

Students also conducted many informal interviews while in the field. Again, the students might have tape recorders or digital cameras, but their primary source of data collection included the scratch notes they took. During the seminar of 2003 students collected oral histories of citizens who were involved in public schooling in Los Angeles during the fifty years following the *Brown* decision. Occasionally, a research participant would agree to speak, but not in front of the camera, so the only source of data collection became the composition notebooks. Students would also happen upon interviews when no cameras or tape recorders were around. Two young women who were collecting oral histories of students who attended schools during the decade from 1954 to 1963 ran into a gentleman in a grocery store who provided an amazing interview. Given that no cameras or recorders were around, they took turns asking questions and transcribing the answers. They were able to refer back to their notes to reconstruct the interview during their data analysis.

There were numerous other field-related tasks requiring students to use their notebooks. For example, during one summer seminar, students visited historical archives where they were not allowed to remove any items from the facility. Any information to be extracted would come only through the recorded notes. Similarly, another group chose to analyze yearbook data from 1950s yearbooks to determine school demographics. As the yearbooks could not be removed from the school archives, students recorded demographic information from a decade of school annuals in their composition notebooks.

During the final two weeks of the seminar the focus turned toward data analysis. In groups students focused on generating analytic memos and data spreads in addition to recording selective transcriptions of taped interviews and annotations of digital video footage. All of these activities were recorded in the students' notebooks. I should add that the students numbered their notebook pages and created a table of contents page at the beginning of the notebooks to ensure easier navigation in the final stages of their research projects. That also made it easier for teacher-researchers to examine the content of the books as well. By the end of the seminar, students averaged over one hundred pages of recorded notes in these composition books. It is also important to note that, as teachers and researchers, we made a conscious decision to return these notebooks to the students, who had become attached to them over the course of the seminar, rather than keep them for research purposes. Each year, a few volunteers would allow their notebooks to be photocopied to allow us to understand how they were learning to annotate and how the notebooks were being used.

Electronic Journaling and Critical Memoirs

Each morning the seminar would begin with the same activity. For approximately thirty minutes students would respond on their laptop computers to a journal prompt. These prompts would then be e-mailed to a writing teacher who would then provide e-mail feedback, thereby continuing the conversation.

The electronic journals served several purposes. First, the journals provided material that the students could draw upon in writing their critical memoirs, a fifteen hundred- to two thousand-word reflexive essay on the process of learning to conduct critical, community-based research. To this end, prompts would occasionally encourage students to reflect on various stages of the research process. For example, after their first day in the field collecting data, a prompt would ask them to share their feelings about the process of thinking about both what they liked and what they might do differently if given another chance.

The journals also encouraged students to reflect on their own personal experiences as they related to the research process. During the summers when students were investigating conditions in schools, prompts often asked them to consider their own educational experiences. During the summer spent at the Democratic National Convention students were encouraged to reflect on their knowledge of politics, their political participation, and their sense of political agency.

Finally, journals asked students to make connections between their changing identities as critical researchers and their plans for the future. Common prompts, especially during the final week, might ask the students to define what it means to be a critical researcher, to consider how they have changed as a result of acquiring the tools of critical research, or to consider how they might live differently in the future. The following journal response was written near the end of the students' experiences at the Democratic National Convention during the summer of 2000:

Natalie's Journal Reflections 8-17-2000

Today was a day of reflections. This week has been filled with many learning experiences and at times that can be overwhelming. There is always a need to take time to reflect and analyze, to learn and to grow. I found myself learning so much just from sitting in the circle today.

Everyone had something of value to say. Hearing everyone's experiences and opinions has enriched my own experience here. I was not at every site all the time, but hearing the account of others has helped me live vicariously every part of the DNC.

I have gone through mixed feelings here this week. It began (I hate to admit), with cynicism. The Democracy Live 2000 seemed like a complete farce, a joke. But maybe that is the way TV is done. Then I experienced frustration at not being able to get into other parts of the Convention Center. I wanted to witness democracy inside those large halls.

But I was not disappointed completely because I found democracy elsewhere. The speakers that visited us this week were all fighting for equality in one way or another. They each had their way of approaching the issues that most concerned them. I discovered that there are people in this world who are really passionate and devoted to making this place better for everyone.

Now I leave cynicism behind but not the anger of the first day. I will take that anger with me everywhere I go from now on, wherever that place may be. It is anger that leads to action, and action to changes. This place needs changes, and someone has to help achieve them.

On this road, which is my life, I continue to walk ahead, going through doors and hoping to someday make positive changes. Someone I really admire said (something like this) "You go through doors in your life, and through some doors you just can't go back." I think this seminar as a whole has been one giant door, and I know, I can never go back.

This student response captures all of the purposes of the journal writing activity in that she is able to reflect on her own experiences, the process of research, and her changing relationship to the conditions that she has been researching. It also conveys the incredible emotions that accompany this type of work for young people. Finally, it shows the tremendous talent and passion that our students have; talent and passion that often go undiscovered during their traditional educational experiences.

Research Papers and Presentations

The culminating products of the seminars consisted of a final research paper and accompanying PowerPoint presentation. Though the format changes slightly with each seminar, the papers and presentations have included an introduction, a review of literature, a methods section, a reporting of findings, and implications for policy and political activism. The PowerPoint presentations average twenty minutes and the reports average thirty pages with the longest being a seventy-seven-page report study of the social and physical ecology of urban schools produced in the summer of 2002.

I briefly share a few excerpts from the student research papers as examples of the quality of writing, the sophistication of the research design and the significance of the research findings of these projects. Each example, in its own way, attests to the powerful academic and critical literacies associated with the project of community-based critical research projects.

The first example is taken from the literature review section of a group studying the multiple spaces for civic learning in Westside Los Angeles:

> Another great example of skills attributed with being a good citizen is being able to "read the word and the world" as in Freire's "First Letter". He states that in order for one to be able to form ones own opinion, he or she needs to be able to build on text that they read and have the ability to relate that to our own world. If we do not interpret and build on things such as theories or problems, then we will all just be another cog in the systematic machine of learning through text.
>
> Some students think that speaking out on issues in their schools is a big skill needed for successful civic engagement. Their methods of speaking out come in the form of petitioning, protesting, walking out, and forming a club. They start off with these examples of passive resistance in hopes that many more will come to grips with reality and face the problem, then they will gather in numbers and hope that they have some sort of impact on their school officials.
>
> Artists play a huge role in civic engagement because they have the power to affect people in numbers. Most artists feel that, because they are so popular and influential (in some cases more than parents or political leaders), they have a responsibility to spread the word to the public. They use their music, murals,

paintings, etc. to express what is in their heads, and being that they do it in such a popular way they feel that if they don't send a message then it has a negative affect on people.

In order to get to the point where the students were able to write this literature review, which subsequently informed their study, the students read the work of philosophers and scholars such as Paulo Freire, Joseph Kahne, and Joel Westheimer (Westheimer and Kahne, 2004), who each offered different definitions of an engaged citizen. They were then able to synthesize these different perspectives with their own lived experiences as students attending schools that offered differing, even competing conceptions of citizenship. Finally the students were able to augment traditional scholarship with an analysis of the role that popular culture plays in transmitting ideas about engaged citizenship to urban teens. The result is a thorough analysis of the pedagogy of civic engagement that combines structural philosophers, educational research, school curricula, and hip-hop music and culture.

The second example is taken from the methodology section of a research group that focused on the experiences of students of color attending Los Angeles area schools during the decade of 1954–1963. In this particular section the students define and then defend an innovative and unique form of data collection, the analysis of old high school yearbooks:

Schools did not have to collect information on the race or ethnicity of students and teachers at schools until the late 1960's, so we acquired this data for our decade by using yearbook analysis. First, we went to each of the high schools and got yearbooks between 1953–1964. We would sit down in pairs with one yearbook and analyze it, inferring the ethnicity of each senior student and faculty member. The researcher looking at the yearbook would go photo by photo and decide which ethnic group the student or teacher appeared to belong to, making an inference by their last name and appearance. The research partner would keep a tally. We all used the same protocol so that we could all record our data consistently and could easily compare them to different schools. On the protocol we categorized the students into five groups: White, African American, Latino, Asian, and other/unknown. These categories use updated terms compared to the 1950 census; we only included categories we thought we could place people into just by looking at their photo and surname so there are fewer categories than the 2000 census. Once we had all the numbers of the 16 yearbooks from 6 schools we decided to convert to percentages. Percentages allows us to compare schools even if they are of different sizes; making bar graphs help us visualize ethnic breakdowns between different years in the same school and between different schools.

The only problem that we encountered was the fact that our methods were not totally accurate. The pictures were in black and white, which made it harder to tell their skin complexion. For example, there were a few people that looked almost white but had a traditionally black last name, so we would discuss these difficult cases with our partners and vote on a category for the person. Even though there was some controversy, the majority of them were easy to group.

After looking at the senior class and the faculty, we also looked at sports teams and other extracurricular activities to assess the group's diversity. We decided to do this because most of our interviewees said that sports were the uniting factor between races. Also, some said that if the school was predominantly white you could find the few minority students in the athletics department and extracurricular activities.

This is a powerful example of critical literacy for a number of reasons. First of all the clarity and level of detail in description are really incredible for novice researchers. The group is able to justify and articulate an innovative approach to data collection, and they are also able to anticipate potential weaknesses in their approach. Additionally, the work is powerful in the creativity that the students employed to develop research methods to explore their chosen topics. These students were one of five groups each studying the lived experiences of students attending Los Angeles schools in the five decades following the *Brown v. Board of Education* court decision in 1954. As the group with the oldest data set, they faced significant challenges that their peers did not. Starting in the 1960s schools were forced to report a great deal more attendance and achievement data disaggregated by race and ethnicity (thanks in no small part to the Civil Rights movement and its impact on thinking about race and ethnicity in the country). Wanting to understand the changing racial demography of the city's schools but not having access to traditional data sets, the group decided to locate and analyze the high school yearbooks from select schools across the city. The sophisticated yearbook analysis yielded very important data not only about the demography, but also about integration and participation within the schools that these students studied.

The third example is also taken from a methodology section of a research paper, from a group doing more traditional empirical work. This particular group studied discrepancies between learning resources available to students attending urban and suburban schools in Los Angeles County:

The group of student researchers visited two high schools and one middle school. These schools and community settings were not chosen at random. Professor Dewey with the assistance of Mr. Genovese was responsible for arranging the site visits through various contacts. One of the high schools was located in a middle class neighborhood while the other high schools and middle schools were located in working class neighborhoods. The reason for visiting two types of schools is to have an equal variety in students, communities, and responses. The student researchers also spoke to community leaders and students in public settings. The educational resources group used two types of assessment tools: surveys and discussion questions for focus groups. The questions for discussion were developed a few days earlier than the survey questions because they were tested on friends and/or relatives attending public schools first. Afterwards, the questions were improved based on practice interviews. The survey questions were developed on the basis of what educational resources students need to succeed in their classes. The protocol for each school visit varied slightly.

What stand out from this section are the scope of the research project and the sophistication of the research design. The students, during the course of this five-week project, were able to visit three different campuses and employ a mixed method design that included surveys, interviews, and observational protocols. What's more, the student research group had the prescience to pilot and refine their survey and interview research instruments. The size, quality, and detail of the data set are what one might expect in a peer-reviewed research article or a Master's-level graduate thesis. The students were able to code and analyze these various forms of data, which, in the end, spoke powerfully to the digital divide that students experienced across Los Angeles County schools.

The final example is taken from the conclusion of a paper in which students studied the basic rights to which all students are entitled. These students consider the implications of their work for educational research and for collective action for social change:

Therefore, we have come to the resolution that credentialed teachers, college prep classes, and clean facilities must be offered to every student regardless of their race or socioeconomic status. According to the 14th Amendment of the U.S. Constitution, no state may "deprive any person of liberty, or property, without due process of law, nor deny to any person within its jurisdiction equal protection of the laws." Therefore, it is unconstitutional for certain schools to provide a better education than others within the same state. This violates the idea of "equal protection of the laws" for all citizens.

Ward Connerly, a UC Regent appointed by Governor Pete Wilson, has introduced a California ballot measure he calls "The Racial Privacy Initiative." The initiative is a measure that would damage California's ability to address racial and ethnic disparities in healthcare and disease patterns, educational resources, academic achievement, hate crime and discrimination. Students will no longer be given the option of providing their ethnic and racial background in California colleges and universities. In addition, "it handicaps community groups, local governments, and the state as they develop solutions to healthcare, education, and other disparities in our diverse state." (Internet http://www.informedcalifornia.org/facts.shtml) The UC Regents voted against this measure in May due to its detrimental effects on university research. This will also have detrimental effects in California because activists and organizations like ACLU will no longer have statistics about the racial make-up of colleges and universities, and educational inequalities may grow. This measure will greatly affect minority communities and low-income communities.

The student writing here is important in its authorial authority; that is, the students envision themselves as a group that has the *right* to intervene in conversations about education reform. In my field notes and in my coding of student-generated texts this demonstration of authority, confidence, or voice by the students came up repeatedly. Students, through their presentations and written production, revealed their changing identities as transformative intellectuals possessing the confidence and the skills to participate powerfully as researchers and as agents of change. This is extremely important when considering the hypotheses of Freire, Fanon, and other critical theorists who recognize the true moment of transformation as occurring when people have a language to describe their oppression as oppression; a following stage occurs when people envision themselves working individually and collectively to challenge oppressive conditions. It is possible to identify both processes playing themselves out in the student writing.

The conclusion is also important because it shows that the students indeed have something powerful to contribute to the conversation about educational equity. They have produced quality work as researchers and they are well positioned as consumers of schooling to make the assertions they do on a moral as well as intellectual level. Finally, the preceding example is just good writing: clear, engaging, emotive, and articulate; the kind of writing that should be published and championed as creative and powerful uses of the written word.

The papers and PowerPoint presentations have as their primary audience a panel of university faculty and community advocates who have expertise either in the research topics or the research methods. The members of these panels listen and then respond to the presentations as if they were at a traditional academic conference in education or the social sciences. Secondary audiences for the presentations and papers include the parents, teachers, administrators, and policymakers who are also in attendance at the final day's activity.

After the presentations, students' papers, PowerPoint slides, and iMovies are published to a website that is accessed primarily by teachers in the Los Angeles area. Papers are also passed on to principals, school board members, state representatives, legal advocates, and community-based organizations. The research from the 2001 summer seminar concerning the composition of an educational bill of rights played a key role in influencing proposed state legislation. Students who researched the potential of hip-hop music and culture to motivate academic literacy development presented to a department meeting at a nearby school and later to a local affiliate of the National Writing Project. Students also lectured to undergraduate and graduate seminars at seven major universities on the west coast. Students have presented their research at the last five annual meetings of the American Educational Research Association as well as the 2001 meeting of the Sociology of Education Association. Two students have co-authored an article that appears in a peer-reviewed research journal and at least one student has expressed her desire to write a book.

IMPLICATIONS FOR EDUCATIONAL RESEARCH AND LITERACY EDUCATION IN URBAN CONTEXTS

There are important implications from the research on the six summer research seminars for methods of educational research and for practices in literacy education. Critical research challenges the who, why, and how of inquiry in education. Whereas traditionally the work of educational research remained the domain of university scholars, the summer seminar encouraged students, parents, and teachers to participate as collaborators in the research process. I have argued elsewhere (Morrell, 2004a) and I continue to advocate that our critical epistemology challenges us as educational researchers to democratize the tools of research; tools that determine ultimately who in our society has the right to speak truth (Foucault, 1972). By opening spaces for young people to conduct educational ethnographies, we can fundamentally change the nature of the practice as well as the knowledge that is produced and distributed in ways that are enabling for these young people, their schools, and their neighborhoods.

Critical research also challenges the *how* of educational inquiry. The work conducted by students and adults was intimate, personal, messy work engaged by interested parties. I call the work unapologetically intimate. Rather than apologize or retreat from the insider perspective, I argue that the benefits for the students of working in schools and neighborhoods close to their own outweigh the supposed challenges of proximity. The nature of the relationships between the students, their subjects, and their communities allowed them to gain access to data that would have been impossible for outsiders to collect. Similarly, my intimate relationship with the students affected, in positive ways, my access to the data I have collected and interpreted from these summer seminars. In both instances, the research has looked different from traditional work, but has been powerful and important work nonetheless.

Finally, the why of critical research has to be tied to personal and social transformation. Rather than seeking to understand the "other" like Margaret Mead, Bronislaw Malinowski, Franz Boas, and other architects of the discipline, this method of ethnographic research ideally helps us to better understand ourselves and our world in the hopes of enabling us to intervene in transforming our relationship to our world and those material conditions we find most unconscionable. Given the present challenges we confront in urban schools, this presents a powerful tool for students, teachers, parents, community advocates, and university researchers who would like to see themselves as agents of change.

I have also argued that any reforms in curriculum and pedagogy targeted at urban populations need to be focused on increasing academic achievement (Morrell and Duncan-Andrade, 2002). Toward this end, I believe that the work of the seminar stands on its own merit as an example of the kind of academic work students are capable of. In a five-week seminar, urban high school students read and wrote in large volumes and produced work that was deemed high quality even by university standards. These students attended schools that were identified as underperforming, yet their textual production in many instances belies their academic records.

I would like to see more opportunities for students to engage in local community-based research as part of secondary literacy courses. The idea of allowing students to draw upon personal interests and expertise in order to develop academic competencies and an empowered relationship to their social world is certainly an appealing one for literacy education. The seminar concentrated on personal essays and research reports, but we also toyed with the idea of having students represent their findings through drama, through fiction, through poetry, or even through film.

I am reminded of Denzin's comments that critical, poststructuralist ethnography is personal and emotional in making sense of the new meanings produced for me as a teacher and as a researcher. I cannot write about these students, the research seminar, or the material conditions confronted in these urban schools without emotion. Nor should I. As an ethnographer of literacy, I continue to learn about the acquisition and usage of language and literacies of power in the service of self and social emancipation; I learn more about how researchers can and should position themselves in relation to the communities and subjects with whom they work. I learn more about what I mean when I use the adjective "critical" as a modifier for nouns like "ethnography," "research," "literacy," and "pedagogy." As a teacher, I learn about the power of stepping lightly, of opening spaces for meaning-making, for authentic praxis as a site for dialogue, reading, writing, and, most importantly, for the manifestation of existential freedom, individual, and collective agency. And I share my story as a teacher and learner, not to demonstrate or convince; but I share my text in the hopes of generating new ideas and entering into your conversations pertaining to the democratization of research tools, the liberation of research methods, and ultimately, the potential of transforming schools, pedagogies, and curricula that socialize and constrain the young to be otherwise.

PRESENTATION DAY

I can think of no better purpose for curricula that include critical writing than to take up the charge of developing writers as engaged citizens and transformative intellectuals who see writing as a tool, if not *the* tool, of social change. For some, this is a radical reconceptualization from composition as fundamentally about helping students to master the discourses of academia and the professions. Certainly this is a worthwhile pursuit and should not be abandoned; though it should be complemented by a more socially oriented focus. Students do not only need the tools to write correctly; they need a purpose for writing that extends beyond scholastic or professional success on one hand, and a better understanding of themselves on the other hand. What students need is an association of composition with advocacy, with activism, with empowerment, and with revolution. Freire has said that the act of studying is, itself, revolutionary. I would add to that that the act of writing, authentic writing of critical texts is a revolutionary act. I contend strongly that writing pedagogies centered upon critical textual production can accomplish these multiple aims.

Consistent with the tenets of critical pedagogy, critical textual production is situated within the experiences of students and uses their experiences and real world problems as a starting point, but it quickly becomes about the business of social justice. It is about naming oppression, certainly, but it is also about eradicating oppression and injustice through the creation of counter-texts, critical texts, that present alternate realities as they simultaneously critique the existing narratives that promote the status quo.

Imagine a high school English course, "Critical Research and Writing," in which the syllabus emanates from critical and liberating dialogue and the classroom becomes the world manifested through real communities engaged in real struggles. And the words created, generated by students in collaboration with community members and fellow cultural workers, are authentic in that they reveal the world even as they rewrite it. The actual process and products of critical textual production in this course are counterhegemonic.

And the process of engaging or even mastering academic discourse is not lost; rather it too is subsumed within the authentic, problem-posing dialogue in that the students contemplate discourses of power as they wrestle with how to articulate effectively to multiple audiences; a goal demanding that they acknowledge and incorporate academic and cultural rhetorics. The continual writing and rewriting are not then requirements demanded by an instructor; they are self-demanded in the process of making the most compelling case or painting the most vivid portrait of a counter-reality possible.

In the process of creating memory through critical literacy—leaving words as legacy, real words, true words, life-transforming words for this and future generations—the need for the writing process is self-evident to students. I have seen this in the writing for the seminar when students are up all hours of the night during their summer vacations working on assignments that are "ungraded." They are not writing for approval or evaluation. They believe, and rightly so, that their words matter. This is nothing new in that many compositionists speak to the importance of creating a meaningful audience. It is different, however, in advocating that literacy educators think first and foremost about a meaningful purpose: active engagement with local and global struggles for liberation and change. When writing is not about preparation for some future outcome, such as a high grade, admission to an elite graduate program, or a well-paying job; rather writing is itself an action of import to the moment; when literacy is life—generative and regenerative, sustaining revolutionary discourse through composers with the courage and confidence to contribute commentary and contestation in chaotic times.

Praxis of Distribution

In addition to the critical consumption and production of texts, the seminar became a place to contemplate the critical distribution of texts; what I call the pedagogy and praxis of distribution. In other words student-researchers and university collaborators needed to theorize a pedagogy and praxis of distribution that considered appropriate audiences for texts, appropriate genres of representation, rhetorical approaches that were significant to these audiences, and mechanisms for disseminating these texts to the various audiences deemed important. I will briefly describe the process for distributing texts to researchers and policymakers, teachers and other school-site personnel, and other youth implicated in the same material, social, and cultural conditions as our student researchers.

Distribution to Researchers and Policymakers

One of the primary audiences for the student-initiated work included university faculty and elected officials. The most compelling genres for these audiences included research papers and PowerPoint presentations. First and foremost, we felt that these populations needed to be convinced of the "merit" of the research before they would even consider the content of the research. To these ends, each research report and presentation included an introduction, a review of the literature, a section describing the methods of research, a section discussing the findings, and a section considering the implications of the research. These are the same sections one would find in a peer-reviewed research article, a dissertation, or even a book. The genre, therefore, would be a familiar one for the academics and for the officials who often consult them.

Similarly, the presentation format mirrored that of a national conference for researchers. I have attended the national conferences of most social science organizations and all follow a similar presentation protocol: a speaker or group of speakers presents for approximately twenty minutes; these presentations are followed by a discussant, usually someone respected in the field, who offers critical commentary on the papers. The session is then open to questions from the audience. All of the final oral presentations for the seminar are accompanied by PowerPoint slides, which add to the rhetorical impact of the presentation. With the aid of the software, students are able to represent their methods and data sections visually, including quotations and images gathered during the research process.

With respect to the distribution, the immediate context is the presentation itself, which reaches an academic audience, all of whom are given access to papers and the PowerPoint slides. These artifacts are made available in hard copy and are posted to a website. National conference presentations are a second prominent method of distribution. For four consecutive years, student groups presented their research at the annual meeting of the American Educational Research Association. Students have also presented at the educational affiliate of the American Sociological Association.

Students and parents, teachers, and university faculty who have represented their work have lobbied policymakers directly through presentations and individual consultations. Prominent politicians are also invited into the haven of the seminar, where they are questioned by students, but they are also able to observe the students at work, providing yet another valuable method of distribution. In the Aristotelian sense, students use variously the *ethos* of the sanctioned researcher, the *logos* of the social sciences, and the *pathos* of near-participants who are directly implicated in the issues that are under research to convince these multiple populations of the validity of their work. All of these practices contribute to powerful scholarship as well as the development of these teens as competent and confident producers of the written word.

6

Cyberactivism

This chapter begins with a unique perspective of critical literacy as the production and distribution of texts via mainstream and alternative media. I begin by pointing toward the multiple successfully subversive uses of cyberspace in the short history of the communication genre. There is no question that cyberspace is a powerful medium of communication with huge potential for local agents who want to participate with larger collectives for social change. I pay particular attention to two cases in which young people were able to use Internet communication to foster larger social movements. These cases include the ongoing revolution of the Zapatista Liberation Army (EZLN) in Chiapas, Mexico, and the successful movements to disrupt the meetings of the World Trade Organization in Seattle, Washington, in November 1999.

The second half of the chapter examines the development of a virtual community of urban adolescents dedicated to using Internet tools to promote social justice. I describe the philosophy of critical pedagogy behind the creation of a critical community of cyberliterate youth. I also describe, in detail, the pedagogy of cyberliteracies that allowed a group of teens with relatively little computer or Internet experience to become proficient and sophisticated users of cyberspace in a short amount of time. I conclude with an analysis of data generated by online fieldwork that documents the myriad critical uses of cyberspace in which these students engaged. I pay specific attention to the development of traditional and new media literacy skills, the development of emergent identities as activists and intellectuals, growing confidence with technological tools, and collective action for social change.

THE SUBVERSIVE WORLD OF CYBERSPACE

Let's face it: we are living in the midst of a revolution. Okay, it may not be a revolution in the traditional sense of the term, with masses storming the capital in arms, but to say we are in the midst of a communications revolution paralleled only by the creation of the Gutenberg press is to only state the obvious. Nothing, in the world of information exchange, is as it was. Cell phones and PDAs now serve as portals to the virtual village; citizens check their e-mail while waiting in line at the airport. Two-pound laptops open to wireless access in New York's Washington Square Park. E-mails dart around the globe at the speed of thought. The libraries of the world and most of the corpus of accumulated human knowledge are only fingertips away for those fortunate enough to afford this access.

Certainly this communications revolution has major implications for the way we now do business: it is possible to conference via webcam and documents that would fill an entire filing cabinet can be sent to a hundred people at once; all at the click of a button. There are also implications for how we entertain ourselves. Children and young adults who used to spend six hours a day staring into the television sets now use half of that time staring into a computer screen and, through that screen, to the world, both virtual and "real." These kids use the Internet to send e-mails, to "Instant Message" friends, to participate in weblogs or "blogs," to seek out information, to play video games against people around the world, to download music and films, or to create their own web spaces or profiles on MySpace (which, at current count, approaches 200 million participants). There are also other unsavory practices of Internet use that do not need to be mentioned, but we know they exist.

Whether for business or for personal entertainment, scholars understand that the uses of cyberspace have changed the relationship of average citizens toward information. Some have argued (Lankshear *et al.*, 1996) that the cyber-revolution has played an important role in democratizing access to information as well as opening up new possibilities for knowledge production and dissemination. Now anyone with Internet access and a knowledge of HTML (Hypertext Markup Language) can be a published author. Amateur websites and blogs receive thousands of hits each month; most of the young people I now work with have MySpace pages that they program regularly, often with sophisticated use of HTML. And countercultural information and practices are supported and proliferated through these new postgeographical spaces. Though these new communications tools can also be used to promote existing hegemonies, I would like to consider their subversive, revolutionary potential by examining the cases of cyberpunks, Zapatistas, and activists involved in the World Trade Organization protests of 1999 in order to develop a grounded theory of cyberactivism that may have major implications for the critical literacy pedagogy of urban adolescents.

CYBERPUNKS

The 1980s witnessed the genesis of cult literary and film classics such as Bruce Sterling's *Hacker Crackdown*, Ridley Scott's *Blade Runner,* and William Gibson's *Neuromancer* as well as the underground phenomenon known as cyberpunk culture. Although the term "cyberpunk" carries negative connotations in the mainstream as a culture of political anarchy, it serves as an example of an empowered youth culture replete with sophisticated literacy practices that bolster subversive activities. The movie *War Games* is an example of this power; showing that a technologically sophisticated teenager could possibly hack into a National Security database. The notion of a savvy teen bringing corporate America to a crawl through hacking into security-encrypted networks and the proliferation of deadly computer viruses is now commonplace. Less understood, however, are the political motives that underlie such activities. The ideology and aesthetic of the cyberpunk are eloquently revealed in this quote from a cyberpunk manifesto:

1/We are those, the Different. Technological rats, swimming in the ocean of information. 2/We are the retiring, little kid at school, sitting at the last desk, in the corner of the class room. 3/We are the teenager everybody considers strange. 4/We are the student hacking computer systems, exploring the depth of his reach. 5/We are the grown-up in the park, sitting on a bench, laptop on his knees, programming the last virtual reality. 6/Ours is the garage, stuffed with electronics. The soldering iron in the corner of the desk and the nearby disassembled radio – they are also ours. Ours is the cellar with computers, buzzing printers and beeping modems. 7/ We are those that see reality in a different way. Our point of view shows more than ordinary people can see. They see only what is outside, but we see what is inside. That's what we are – realists with the glasses of dreamers. 8/We are those strange people, almost unknown to the neighborhood. People, indulged in their own thoughts, sitting day after day before the computer, ransacking the net for something. We are not often out of home, just from time to time, only to go to the nearby radio shack, or to the usual bar to meet some of the few friends we have, or to meet a client, or to the backstreet druggist. . . or just for a little walk. 9/We do not have many friends, only a few with whom we go to parties. Everybody else we know we know on the net. Our real friends are there, on the other side of the line. We know them from our favorite IRC channel, from the News-Groups, from the systems we hang-around: 10/We are those who don't give a shit about what people think about us, we don't care what we look like or what people talk about us in our absence. 11/

The majority of us likes to live in hiding, being unknown to everybody except those few we must inevitably contact with. 12/Others love publicity, they love fame. They are all known in the underground world. Their names are often heard there. But we are all united by one thing – we are Cyberpunks (Kirtchev, 1997).

We see the image of the lonely intellectual using cybertools to escape a desolate postindustrial wasteland, finding solace and new definition in a virtual reality. The cyberpunk is an alienated member of society, but not a powerless one. S/he is an intellectual and a knowledge producer. As the manifesto and other literary classics (such as the work of Sterling) suggest, cyberpunks are dreamers and revolutionaries. They see in the world what "ordinary" people are unable to see. And not only do they see the dystopian vision of the future, they have developed the technological sophistication to act against it. Again, I quote at length from Kirtchev's manifesto:

5/We are in the middle. We are interested in what happens now, but in what's gonna happen tomorrow as well. 6/We look in the net, and the net is growing wide and wider. 7/Soon everything in this world will be swallowed by the net: from the military systems to the PC at home. 8/But the net is a house of anarchy. 9/It cannot be controlled and in this is its power. 10/Every man will be dependent on the net. 11/The whole information will be there, locked in the abysses of zeros and ones. 12/ Who controls the net, controls the information. 13/We will live in a mixture of past and present. 14/The bad come from the man, and the good comes from technology. 15/The net will control the little man, and we will control the net. 16/For if you do not control, you will be controlled. 17/The Information is POWER!

Cyberpunks have been conscious and reflexive of their power as anarchistic, technically competent social dissidents, a fact lost on much of the larger population. In a time when critical theory is largely defined by proximity to neo-Marxist or poststructuralist agendas, the cyberpunks offer an interesting counterpoint, demonstrating an alternative trajectory for informed anti-capitalist praxis. These alienated youth have explicit critiques of dominant hegemony, of capitalism, of the alienation of the "everyday person"; they envision new virtual spaces as a logical site of battle; and, most importantly, they envision themselves as informed and empowered participants in this battle against the dominant forces at work in society.

There is much here in the narrative of the rise of the cyberpunks to inform a grounded theory of literacy praxis in urban classrooms. Cyberpunks are helpful in informing our thinking about the relationship between nascent communications technologies and the ways in which power is wielded in Western postmodern democracies (here we can turn back to the work of Baudrillard and virtual technologies being used to promote late capitalist hegemonies). However, the cyberpunks are disinct from most postmodern theorists in that they see themselves as being able to contest against these virtual practices of hegemony; in other words, they have theorized their own counterhegemony. The ideas of youth-led social activism and the Internet as a worthy site of ideological/revolutionary struggle are important outcomes of the cyberpunk movement.

We should also learn that, when "the people," in this case young cyberpunks, create their own revolutions, they rarely look like what we would envision. Rather than express rage and disgust at the computer intellectuals for not conforming to our pre-existing (and probably outmoded) aesthetic, as theorists and educators we would be better served to understand the genesis and workings of this underground countercultural phenomenon. We are also well served to learn from these youth how to use the Internet to advocate for social justice, however we choose to theorize that term. The next two movements I describe, the Zapatista revolution and the 1999 protests against the oppressive practices of the World Trade Organization, have done just that; each of these movements has taken this revolutionary concept of virtual activism for personal freedoms, economic, and social justice to apply to more "traditional" social movements.

THE ZAPATISTA EXAMPLE

In *The Road Ahead*, Bill Gates, CEO of Microsoft and philosopher of the communications revolution, claims that access to information will determine ultimate power in the new millennium. Virtual wars will be fought over who has control of information systems that drive the postindustrial economy and, in turn, politics and social life. Not only will wars be fought over access to these communications technologies; it is now possible that actual wars will be fought utilizing these communications technologies. We see that now as we witness the image of the soldier in a camouflage tent staring at a laptop screen.

Witness as a case in point the Zapatista uprising of 1994. The ELZN, or Zapatista Liberation Army, is a modern movement of Mexican peasants modeled on the movement of Emiliano Zapata during the Mexican Revolution. In 1994 these land-tilling revolutionaries seized power in Chiapas and other portions of southern Mexico in order to call for the same reforms that Zapata had fought and died for so many years earlier. Righteous enough. Now normally the Mexican government and its forty thousand troops that continue to surround the revolutionaries could just bulldoze its way into the compound and end the hostilities without much effort. Only they couldn't because the eyes of the world are on the Zapatistas as they watch the standoff virtually and communicate with one another through the Internet. Activists and interested spectators throughout the world could not only watch and keep abreast of the activities of the EZLN, they could also email their righteous indignation to national and international officials, including the Mexican government. With so much international attention garnered primarily through virtual communication channels, the small band of Mexican farmers was able to hold off a powerful national army. Without the assistance of the Internet, they might not have had nearly the same chance (Russell, 2005). In 1998 the RAND corporation submitted a report to the United States army in which they referred to the Chiapas uprising as an information "netwar" where new communications technologies were more powerful than military might (Ronfeldt *et al.* 1998). In a superb media analysis of the Chiapas uprising and impact on social movement theory, Russell (2005) found literally thousands of websites and active listservs that helped to propel this local indigenous struggle into an international phenomenon.

When taking a virtual trip to one of the more popular EZLN websites, one is greeted by a statement (in Spanish) that in ten years of existence the website has received over five million visitors. Through simple navigation of the sidebar icons, one is also able to locate a ten-year archive of seminal declarations and recent communications, the five declarations of the Lacandon Jungle, interviews with Subcomandante Marcos and other leaders, a historical timeline of events between 1994 and 2005, photos of the movement, opportunities to join listservs and discussion groups, and links to other important websites associated with the struggle for indigenous rights and universal social justice. For example, at the time of this writing, on the page maintained a large link to *Radio Insurgente la voz de los sin voz* (Insurgent Radio, the voice for those without voice). Additionally, there is a link to a University of Texas website that contains important documents chronicling the eleven-year EZLN "Revolution." One is also greeted by this important message from the English Webmaster:

- The domain name was registered for this site with the permission of the EZLN leadership.
- You are encouraged to continue to disseminate/reprint/translate the communiqués of the EZLN assembled at this site; they are the work of the General Command of the EZLN, and neither this site nor the webmaster hold any copyright claims to them.

- Many people contribute to the presence of zapatismo on the Internet—through this page and many others, as well as through other Internet media (e.g. ftp and gopher, various mailing lists, etc.). See the links page.
- Subcomandante Marcos does not have a direct e-mail address, but the EZLN can be contacted *regarding the 2001 march to Mexico City only* via [URL deleted] (PLEASE do not misuse their email service!)
- The crisis in Chiapas will not be solved in Cyberspace; yet, the Internet can be a powerful tool for activism and information dissemination (hence, the page's existence). (URL deleted)

It is important to note that the current (at the time of this writing) hosts of the site hail from a very popular graduate-level university department at an elite institution in the United States. Elements of the site are maintained in at least five different languages including English, Spanish, French, Italian, and Portuguese, signaling both an intellectual effort and a global struggle to support the cause of the EZLN and to utilize cybercommunications for subversive and revolutionary purposes.

The website was put together in the spring of 1994 in order to provide reliable information on the Zapatista uprising and serve as a mouthpiece for the Zapatistas in cyberspace. The page is always growing, and well over five million people from Mexico and elsewhere have used it as a resource. During the late 1990s, for example, I used the site to keep abreast of the events in Chiapas, but also to learn about struggles for social justice worldwide. I could gather information that I trusted and I was even provided with emails of important officials to whom I could write in support of particular causes. It was largely through my legitimate peripheral participation on the website that I learned about the power and importance of cyberactivism. It was also at this time that I became involved with the Futures Project at South High and contemplated the critical and subversive uses of cyberspace. I will talk later in the chapter about how we employed lessons from the Zapatista and the WTO rebellion to theorize and implement a critical cyberpedagogy among these urban teens.

WTO PROTESTS 1999

From the postponing of the opening ceremony to the declaration of martial law and the firing of tear gas and rubber bullets, between 40,000 and 50,000 protesters took to the Seattle streets to oppose WTO power and practices. This resistance, both focused and dispersed, may have seemed like a spontaneous movement when seen through the mass media lens. In truth, preparations had started months prior to the summit with considerable mobilization conducted through the Internet. (Eagleton-Pierce, 2001, p. 332)

How was it that thousands of youth activists were able to converge on the streets of Seattle, Washington, during November of 1999 in efforts to halt or disrupt the activities of the World Trade Organization, which was scheduled to meet there? How were these youth able to be so successful with such limited resources at their disposal? Although public radio (Pacifica Radio in particular) played an important role, I argue that much of the organization and substance of the protest emerged from a core of coordinated and sustained Internet activism.

There was no mainstream coverage to speak of pertaining to the growing restlessness that was working its way into an international movement until after the protests were under way, and even that coverage was uneven and biased against the mobilized youth. Even in the absence of mainstream media sanction or traditional public spaces such as churches, town squares, and town halls, these youth still managed to coalesce themselves into a unified and well-informed collective of dissidents to global capitalist domination.

I participated in this virtual movement on many levels: as a viewer and reader of the emergent counter-discourse; as a signer of petitions; as a writer of e-mails and letters to public officials and corporate elites; and as a teacher to adolescents who were willing and able to participate virtually in the protest movement from the classrooms and neighborhoods of southern California.

I was pleasantly surprised at the amount of critical information that became available through cyberspace for those of us whose instincts told us there was something terribly wrong with the narrative of globalization being articulated via mainstream media outlets. Through the work of cyberactivists and the radio activists at Pacifica I learned about the growing differentials between the salaries of the average worker and the average CEO and how this differential had grown exponentially since the conclusion of World War II. On some Internet sites, these CEO salaries were actually published!

I also learned about these corporations' treatment of workers around the globe; their mistreatment of the environment; and their manipulation of national and international laws in order to maintain a corporate hegemony in the West and an intricate neocolonial relationship with the non-West.

Additionally, I learned a great deal about how to participate as a virtual activist. I learned, for instance, how to keep friends informed on the issues via email groups and listservs; how to put pressure on key stakeholders through a bombardment of virtual texts; and, yes, even how to mobilize physically at the local level; how to arrange travel and lodging for the Seattle protests; and how to coordinate meetings and activities at the Seattle event. Certainly activists were able to coordinate such activities before the advent of the Internet, but recent assaults on public spaces have made organizing on this scale difficult.

Further, I argue that the cyberactivism is unique in the amount of previously withheld information that the average citizen can obtain (of course one needs access to the Internet to read this information). Also unique are the myriad opportunities for active participation for those around the Western world who wanted to show solidarity with their *compadres* who were actually able to take to the streets of Seattle.

Some critics might rightly contend that information transmitted via the Internet has no external regulation for accuracy. Anyone who is able to purchase a domain name and has even a rudimentary knowledge of HTML can become an Internet publisher with access to hundreds of millions of visitors. Given this reality, one might question whether it is possible to trust any "critical" information transmitted. I argue that one must be discerning and must seek, when possible, to corroborate or triangulate data with other sources; that is just smart investigation. What is surprising is that the public generally doesn't question the information that it receives from mainstream print and media sources. If the original source is CBS or the *New York Times*, then it must be accurate. Of course, recent events have taught us how erroneous these assumptions really are; reporters and journalists from the powerhouse media outlets can outright lie or get their facts confused. As an ideological state apparatus (Althusser, 2001) the mainstream media must function as dispensers of absolute unquestioned truth. To question our basic sources of information about the world might lead to the sort of unrest and public questioning that could foster social transformation (Apple, 1990; Loewen, 1995).

Basically, given the media hegemony that exists (corporate elites control most mainstream media outlets) the only strategy for accessing and producing information that is critical of that hegemony is to develop or take advantage of outside channels such as those provided through cyberspace. For all of the federal attempts to control it, the Internet remains largely a virtual web of houses of information exchange that are virtually impossible to regulate. For all of its shortcomings (such as the digital divide, the lack of external fact-checking or peer-review, and the loss of the "real") cyberspace remains a vital source of counter-information and mobilizing for action in our postgeographic world.

In the spirit of poststructural ethnography, it is my own relationship to cyberactivism during my formative years as a graduate student and teacher that shaped my own praxis as a scholar and my work with the South High

Futures Project to establish a vibrant community of practice centered, in part, around becoming cyberactivists. The second half of this chapter focuses on the Futures Project and how the students learned to become cyberactivists, and the various social, cultural, and academic outcomes associated with this practice.

CYBERACTIVISM AND URBAN YOUTH

Lankshear, Peters, and Knobel (1996) project practices of critical pedagogy into cyberspace and consider the viability of critical pedagogy within an environment where a range of new technologies and practices have converged to produce a communications revolution. The authors argue that critical pedagogy is a viable enterprise within cyberspace. Lankshear, Peters, and Knobel begin their work by laying out the tenets of critical pedagogy as it was defined in modernist spaces before critiquing some of the contradictions or limitations that resulted from this juxtaposition: (i) critical pedagogy in modernist spaces remained strongly teacher-controlled; (ii) practices of critical pedagogy within formal settings remain bounded by curriculum and syllabus demands and have failed to account for multiple, contradictory, overlapping social positions. These problems, the chapter argues, originate in spaces of enclosure that characterize the modernist institution of schooling. The book, the classroom, and the curriculum can be viewed as intermeshed fixed enclosures.

Practicing critical pedagogy in cyberspace, they argue, can force educators to account for sophisticated notions of multiplicity. Cyberspace calls into question the stability and coherence of the book and forms of narration enacted upon it. The distinction between the reader and the writer disappears as the reader can add, delete, edit, and modify the text in so many ways as to make her or him the manifest creator of meaning. Also, the social spaces of cyberspace enable subjects to re-examine, play and experiment with, and ultimately transform their own multiplicity. Cyber "space" allows for more democratization, as it is constituted by a logic that is both participatory in nature and interactive in terms of format. The electronically mediated communication tends to break down spaces of institutional enclosure and subvert their mystification of the word–world relation. The radical interactivity and convertibility of digital text undermines at the level of lived textual practice the very notion of a static, immutable, transcendent reality pictured by the book. When looking at the potential for critical pedagogy in cyberspace, the authors point to the possibility of digital text exploding the notion that meaning is encased within texts. A critical pedagogy of cyberspace might also foster the creation of safe places for learners to develop and discover commonalties across difference, and the establishment of a more egalitarian relationship between students and teachers in which the students may actually have expertise over the technology and teachers become experts at maintaining an ethos of interrogation and assisting students in conceptualizing and framing their questions and ideas (p. 178).

In the South High Futures Project, we were very much influenced by the work of Lankshear, Peters, and Knobel in considering the use of cyberspace to promote the goals of the project. We were also influenced by the anthropology of cyberculture that seeks to understand new forms of social construction of reality (technoscapes) and new forms of negotiation of such construction are introduced by new technology. Also anthropologists are concerned with ways that people engage these technoscapes routinely and the consequences of doing so in terms of the concomitant adoption of new ways of thinking and being.

According to Escobar (2000), the emerging cyborg anthropologists adamantly claim that human and social reality is as much a product of machines as of human activity, that we should grant agency to machines, and that the proper task for an anthropology of science and technology is to examine ethnographically how technology serves as an agent of social and cultural production. As critical educators interested in the intersections of new media technologies and education for social change, the project teacher and I participated in various ways to promote and facilitate these critical literacy practices in cyberspace. In this chapter I talk about four strategies that we employed in order to promote a culture of cyberengagement: developing cyberliteracy skills, encouraging communication through cyberspace, alerting students to critical content on the Internet, and modeling critical uses of cyberspace ourselves.

Developing Cyberliteracy Skills

When the South High Futures Project purchased home computers for the students in the spring of 2000, most students had very little experience with the tools themselves, let alone with the Internet as a virtual space for engagement, production, and praxis. It was our responsibility, then, to help the students to develop basic cyberliteracy skills before we could expect them to access cyberspace for academic or critical purposes. Toward this end, we developed a pedagogy of cyberliteracies that included everything from helping the students to choose Internet service providers to helping students learn how to send e-mails with attachments to learning how to use online search engines such as Google to quickly obtain desired information.

One of the great benefits of a pedagogy of cyberliteracies is that the natural activities fit very well with a sociocultural model of learning that we attempted to honor in all other activity systems of the program. That is, rather than viewing learning as the transmission of discrete facts from a knowing other, we viewed true learning as occurring only when students were engaged in meaningful participation in culturally meaningful activity (Cole, 1996). One way to assess learning, then, was to follow Lave and Wenger's model of situated cognition, through which we were able to evaluate changing participation over time in a changing community of practice (Lave and Wenger, 1991). When teaching the cyberliteracy skills, we were able to have students actually engaged in Internet activity as a part of their growth and development as technology users, as literate beings, and as agents of social change. This made the learning space a richer one, it increased student motivation to learn, and it actually facilitated the development of fairly sophisticated cyberliteracy practices in a relatively short amount of time. I will document and analyze some of these literacy practices later in the chapter.

Our pedagogy of cyberliteracies is also resonant with recent practices in composition studies that focus the emphasis of pedagogy to one that honors process over product and production of texts over textual consumption (Villanueva, 2003). Rather than owning a body of content, what we were really after was helping students to develop a mastery of a series of processes (Murray, 2003) and a sense of reflexivity about their own learning and identities as technology users and cultural producers. This included the development of technical competencies, but it was an enabling pedagogy, a pedagogy of freedom that ultimately makes the students the experts, not over a body of ideas, but over a set of strategies that would allow them to become continual learners and continual producers in socially meaningful literate activities while using the unique tools and arenas cyberspace affords.

Encouraging Communication in Cyberspace

Once the students were all plugged into the Internet (this particular intervention preceded the wireless boom) and were in possession of their home computers (purchased by the project), we began to disseminate certain course content only via the Internet. Additionally, certain student assignments were to be sent in via email. We also attempted to develop parallel conversations to the course themes of youth-led critical research, civic engagement, educational equity, and social justice that would allow continued conversation between official class sessions. This form of communication took some time, given that the students lacked the schema for casual electronic communication with teachers. Students did pick up the AOL Instant Messenger capability rather quickly and Instant Messaging became a favorite form of communication among the students and ultimately between students and teachers. Ultimately, I began to conduct virtual office hours for students when they would visit for homework help via Instant Message.

Alerting Students to Critical Content of Cyberspace

As part of the major activity throughout the eleventh grade year, the Futures students were actively engaged in their critical research projects. Many students were developing their own research while others were continuing with projects started in the summer seminar. By their junior year, many of the students had become accomplished researcher-activist arranging their own protests and developing research as a tool for advocacy. Also, during their junior year, the Internet became a flurry of activity as students used cyberspace to participate virtually in the WTO protests and to follow the buildup to the Democratic National Convention, which was being hosted in Los Angeles the following summer. The role of the Internet in contributing to the rising climate of social activism in the city and around the globe provided opportunities for us to alert students to the sheer amount of critical information available on the Internet and the possibilities of being involved in activism via the Internet. When seeking out or sharing this information, the students could cut and paste URLs into emails and Instant Message conversations. It wasn't long before students began to share critical Internet content with one another as well as with the course instructors.

Modeling Critical Use of Cyberspace

Providing spaces for students to learn through apprenticeship (Rogoff, 1991) was an important component of the critical literacy pedagogy that I envisioned and hopefully enacted with the Futures students at South High. I and the other course instructor took advantage of opportunities to model the form of cyberactivism that we were learning via our own authentic participation in the practice. For example, I could use the technology to "carbon copy" (or "cc") students on emails that I sent to politicians or send them petitions and action alerts that were being circulated for WTO and DNC protesters. Additionally, there were opportunities in class for students and instructors to watch each other navigating and producing in cyberspace. In this unique learning space I could talk students through my various Internet activities showing them how I could locate esoteric information or triangulate sources.

Using the Internet as a learning and communication tool was vitally important to the students' development of new media literacies and to their emergent identities as cyberactivists. Ultimately, however, we realized that the most critical use of cyberspace probably entailed creating a website of our own, and this became the collective project for one semester of the course. In retrospect, we should have found students or teachers with more expertise in webpage design, but the process of creating even a basic webpage for the Futures Project was instructive.

The students managed to publish a website that year, although it admittedly left a lot to be desired. The shortcomings were all attributable to the course instructors (us) not providing sufficient modeling or access to expertise to create more sophisticated web pages. In reality we didn't possess that expertise and we couldn't afford it. Only a few years later it is possible for even amateur web designers to produce professional-looking web pages through the use of software programs like Dreamweaver, which simplify the process as much as is possible; and almost all of our students now have basic MySpaces. The ante is always being upped, however, and technology advances at the speed of thought, or so it seems.

Even though the site was "lacking" in aesthetic quality, the students did get to see their work published to a site that was accessible by friends and other interested parties such as teachers and researchers. The students learned about HTML and web design, and they took extreme care in the content that was going to be published. There is something about telling adolescents that their work will be made public that makes them tougher on themselves than teachers can ever be. In the end, we achieved our goal of helping the students to transition from complete novices to competent cyberspace users and producers in a short amount of time. Though they didn't acquire complete expertise over the practice, they learned many valuable tools that helped them in their research endeavors, in their other coursework, and in their literacy development.

Critical Literacy Development in a Cybercommunity of Practice

To better understand the emergent cybercommunity of practice and its implications for revolutionary praxis, I engaged in online and offline fieldwork (Escobar, 2000) in which I monitored and collected electronic communication over an eighteen-month period (from January 2000 to June

2001). These communications included over three thousand pages of e-mails, Instant Message conversations, and chat sessions. I also recorded observations of students negotiating cyberspace during project class. Finally, I examined data from student work and student conversations that refer to cyberspace. In my ethnographic investigation, I identified several literacy practices associated with critical pedagogy in cyberspace including sending e-mails for political purposes, engaging in critical online research, and virtual lobbying of politicians and other power brokers.

Initially all of the emails that the instructors received pertained to academic questions. Students wanted clarification on the homework or students needed help with other courses. For example, several students learned how to send attachments because they wanted feedback on an essay that they were writing for an English class. Other students participated simply because it was an assignment. Here is one example of a typical email received that first month:

> Hi Ernest, this is [name of student]. I have an English assignment due this Friday and I was wondering if you could please edit it before I turn in. The topic is: A conversation between Gatsby and Daisy when they meet at Nick's house in Chapter V.
>
> The new conversation has to weave in details from the rest of the novel, assure that the style remains consistent with the rest of the novel and to use the same vocabulary. I'll include the conversation, however, I'll understand if you can't edit it, I know you're a busy person.

Consider the following example, taken from an Internet chatroom, less than two months after the students received their computers. For all of the students except Student 2, this is their first significant experience with computers or the Internet. I use an extended example because it is indicative of the culture that developed around cyberspace and it shows the multiple literacies being developed in the process:

Teacher:	are you still thinking of taking the AP history exam?
Student 1:	it was terrible
Student 1:	no
Teacher:	The essay question was terrible?
Student 1:	yes
Student 2:	I still need to do chemistry and US history
Morrell:	S1 and S2, you need to think about your proposal
Teacher:	So, I could have worked with it through with you . . . . Is there any way you can start working?
Student 3:	I am doing it with A [another student] tomorrow
Teacher:	with C [another student] dealing with History

Student 2:	ok bye everyone this time it's for real
Morrell:	see ya
Morrell:	ok [Student 2], you're off the hook
Student 3:	[Student 1], www.?
Student 2:	thanx [teacher]
Student 2:	I know what I want to do [Morrell]
Morrell:	what's that?
Student 2:	hip hop Ern
Morrell:	cool!!
Morrell:	I'm down for hip-hop
Teacher:	when was it due?
Student 2:	week ago
Teacher:	how many points are you going to miss?
Student 2:	50
Teacher:	You know grades are due on Friday . . . actually we have to turn them in on Monday . . .
Student 2:	I have an 85.9
Teacher:	It would be in your best interest to do something . . . .
Teacher:	So even if you have 25 points added on, it may put you at an A–
Student 2:	Well I'll talk to him
Teacher:	85% is good, but it is not your best, and not what you want to go to the schools you keep
Student 1:	Do you see it [Student 2]?
Teacher:	Telling me about . . . . no one thinks it is possible to get an A in his class
Student 2:	I think its possible
Student 2:	His class is easy
Student 1:	Think about it Student 2
Student 2:	What Student 1?
Teacher:	Looks like
Student 1:	Good idea [teacher] they should start a history group
Student 1:	read it again Student 2
Student 2:	Huh?
Student 2:	So [Morrell] I was planning to do hip hop for the proposal
Morrell:	What about hip-hop?
Student 2:	Run DMC to Gangstarr to BIG

At first glance the conversation appears disjointed until one understands that five distinct participants (three students and two teachers) are having parallel and interweaving conversations. The teacher is trying to convince Student 2 to hand in a US History assignment, Student 1 and Student 2 are collaborating on a proposal (which is actually a piece of critical research), and Student 2 is trying to share with me his ideas for a paper on hip-hop activism that he wants to complete for an English assignment. More easily discernable are the multiple literacies that are both accessed and developed throughout this interchange and within the community of practice. Students and teachers are able to communicate freely within a virtual realm as they simultaneously share texts and resources through emails and the sharing of websites. Further the students are able to use their emergent cyberliteracies within a space of an Internet chatroom for mundane activities like homework, but they are also able to collaborate on research projects and affirm one another as critical intellectuals within a school where they are often not viewed this way. Finally, it is important to acknowledge that all of this communication is mediated through the written word; the students must develop as writers if they are to adequately access these cyberspaces. Without being consciously aware of their production, students produced dozens of pages of writing through their normal cybercommunity activities. The same, obviously, can be said for reading development.

As a result of their participation in this emergent cybercommunity of practice, students gained access to information online that assisted them in their school and research activities (as the previous example articulated). Students also lobbied politicians, forwarded political messages, joined activist listservs, signed online petitions, and submitted work to online publications furthering their political causes, affirming their identities as citizen-scholars, and developing their academic, critical, and cyberliteracies in the process.

CONCLUSION

During the year and a half of the creation and growth of the cybercommunity of practice, I was able to substantially document how the students used the Internet for a variety of social, academic, and activist-oriented purposes. With each of these uses came evidence of academic and critical literacy development. Its not insignificant that the students used cyberspace to trade drafts of papers and to study for tests, especially given that these students lived far away from each other in a major city where it was not feasible for most of them to travel at night. The online writing community helped the students to develop as academic writers; most of the students took papers for class and articles that they were writing for school newspapers, online journals, and college scholarships through multiple drafts that simply would not have happened without the existence of the community in cyberspace.

Additionally, the students certainly used the Internet to consume the work of other cyberactivists. The focal points of this consumption entailed the monitoring of the indymedia.org website prior to and during the Democratic National Convention. Individually students found their own cyberactivist communities to join and monitor throughout this process: sites that ranged from underground hip-hop to Movimiento Estudiantil Chicano de Aztlán (MEChA) organizations at high school and college campuses, to the websites and listservs supporting the Chiapas resistance. The beauty of cyberspace for literacy educators is that it demands that all active participants become readers and researchers who must sift through and synthesize large amounts of written information making decisions on what sources they choose to engage and which sources they dismiss. What's more, for critical literacy educators the beauty of the Internet is that reading critical content brings additional demands, even if they are as simple as cutting and pasting a link or responding to an email. The reading of cyberactivism fosters cyberactivism.

Finally, I would contend that the students serve as a model of cyberactivism because they clearly became activists and cyberspace became a primary site of learning and engagement: a space for developing and disseminating critical ideas and critical content. Certainly these students were published on various Internet sites and they participated vicariously and directly in some major virtual social movements during these years as well. Mostly, however, this cyberactivism occurred at a very local level where these twenty-five students used cyberspace to inspire one another and their teachers and to put genuine fear into a school and district administration. At both the local and the global level, there is evidence that these students became a part of something larger than themselves, something in which they took obvious pride. The beauty of the virtual movement is that, even when you are by yourself, you don't have to be alone.

It is also obvious that the Futures students developed a wealth of traditional and new media literacies. The sheer number of words that the average participant read and wrote would be difficult to quantify, because it would be so large. As I said, I have three thousand pages of notes and excerpts from the Internet, and that is only communication to which I was privy! Educators and researchers who choose to ignore the intellectual nature of cyberspace participation do so at their own peril; and they miss a golden opportunity to bridge the old and the new, and to connect with the new generation of activists and intellectuals who have grown up witnessing the power of the new-media social movements and whose seemingly endless reservoir of ideas the world has only begun to understand. There is so much possibility if only we allow ourselves to think outside of the box—unless that box happens to be a computer screen.

7

Critical Media Literacy

> Due to the dominance of mass media forms such as popular music, fashion, television, the Internet, and video games in the lives of young people in industrialized societies today, it is fair to say that mass media forms constitute their primary cultural resource. Teens in the United States, for example, spend up to half their waking hours engaging with some form of media. As such, it is also fair to say that however varied the experiences of individual adolescents may be, their lives are mediated, to a large extent, by the mass media. (Mastronardi, 2003, p. 83)

In the article "Saturated in Beer" researchers found that children as young as fourth grade were being repeatedly advertised to by beer companies. These children could identify many of the popular beer advertisements, which included characters and practices that seemed targeted at youth. Even though the ninth graders in the study admitted to liking the advertisements more, the fourth graders were actually exposed more often to the beer advertisements (Collins *et al.*, 2005). Along these lines, medical research has demonstrated a link between media watching and youth smoking, dietary habits, and attitudes toward sex and sexual behaviors (Escobar-Chaves *et al.*, 2005).

We also know that youth are the targets of mass media campaigns that seek to develop loyal consumers at increasingly younger ages. Understanding the links between children's desires and parents' wallets, these corporations target the former without reservations. As the introductory quote attests, youth involvement with corporate media is varied. When analyzing the relationship between youth and the media, for example, it is important to simultaneously think about media advertising, television watching, music consumption, film viewing, and video game purchases, to name a few. As the Mastronardi

(2003) quote also attests, however one defines youth involvement with the media it is difficult to argue against the reality that media are, for today's youth, their primary cultural influence, surpassing the family and the school. Rather than dismiss or denigrate the media and the young people involved, it behooves educators, educational researchers, and others involved with youth to understand youth involvement with the media. More importantly, it is important to develop educational programs that help young people to become more informed consumers and producers of media.

It is important to note, for example, that not all uses of the media are negative. The same medical research community that decries the effects of beer and cigarette advertising to teens has also shown that positive advertising can have a beneficial impact on children's choices to stay away from drugs, to eat healthy foods, and to exercise more. Additionally, youth-produced media have played an historical role in raising young people's awareness of injustice, and their commitment to working for social change. Powerful films such as *Schindler's List* and *Malcolm X* have introduced new generations to historical events and people. And concerts like Live Aid in 1985 and Live 8 in 2005 have brought the world together to unify against global challenges such as hunger, poverty, and AIDS.

There is no doubt that young people need a media education that exposes them to the dangers and possibilities associated with the institution. I argue that urban youth are even more in need of such an education, given the stakes associated with the negative outcomes associated with uncritical media consumption. I offer in this chapter both a theoretical foundation for the critical media education that I imagine as well as the examination of several cases of critical media pedagogy with urban youth. In these cases I make sense of how the young people have come to understand dominant media, how they have come to see themselves as media producers, and how each of these projects produces powerful and empowered literacy learning. To begin, however, I turn to the field of media and cultural studies which has, for seventy years, made important connections between the power of media industries and the social construction of knowledge in industrial societies.

CULTURAL STUDIES, MEDIA STUDIES, AND CRITICAL MEDIA PEDAGOGY

Cultural studies is an interdisciplinary field that appropriates theories and methods from sociology, anthropology, linguistics, literary criticism, art theory, philosophy, and political science. It aims to examine its subject matter in terms of cultural practices and their relation to power. Its objective is to understand culture in all its complex forms and to analyze the social and political context within which it manifests itself. From its beginnings in Britain in the 1960s with the Birmingham Centre for Contemporary Cultural Studies, its progenitors categorized cultural studies as both an intellectual and political enterprise. One of the primary aims of the discipline is to understand the structures of dominance everywhere, especially in industrial capitalist societies (Sardar and Van Loon, 2000).

Theorists and practitioners of media studies understand that media culture has become a dominant force of socialization, with media images and celebrities replacing families, schools, and churches as arbiters of taste, values, and thought, producing new models of identification and resonant images of style, fashion and behavior (Kellner, 1995, p. 24). Along these lines, Kellner (1995) contends that media cultural studies undertakes the project of analyzing the complex relations between texts, audiences, media industries, politics, and the sociohistorical context in specific conjunctures.

The Italian social theorist and communist activist Antonio Gramsci was one of the first to truly study the role of media in proliferating dominant hegemony. Gramsci was interested in analyzing the agencies by which culture is shaped (i.e. media, literature, theatre, schools, politics) and to what extent culture could be guided by conscious political agency (Gramsci, 1985). Gramsci arrived at the same conclusions that the Frankfurt School theorists would a few decades later: that the media were powerful instruments of knowledge production that would be used by the powerful in society to configure social thought.

Gramsci, however, was ahead of the Frankfurt School media philosophers in that he understood the potentially positive role of media in bringing about revolutionary consciousness. That is, Gramsci not only theorized media hegemony; a key component of Gramsci's theory entailed a pedagogy of the proletariat. A goal of the Gramscian pedagogical project was to create citizens who were able to wrest the class privilege of culture away from the ruling class by expanding and restructuring the educational system. Additionally, Gramsci sought ways to create citizens that were better critical consumers (of dominant culture) and producers (of proletarian culture) (Gramsci, 1919/1985). Gramsci understood that media outlets could become tools used by the proletariat to promote radical changes in society.

The theory of critical media pedagogy as media production draws from the work of Gramsci, the Frankfurt School, the Birmingham Centre for Contemporary Cultural Studies, and American critical cultural theorists such as Kellner, Giroux, Lipsitz, and McLaren. According to this theory, critical media pedagogy involves counterhegemonic instruction aimed at developing a consciousness of the role of the media in configuring social thought. This pedagogy also intends to foster engaged citizens who are able to critique these master media narratives and who also have the skills to use new media technologies as tools in the struggle for social and educational justice.

Further, a critical media pedagogy targets populations that have been targeted by media industries. Finally, critical media pedagogy involves critical consumption, production, and distribution of new media texts. The addition this makes to the field is the heavy emphasis on critical media pedagogy as media production. Rooted in the Gramscian project of cultural production and the Freirian project of conscientization, the critical media pedagogy translates the media consciousness into the creation of new/critical/counter media artifacts that are themselves a part of the pedagogy of others. Producing counter-knowledge through the manipulation of media tools is the mission of the critical media pedagogical project as I envision it. This is consistent with other work where I have imagined critical pedagogy as knowledge construction and as skill building. Just as a fundamental outcome of Freirian pedagogy encompasses the learning of languages and literacies of power, the critical media pedagogical project must entail the development of skills with the tools associated with new media technology. Acquiring the critical language to deconstruct media narratives is important, but not enough. Students as agents of change must also develop the skills of digital video filmmaking, web design, and musical production, to name a few. The model also suggests a "who", a "how," and a "why" of critical media pedagogy that are important for practitioners and researchers in this nascent, yet potentially transformational field.

Media Literacy as Media Production

Much of the work in media and cultural studies focuses on the consumption of mainstream media. Particularly, the work of critical media literacy usually entails a critical reading of how dominant media texts promote problematic values. Certainly these are valuable decoding skills of use to any critical citizen. For example, as an English teacher and as the co-director of the summer research seminar, I would have students read the newspapers, magazines, and television news footage to examine problematic messages sent along the lines of race, class, gender, religion, nationality and age.

Although I would not dismiss this kind of work, I advocate that critical media literacy needs to be more theorized around production and distribution. This holds true for media literacies as well. Critical media curricula, then, need to focus more on how urban youth can produce and distribute via new media genres. Whether through the production of websites, digital video documentaries, hip-hop CDs, or digital photojournalism, literacy educators are challenged to open up spaces for critical production across the new media genres (Buckingham, 2003; Goodman, 2003).

The production of new media artifacts can also serve a critical function in creating empowering counter-narratives of reality. Gramsci (1971) contends that every class has its organic intellectuals that are responsible for knowledge production and dissemination. I would argue that new media technologies are the tools of the new "class" of urban youth public intellectuals who may stand in opposition to the dominant classes who use mainstream, corporate wheels to promote a hegemony—a domination of ideas—that reinforces the neoliberal values of capital accumulation and individual achievement.

Toward these ends I talk about two projects in which urban adolescents were involved in critical media consumption and distribution. In the first example, teens investigated the various ways that urban youth are portrayed in the media and the politics behind these portrayals. They interviewed participants in the media and employed a critical discourse analysis of major daily newspapers to understand the associations made with urban youth or any other young people involved in social action. In the second example, teens created a short film that documented the various learning spaces for civic engagement in South Los Angeles. As a part of this project, the students investigated the lessons that students learn from popular media about youth civic engagement. More importantly, though, they wanted to relay their findings through a popular media that would itself engage these same youth.

YOUTH INVESTIGATING THE MEDIA

Given young people's engagement with the media and the media's fixation on the young, we decided to have a major focus of the summer seminar devoted to developing critical media literacies among the adolescent participants. During the summer of 2000, the Democratic National Convention was held in Los Angeles. As seminar organizers, my colleague and I thought that the political climate in the city that summer served as the perfect backdrop for critical research. In the neighborhoods around the city where we worked, the conversations revolved around access. The poorest neighborhoods nearest the convention were denied access to the transportation they needed to get to work. A thirteen-foot concrete barrier was placed around a perimeter that denied activists reasonable access to the convention space. Within this context we began considering the access that young people had to their city on a daily basis. We also questioned the access that young people had to the spaces and resources they needed to become engaged and empowered citizens and professionals. Finally we questioned the access youth had to the very political processes that were occurring in their home city.

Of the five student groups, we dedicated one group to investigating youth access to the media and the media's portrayal of urban youth; particularly those youth engaged in social activism. As part of their work for the seminar, students read works about media literacy from theorists such as Douglas Kellner and Peter McLaren while also designing a study intending to understand the complex relationships between urban youth and the mainstream media industries.

The study that the students designed included interviews with representatives of the mainstream media, a survey distributed to media personnel working the convention, and an analysis of daily newspapers' coverage of the week of the convention. The students employed an analytic framework that drew upon cultural studies, critical discourse analysis, and Gramscian hegemony theory to understand the media discourse as it pertained to urban youth and young people engaged in political activism. The adolescent researchers also employed analytic techniques from semiotics and visual sociology to study the photographic images associated with the news stories.

The findings of the study are not surprising. The interviews with reporters and media personnel corroborate the analysis of the newspapers: that urban youth and youth who participate in activism are caricatured as violent and deviant individuals that need to be heavily policed and restrained for the public good. For example, in all of the feature stories from the daily newspapers, "weapons" and "police" were among the two most prevalent terms. Additionally, every accompanying image to the news stories either shows youth engaged in "deviant" activities or else shows disruptive youth being justifiably policed.

Only one small, local Spanish-speaking newspaper made any attempts whatsoever to present the core issues around which the youth were protesting. This was also the only newspaper to show any humanizing images of the young people; portraying them as committed citizens marching in unity and peace displaying images of people whose actions should be celebrated instead of policed. As a researcher and participant, I can certainly attest to the prevalence and veracity of these images (of peaceful protest) as opposed to the images pasted on the front pages of the national newspapers.

These incongruities led the adolescent researchers to ask questions about what counts as newsworthy when it comes to youth organizers and the young and poor. Why, for instance, is a successful, peaceful protest not news? Why are the fundamental issues that bring together ten thousand people on a sunny summer day not news? What common narratives of youth are reinforced when newspapers run stories such as they did during the week of the convention? What policies get enacted and what practices get accepted when the public embraces the narrative of its young as a deviant and potentially violent species?

These questions and more are at the heart of a critical media literacy, at least the consumption-related aspects of the concept. Student participants learned to critically read newspapers as ideological texts rather than as objective and neutral ones. They also learned to see the media stories as narratives rather than as essential truths. Freire and Macedo (1987) identify this reading against the text as an act of counter-hegemony. I argue that these literacies are vital for our young people who are inundated with such bad and dehumanizing information via mainstream media outlets on a daily basis. These critical media literacies can serve as protection against alienation, depression, eating disorders, violence, and a host of other ills that can be linked, at least in part, to the uncritical consumption of mainstream media texts.

The media literacy project entailed much more than just the critical consumption of mainstream texts. Although this type of decoding of texts is certainly important to any academic or critical enterprise, in and of itself it is not sufficient. We also wanted students to be able to access different information, or even to produce and distribute their own countermedia texts. It was important, for instance, to ask students how they might locate "good" information, "accurate" information, or at least information that called into question or challenged dominant media narratives proliferated via newspapers or the evening news. It became important for students and teachers to identify sources such as Pacifica Radio, the *LA Weekly*, indymedia.org, salon.com, and *The Nation* magazine as alternative sites to access information about current events. Students were also able to identify a small progressive newsletter that targeted local neighborhoods in the city. These texts were often available in churches, barber shops, and shopping centers. From this process, we theorized that an important component of critical media literacy involves seeking out critical media texts to consume.

Another important component involves becoming participants in the production of critical media. I have argued throughout this text that the production and distribution are central to my conception of critical media literacy. For example, the student research report on youth access to media served as an empowering literacy practice for the adolescents who were involved. Creating a research presentation to distribute to multiple audiences, posting the PowerPoint and paper on an online journal, and writing editorials and articles for school newspapers were production-oriented critical literacy practices associated with the media project.

iMOVIES AND CRITICAL PUBLIC HISTORY

In chapter 3 I talked at length about the role of documentary filmmakers as critical media philosophers who were making important contributions to critical social thought. I focused in particular on the documentaries *Super Size Me* and *Fahrenheit 9/11*, which confronted, respectively, fast food corporations and the United States government and military. It is important to document what these have meant to the way that we think about the world. In this section, however, I want to comment on what these films represent to the way we think about the filmmaking itself as a political tool. I also want to talk about a larger movement that these documentaries are situated in, the guerilla filmmaking revolution.

For many obvious reasons, movies are very expensive to make. Hollywood blockbusters cost in the tens of millions of dollars. Cameras are expensive, actors are expensive, sets are expensive, and the explosions are expensive. Until the mid-1990s, the prohibitive costs made it essentially impossible for anyone but Hollywood studios to make pictures. Whereas a young fifteen-year-old could put together a band and make professional sounding rock or hip-hop music, the aspiring filmmaker had very few resources available to match that accomplishment in film. Of course people tried; but very few low-budget films had managed to capture the popular imagination the way that the grunge and hip-hop movements had during the 1970s and 1980s.

In 1993 the director Robert Rodriguez made a movie entitled *El Mariachi* for under $10,000; the movie was wildly successful. Not only did the film itself capture the public imagination, but also the idea that a film could be made that cheaply captured a generation of would-be filmmakers and spawned the rebirth of independent filmmaking. Books emerged to help budding filmmakers make films for "used car prices," and Rodriguez even made short films on the subject. There were still two major challenges for these artists, however: the cost of cameras and film and the limited avenues for film distribution. Within a matter of years, all of this would change profoundly.

I once heard a media professor pronounce that cyberspace and the digital camera had democratized media production. That seems the perfect way to describe what began to take place in filmmaking in the late 1990s. The advent of the digital video camera essentially made it possible for anyone to be a filmmaker and the Internet made it possible for any film to be published to a potential audience of thousands. Digital video cameras could be purchased for a fraction of the cost of traditional 35 mm cameras used by the big studios. Computer software programs such as iMovie, Final Cut Pro, and Adobe Premiere made it possible to edit digital film on a basic personal desktop computer. DVDs also became easy to mass produce, but short films especially could be uploaded and viewed on the Internet by surfers with high-speed access.

It was the proliferation of digital filmmaking and Internet distribution that set off the explosion in guerrilla filmmaking. Amateur filmmakers could create home movies, but they could also document the youth popular culture of the time and publish these homemade films to an unlimited audience. As would be expected the Internet became home to a large array of concert documentaries, surfing and biking movies, films of insufferable conditions, of social protests, and films covering the everyday lives of young people in America. Wherever the young people could go, so to could their cameras. Internet sites like YouTube.com, which hosts amateur video films, counts its hits in the tens of millions.

I argue that this led to the simultaneous rise of documentary films and digital films in our culture, and the amazing social impact of the documentary films such as *Fahrenheit 9/11*, *Super Size Me*, *The Corporation*, and *Bus 174*, in the past decade alone. It is important to note that many of these films were made with 35 mm cameras and some had larger budgets, but I still argue that they were able to thrive largely because of the movement that they emerged out of and they still stand as exemplars for young people with cameras, a social conscience, and an imagination.

In our work with young people we knew that they possessed the social conscience and imagination. They didn't necessarily have access to the cameras, the computers, or the expertise needed to learn how to make short documentary films. I was inspired by my work in media studies and the work of Norm Denzin in poststructural ethnography to think about the possibilities of short documentaries as authentic and important research products. I knew that the students would be motivated to learn how to make documentaries and that the visual images would be powerful, especially in capturing the inequitable conditions in urban schools and communities. I also had an unformed hunch that the process would yield powerful learning of traditional and new media literacies. With these ideas in mind we purchased some relatively inexpensive digital video and still cameras, loaded the computers with software, and petitioned our resident filmmaker to put on a few seminars for our students.

Making iMovies

It was during the summer seminar of 2003 that we officially added iMovies (short documentary films edited on Apple iMovie software) to the list of "textual products." As researchers and teachers, we wanted to expand notions of text and literacy to encompass more new media. In previous seminars students had used laptop computers; they had performed Internet research; and they had created PowerPoint presentations of their research. The summer of 2003 was the first to focus on digital video production as a form of textual production.

The students, who were accumulating oral histories of participants in Los Angeles public schools, used digital videos to record as many interviews as possible. Each research team was issued a digital video camera, a tripod, and a supply of mini digital videotapes. Additionally, a professional filmmaker offered a workshop to help the students become acquainted with the cameras. The workshop also provided students with techniques for composing shots and keeping the camera steady. The filmmaker then sent students on assignment to capture images around the campus. Each group's footage was critiqued and students were given a short list of reminders concerning camera care and operation.

For three weeks student groups traveled around Greater Los Angeles interviewing students, parents, teachers, administrators, ministers, activists, university researchers, and politicians who had some measure of involvement with Los Angeles public schools during the period of 1954–2003. During the final week and a half students reviewed their digital footage for clips they could use to create their iMovies. Then, with the assistance of the filmmaker and university staff, student research teams put together five-minute iMovies. Each team created iMovies complete with music, transitions, and graphics. Copies of the interviews were also transferred from digital masters to VHS tapes and donated to a community-run historical archive.

YOUTH MEDIA PRODUCTION AND
CRITICAL LITERACY

It is impossible, in these days and times, to imagine critical literacy education outside a context of media education. And it is not advisable to imagine a critical media education outside of the context of youth media production. That being said, there are logistical, economic, and experiential barriers to generating sophisticated media production in urban schools. The logistical concerns are of two sorts. First of all, given the way schools are structured it is difficult to imagine how to create spaces for all students to be able to create media artifacts like web pages and documentary films. The process one must go through to create these products is not one that fits easily within the fifty-five-minute class period. Our students in the summer seminar were able to produce quality films because they were able to work five to six hours at a stretch on the site location, shooting, and editing. They were also able to travel about the city to collect footage for their films. The limiting logistics of schooling would make it difficult to do so.

The second logistical limitation concerns the rightful location of media education within the currently articulated disciplines. Surely, we can imagine other iterations of course structures, but I can imagine teachers who are positively predisposed to this sort of pedagogy wondering how it would fit into their classes. If, for instance, one decides to create a unit on film production in an English class, what happens to the teaching of expository essay writing and all of the other standards to which teachers and students are held? This presents a very real challenge to our teachers, who must work within definitive frameworks in their disciplines.

There are also economic barriers to a pedagogy of media production in urban schools. Although schools and districts are willing to spend thousands, even millions of dollars on state-of-the-art security systems and textbook packages, they seem less likely to be willing to purchase high-end digital video cameras or software packages. In their defense, these technological products can be costly, they can easily be broken, and they usually need to be upgraded or replaced every couple of years. When one considers that many students in urban schools across the nation do not have adequate basic learning materials, the idea of equipping them with sophisticated technical tools can seem daunting.

Finally there are experiential barriers that need to be considered when thinking about media production in K-12 classrooms. Whereas newly minted credentialed teachers are required to have technology as a component of their credentialing process most teachers, new and old, do not have the skills or experience to help students to become sophisticated media producers. Teachers without expertise in web design and digital video production, for instance, will be understandably less willing to create classroom projects that have their students actively engaged in these processes, and, if they do take the plunge, it is unlikely that novice students will be able to create superior media products.

These logistical, economic, and experiential barriers to meaningful media production in urban K-12 classrooms are substantial. They do not, however, diminish the very important reality that media literacies will be an important component of the literacy repertoire of engaged professionals and citizens of the twenty-first century. As literacy researchers and educators, we'll have to keep reminding skeptics and opponents of this fact even as we continue to find creative ways to incorporate media production into our standard courses, as we create new courses and programs of study that foreground media production, as we advocate for additional funding for urban classrooms, and as we find multiple pathways for beginning and practicing literacy teachers across the content areas to gain proficiency with multimodal production tools.

8

Critical Literacy as Care for the Self

This brings us to the final section of the book. In the first section I argued for a broader definition of the "critical" in critical literacy: one that encapsulated the entire Western philosophical tradition as well as several important "Othered" traditions ranging from postcolonialism to the African-American tradition. In the second section I looked at four cases of critical literacy pedagogy with urban youth, which included teaching popular culture in a high school English classroom, conducting community-based critical research, cyberactivism, and critical media literacy education. In this final section I return to theory. First I consider two areas of critical literacy pedagogy that are still relatively unexplored in our discourse. This chapter considers the importance of critical reading and writing in constituting and reconstituting the self. I argue that reading and writing can play a crucial role in self-healing and self-definition for urban youth. In the next chapter I talk about critical writing that is not just about coming to a critical understanding of the world, but that plays an explicit and self-referential role in changing the world. The final chapter outlines a grounded theory of critical literacy pedagogy and considers the implications of this pedagogy for literacy research, teacher education, classroom practice, and advocacy work for social change.

I begin by examining theories of reading that are consonant with my view of literacy as care for the self. Particularly I draw upon Louise Rosenblatt's aesthetic reading as care for the self. I then draw upon Foucault's discussion of the *hupomnemata* (Foucault, 1997) and Sartre's conception of committed writing as an exercise of freedom for the author (Sartre, 2001), to consider how critical literacy can promote important transformations of the self. In contrast to most of the work on critical literacy that examines larger social outcomes, I think about how critical literacy can be about repositioning oneself with oneself.

WHY WRITE?

It makes sense that, in schools, we generally conceive of writing as a method of demonstrating knowledge; both in form and in content. That is, in the language arts classroom, attention is paid to spelling, grammar, punctuation, etc. as well as the ability to use words to make a thoughtful argument. In the early elementary grades teachers focus on the basic structures of language, how to write sentences and paragraphs, how to learn the parts of speech, how to make subjects and nouns agree, etc. At the secondary level, teachers continue to focus on grammar, spelling, and vocabulary building, but they also focus on writing to persuade an audience of ideas: how to write a thesis statement; how to begin paragraphs with topic sentences that are supported by information, either facts or logic. Students write essays to demonstrate their ability to use written language and their ability to argue coherently through this medium.

In the content area courses, writing is usually used to demonstrate knowledge. In science classes, students are required to write up their experiments in lab books; in a social studies classroom, students may write a report on the causes of the Civil War, or they may use writing to provide short answers to factual questions about the Civil War, etc. In a mathematics course, students may write out their explanation for a solution to a particular problem. Although there has been an increasing attention paid to content area literacy, once students have passed the elementary level, writing ability is usually taken for granted in content area courses. However, at secondary and postsecondary level, content area teachers have become increasingly interested in writing instruction, as it pertains to the ability of students to demonstrate their knowledge in these respective disciplines. At the postsecondary level, for instance, there is an ongoing debate over who is ultimately responsible for the teaching of writing. At heart, though, this ongoing debate is framed with the dual purposes of writing that I laid out earlier; either students from elementary to postsecondary levels are using writing to demonstrate their mastery of the language or they are using writing to demonstrate their mastery of content. The major aims are to communicate to others, whether a teacher, or some larger audience external to themselves. I do not want to critique these purposes of writing instruction or these desired outcomes; of course it is important for students to have a mastery of written language (what some have called the Language of Wider Communication (Smitherman, 1999). It is also important for students to be able to use their writing to communicate valuable information to others. Even within a critical literacy framework, I have demonstrated the various ways that students can use their writing to communicate important messages to others about issues of inequity and injustice in society. In the next chapter, as well, I will talk at length about how critical literacy, and in particular critical writing, can serve as an important component of engendering revolutionary praxis.

In this chapter, though, I would like to put forth a different consideration for the purpose of writing that is not often part of the discussions I alluded to earlier. That is, I would like us to consider the role that writing can play in identity development or as poststructuralist Michel Foucault might say, that writing can play a role in the care for the self. Many genres of writing and purposes of writing can be internal more than external. For instance, as a scholar and as a citizen, I often write down ideas to know how I feel about a certain issue; writing, therefore, becomes an important process in excavating my own thoughts. Often I do not know what I am or have been thinking until I see the actual words on the page. Writing, at this moment, literally becomes staring at mental activity.

Others may write to relieve pain, or to deal with stress, loss, anger, etc. It is possible to use personal writing as a strategy for coping with great stress or great loss, and even to use writing as part of the healing process, when the actual words can assist us in transcending difficult moments in movement toward brighter ones. At a particularly low moment, I wrote a poem that contained these two lines:

I am writing to heal
I am writing wings and shields

It is quite possible, at this moment, that writing becomes a catharsis, a letting out of emotions that become painful or even dangerous if they remain internalized. I am convinced that much of great literature begins this way; even though it can ultimately be shared with others, it began as a strategy to help the authors to successfully cope with otherwise overwhelming emotion.

Writing can also function as the expression of feelings of immense joy, and the writing itself can be a pleasurable experience secretly recounting the joys and triumphs of life. Some of the various genres that encompass these forms of writing that I have laid out include journal or diary entries, memos, notes to self, poems, or stream of consciousness writing in errant notebooks or scraps of paper. Each of these purposes of writing challenges the dualism that manifests in most curricula. This is not about a mastery of the language, nor is it primarily to demonstrate or disseminate knowledge, though these texts can and often do become public documents. As internal, personal pieces, they are not concerned with grammar or coherence per se; they are functional texts, they are emotional texts; they are living texts. Unfortunately, there are very few spaces within the academy where students have the opportunity to develop this form of writing or to practice it if they already have some experience. It's likely that many students will never learn that they can use writing in this way. I associate these writing practices with critical literacy because they are potentially empowering writing practices, particularly as they help to develop empowered identities and help students to cope with fear, alienation, and other negative outcomes associated with being a member of a marginalized group in society or those associated with taking unpopular stances or holding unpopular views. This self-writing is also critical in that the processes of reflection and metacognition are important to developing a critical epistemology.

I will talk more in this chapter about various ways that other scholars have envisioned utilizing writing as care for the self, but I first begin with a detour where I theorize how the other literacy practice, reading, can function in this process as well. I will conclude the chapter with some implications for literacy scholarship in helping literacy educators and literacy scholars to envision a critical literacy praxis as care for the self in urban schooling contexts.

EFFERENT VERSUS AESTHETIC READING: READING AS CARE FOR THE SELF

In a similar way to writing, reading too has been framed in dualistic terms throughout the elementary, secondary, and postsecondary levels of education. In the early grades a great deal of focus is placed on decoding and comprehension skills; that is the actual process of learning to read itself. Generally the upper elementary grades and secondary grades are focused on reading to learn. This is a crude dichotomy because early elementary students are certainly reading to learn and secondary (even postsecondary) students are still, in many ways, learning to read. At each level, for instance, students need to acquire more sophisticated skills to handle the content and genre-specific texts that they encounter. Again, content area literacy teaching helps educators think about the various strategies students need to acquire if they are to successfully navigate the content of disciplines. Successful teachers encourage students to move from summary to analysis; and they impart strategies for using what students know in order to learn what they don't know: active reading strategies such as highlighting, underlining, writing notes in the margin at the postsecondary level as well as a host of other strategies such as creating annotated bibliographies, reading summaries, and literature reviews, to name a few. These educators realize that reading a chemistry book is fundamentally different from reading a Dostoyevsky novel even though some of the decoding and active reading strategies may transfer from one text to another.

Again it is important to underscore the importance of decoding and comprehension, reading to learn, within the critical literacy framework of the book. If students are going to develop into citizen-activist-scholars, they need to be able to read a variety of texts to obtain information about the world. These texts include novels, poems, plays, research reports, business reports, data spreadsheets, stock market indices, encyclopedia entries, websites, memoranda, constitutions, essays, newspaper articles, and legal briefs. The only way that these students will be able to transform the world is if they are able to access dominant information in a way that will allow them to form a sophisticated critique of the world. Part of our mandate as critical literacy scholars is to brainstorm effective methods to assist students in acquiring these traditional and critical reading skills. I have talked at length in earlier chapters about various ways that I have attempted to accomplish this goal in my work with urban adolescents, and I will talk in the following chapter about the role of critical reading in precipitating social praxis.

As with writing, however, I also feel that there are important purposes for reading that are not necessarily addressed much in schools, yet are fundamental toward a complete critical literacy perspective: what I will call reading as care for the self. Many of the reading practices that I describe at the secondary and postsecondary levels can be described as reading for information; students are required to read texts in order to derive meaningful information from them. Even the artistic texts that students confront in English courses are read primarily for information. Students are generally graded for their ability to interpret, dissect, and critique these literary pieces. The same rule of thumb applies across the content areas: students read texts in order to comprehend, interpret, critique, and demonstrate mastery of information. These are what the theorist Louise Rosenblatt refers to as *efferent readings* or reading for information. Rosenblatt, too, envisioned an additional purpose for reading, what she called *aesthetic readings* of texts. Aesthetic reading is reading to explore the work and oneself. Here, readers are engaged in the experience of reading, itself. Rosenblatt states, "In aesthetic reading, the reader's attention is centered directly on what he is living through during his relationship with that particular text" (1978, p. 25). It is to the aesthetic reading and its relationship to care for the self that I now turn.

The poet William Wordsworth defined a poem as a spontaneous burst of emotion. The poet Pablo Neruda spoke of the importance of poetry and all art serving to create emotions that inspire greater humanity. Nearly all great writers have talked about the pleasure of the text: the importance of literary works as entertainment and inspiration. The hip-hop artist KRS One refers to this process as *edutainment*, fostering the idea that texts are intended to inspire even as they educate. I argue that the pleasurable and inspirational readings of texts are largely absent from basic literacy instruction. For some reason we have decided to take some of the most beautiful words ever written and treat them specimens to be studied and pulled apart. We have taken the most politically charged words ever written and treated them in the disinterested way that an Olympic judge regards a figure skating performance. It is no wonder, then, that students treat many of the academic texts they read in the same disinterested manner.

What is lost when we do this? I contend that students lose the essence of the creation of the texts in the first place. Most poems were not written to be studied in courses; they were meant to be read and enjoyed. Neruda often claimed to be unable to understand the graduate theses that were being written about his own poems (Epstein, 2004). Most political and philosophical tracts are also written in a context with a passion and emotion that are generally lost in the dry and factual readings promoted in schools. Similarly, we miss the excitement, zeal, and passion that informs the quest for knowledge in math and in the sciences. As a result of this, students miss the purpose of writing, but even more they are also not taught how to emulate this emotion in their own writing, nor do they actually have the opportunities to produce in the very genres that they read.

A critical literacy framework that allows students to experience aesthetically the texts that they read opens up spaces for students to be inspired to a fuller humanity. This is critical literacy in that it promotes transcendence over the mundane, the ordinary, and the taken for granted. It gives students permission to dream through texts, to read in ways that allow them to repeatedly discover and rediscover themselves through the texts that they read. It also allows them to experience legitimately the emotions that accompany the creation of the texts that they read. These experiences hopefully increase the motivation that students have to become avid consumers of written texts; a development that can only help in facilitating critical and empowered, identities as unique individuals and transformative citizens. Finally, the aesthetic reading that I am promoting as reading as care for the self has potential to help students become more thoughtful and energetic writers in that they will be better able to understand the multiple purposes of writing on a purely human and emotive level; they too will become more willing to write to politicize and to convey the powerful and myriad emotions that are the core of the human spirit. I now transition to discuss some concrete manifestations of how scholars and artists have used reading and writing to care for the self as a pathway into my own developing grounded theory of critical literacy praxis in schools as care for the self. I talk about Foucault, the authors of slave narratives (particularly Frederick Douglass and Harriet Jacobs), and Che Guevara's published diaries *The Motorcycle Diaries* and *Back on the Road* (also known as *Otra Vez*), and I speak from my own experiences as an emergent scholar and writer before concluding the chapter with thoughts for the field to consider.

FOUCAULT'S HUPOMNEMATA

In his candidacy for the Collège de France, Michel Foucault described himself as an historian of systems of thought. In his lectures and in the description of his courses, he described his goal as understanding the knowing subject, or even separating the subject from the will to truth. As a criticalist, I interpret this to mean that Foucault wanted to understand who we were as humans outside what we were taught to believe; or separate from the discourses that shaped our realities. As part of this project, Foucault studied self-writing through the Western philosophical era as part of the care for the self and as a way of coming to know oneself that would allow for navigation of oppressive discourses. Foucault found that self-writing played an important role in helping citizens to master the art of living. Various traditions identified self-writing as playing an important role in helping ascetics to understand the impulses of their soul, or to subject one's life to an all-important personal gaze in a way that would lead to a more perfect existence. Foucault saw the pre-Christian literature of the first millennium B.C. as theorizing writing as playing a role in the philosophical cultivation of the self. Specifically he identifies how Pythagoreans, Socratics, and Cynics attached importance to self-writing in helping citizens to master the art of living. In summing up the role of writing in this era, Foucault comments:

> writing constitutes an essential stage in the process to which the whole askesis leads: namely, the fashioning of accepted discourses, recognized as true, into rational principles of action. As an element of self-training, writing has, to use an expression that one finds in Plutarch, an *ethopoietic* function: it is an agent of the transformation of truth into ethos. (1997, p. 209)

Foucault focuses on the hupomnemata, what he defines as the account books, or notebooks serving as memory aids, that facilitate the development of critical reflexive thought on discourse, particularly as discourse manifested itself in dominant texts, usually books. These notebooks constitute a material record of all things read, heard, or thought; serving as a meta-text that subjects could continually reread and meditate on as they came to know, even to fashion themselves as true selves. About these texts Foucault writes:

> They do not constitute a 'narrative of oneself'; they do not have the aim of bringing to the light of day the arcane *conscientiae*, the oral or written confession of which has a purificatory value. The movement they seek to bring about is the reverse of that: the intent is not to pursue the unspeakable, nor to reveal the hidden, nor to say the unsaid, but on the contrary to capture the already said, to collect what one has managed to hear or read, and for a purpose that is nothing less than the shaping of the self . . . such is the aim of the hupomnemata: to make one's recollection of the fragmentary logos transmitted through teaching, listening, or reading, a means of establishing a relationship of oneself with oneself, a relationship as adequate and accomplished as possible. (1997, p. 211)

Ultimately Foucault felt that these imminently personal texts could form the core of correspondence: critical texts to be shared with others; but only after going through the process of intense self-exploration through writing. After this process, however, the correspondence that would emerge from the hupomnemata would constitute a unique and powerful way of manifesting oneself to oneself and to others; in this way the writing that results is a showing of oneself or a projection of oneself into view of others. The creation, reflection upon, and dissemination of the hupomnemata constitutes a powerful critical literacy praxis on two levels: it allows subjects to know themselves more fully as complicated and unique human beings, very consonant with Freire's (1970) call for humanization as an ontological necessity. On another level, the dissemination of these texts allows for a more honest and human exchange between authors, texts, and readers that is mutually empowering. The more I come to know another, the more I am able to appreciate and know and love myself, with all of my faults and unique gifts. Further, the more I see critical reflection on institutionalized discourses modeled, the more I will be able to apply these types of analytic tools to my own living, my own rereading and acting upon the world.

In my own work as a teacher, scholar, and writer I tried to envision how this hupomnemata most paralleled my own writing, and I also wanted to consider what existing genres might be tweaked or new genres imagined as a result of reading Foucault's study of self-writing. Certainly the personal journal and memoir come to mind as examples of genres, but the hupomnemata seems a step prior even to the more polished personal reflection contained in a memoir; it is an elemental text that exists, I imagine, in fragments, at the level and substance of thought. It necessarily needs to be choppy and discursive, as thought normally is. It is writing that needs to be brutally honest with the self and the world. It is a continual writing, a spur-of-the-moment writing; the pen and the notebook must always be near. I think of the poet or screenwriter who carries the small 3" × 5" notebook and pen in the purse or back pocket, always ready to capture an idea, an image, or a thought.

It is important to add, though, that the hupomnemata is not only personal, but it is critical as well. It is a personal text that asks tough questions about texts and the world. It exists as a text to be read, reread, and reflected upon, even acted upon. In this way, it is necessarily different from a diary or journal, which may or may not add the reflexive component. At any rate, it is a compelling genre to be studied and incorporated by teachers, students and scholars interested in the relationship between critical literacy, personal development, and social praxis.

SARTRE AND COMMITTED WRITING

The French Existentialist philosopher Jean-Paul Sartre felt that one of the chief motives of artistic creation is to feel that we are essential in relationship to the world. On this topic, Sartre writes:

> If I fix on canvas or in writing a certain aspect of the fields or the sea or a look on someone's face which I have disclosed, I am conscious of having produced them by condensing relationships, by introducing order where there was none, by imposing the unity of mind on the diversity of things. That is, I feel myself essential to my own creation. (1998, p. 624)

Sartre, like many other critical philosophers, uses philosophy to theorize dysconsciousness and inaction in humanity while also working to challenge and reverse these real, but unnatural human conditions. For him, the process of writing was, at once, a consciousness and an action upon the world. For it is in considering one's text through the eyes of others (potential readers of the text) that the writer becomes conscious of the productive activity, of him or herself as a producer of consciousness; as a shaper of the world, and of thought. Sartre further writes:

> To write is thus to both disclose the world and to offer it as a task to the generosity of the reader. It is to have recourse to the consciousness of others in order to make one's self be recognized as essential to the totality of being; it is to wish to live essentially by means of interposed persons; but, on the other hand, as the real world is revealed only by action, as one can feel [themselves] in it only by exceeding it in order to change it, the novelists universe would lack thickness if it were not discovered in a movement to transcend it. (1998, p. 632)

The idea of being essential and of truly acting in the world are essential to Sartre's existentialism, to the critical project of the twentieth (and now twenty-first) centuries, and to the work of many progressive writers, artists, and intellectuals, among them Pablo Picasso, Pablo Neruda, Simone de Beauvoir, Paul Robeson, and Jean-Paul Sartre himself. On this topic critical literary theorist David Macey (2000) comments:

> For Sartre to write is to name and unveil the world, and to project an image of being in the world. The writer thus assumes a specific position within the context of a sociopolitical reality and is said to be committed to the extent of being lucidly conscious of involvement in the world. He or she is also under a moral imperative to disclose to the reader a reality in which the individual can be seen to be a historically situated being who is committed to a quest for authentic freedom. The idea of commitment establishes a full circuit between reader and writer. (p. 66)

Sartre's committed literature speaks to the role of writing as social praxis, but he also theorizes the role of committed writing on the writer her- or himself. Committed writing is the manifestation of a way of being in the world. It is an expression of existential freedom. In that way, writing engaged literature is a part of the process of a continual becoming; becoming ourselves in a world where external forces are constantly seeking to alienate us from our true selves. Sartre's main contention with humanity was that too many of us acted in bad faith (Sartre, 1984). That is, we failed to acknowledge our existential freedom, choosing instead to see ourselves as tied to external social and cultural constraints that constantly prevented us from acting, or being, our true selves. The acting in bad faith, then, is a process of alienating the self from the self, and it causes self-loathing and shame. Writing to share with humanity the potential of freedom, then, could serve as a liberating act for both the reader and the writer. For the writer, it is in that moment of creation, when she or he is putting the ideas to words, to texts, that the first true being in the world occurs. This committed writing can be seen as self-fulfillment or self-humanization even as it is also clearly social activism.

It is through this writing for others, a writing for the world, that we come to know and love ourselves, that we come to be empowered over our own texts and ultimately, our own lives. In this way, committed writing becomes the care for the self in that it is a process that allows the writer of committed texts to know and become themselves. I can remember the first committed texts that I created in college. I wrote for an underground publication with a circulation of several thousand. I wrote poems and journalistic pieces that encouraged students to rebel against injustice in the educational system and society at large. Those texts, although meant for others, were also my first true acts of being in the world. I became a different person for writing those texts even before they were ever read by outside eyes. The texts were, for me, an act of freedom, and a license for me to see myself as an agent in my own destiny.

In schools or classrooms, teachers can allow students an opportunity to become themselves more fully by presenting opportunities for students to create committed literature. As with the hupomnemata, the movement toward the production of committed literature explicitly challenges the genres of production currently prevalent in most literacy classrooms. Sartre felt that the true genres for committed writing were prose fiction and drama. He later conceded, during the Negritude movement, that poetry could also be a genre of committed writing. I would add the creative non-fiction texts of journalists and essayists such as Edward Said, Joan Didion, Alma Guillermoprieto, and Hunter Thompson to this list as well. Either way, there are few opportunities for students to produce in these genres and to write texts that allow them to feel and act more fully human in the world. As I have argued in previous chapters, it is rare that students see themselves as producing texts that will even be relative to the world, given that the sole audience for most of their work is the waiting gaze of the teacher, who serves more as a judge of the merits of the text than as an authentic audience for the text. I will talk more about process and production in the final segment of this chapter when I consider the implications of writing as care for the self on the teaching of literacy to urban adolescents.

SURREALIST AND AUTOMATIC WRITING

André Breton (1896–1966) is the founder of Surrealism, a French avante-garde literary and artistic movement prominent in the 1930s and 1940s known for its revolt against all forms of realism and rationality and its attempt to unleash unconscious creative forces. For Breton and other Surrealist writers, writing became an activity that, when done correctly, could put one in touch with one's very soul. In many ways, the Surrealists borrowed the spirit of Romantics such as Wordsworth and Coleridge who also felt that writing was, at its best, a spontaneous burst of emotion. In the late eighteenth century, Wordsworth and Coleridge embarked on a two-year experiment to produce conversational poetry that would resonate with everyday working people and evoke powerful emotions. For the two poets the emotion evoked by the poem was more important than the poem itself. In order to produce emotional poetry the authors devoted themselves to inhabiting the emotional states they wanted to inspire in their writing. Resulting from this powerful collaboration and composing process are a set of classic texts and a movement that would change forever the face of poetry and the aesthetic of the poet.

In order to maximize their literary creativity, Breton and his Surrealist associates engaged in what they called Automatic Writing, a form of textual production in which participants write as quickly and openly as they can, without conscious thought, in order to produce voluminous heartfelt and authentic texts that defy the social and literary conventions of the time. Consider this passage, from the first Surrealist Manifesto (Breton, 1972), in which Breton describes an Automatic Writing event:

> Suddenly a few good fragments came to mind, quite suitable to be used in a rough draft, or serialized; all of a sudden I found, quite by chance, beautiful phrases, phrases such as I had never written. I repeated them to myself slowly, word by word; they were excellent. And there were still more coming. I got up and picked up a pencil and some paper that were on a table behind my bed. It was as though some vein had burst within me, one word followed another, found its proper place, adapted itself to the situation, scene piled upon scene, the action unfolded, one retort after another welled up in my mind, I was enjoying myself immensely. Thoughts came to me so rapidly and continued to flow so abundantly that I lost a whole host of delicate details, because my pencil could not keep up with them, and yet I went as fast as I could, my hand in constant motion, I did not lose a minute. The sentences continued to well up within me; I was pregnant with my subject.

Now to the literary purist, Breton, the Surrealists, and their style of textual production can all easily be written off as nonsensical. Much writing that bears the label "surreal" breaks most of the rules that we teach about writing with respect to process and product. What it does, however, is restore spirit and passion to the writing process. In the excerpt from the manifesto, Breton describes a productive writing encounter that is intense, free flowing, and filled with passion and joy for the subject of the writing, but also for the process itself. In urban secondary literacy classrooms, where so much writing is deliberate, methodical and even intentionally distant, it is easy for students to never have the experience of writing in this way. Even in critical literacy pedagogy, when students are ostensibly writing socially oriented texts, their composition processes often lack this component. It is important for critical literacy educators to consider how to make spaces for exercises and texts that resemble the automatic writing of the Surrealists.

A grounded theory of critical literacy praxis holds space for challenging the very nature of writing and text. In the spirit of challenging, students need to have the experience of producing texts that challenge the genre, but they also need the opportunity to produce texts that challenge their very beliefs about themselves and the world. Automatic writing can do this. It goes without saying that certain texts do not lend themselves easily to peer-reviewed writing groups or even the pen of the teacher. Should there be texts produced by students that are read by no one but the students themselves? What might they write given the space and support and freedom to write without rules or walls? How might they think differently about writing, about texts, about themselves, or about the world? I argue that a critical literacy pedagogy needs to seriously explore these questions. Given that the focus of this chapter is on critical writing as self-healing, self-awareness, and self-actualization, it only makes sense to advocate that students be given the license and the structures that allow them to write to themselves and for themselves and to write "automatically" without inhibition; to write with reckless abandon and disregard; and to surprise even themselves with what comes out on the page.

This type of production lends itself to the literacy instruction of urban adolescents, given that adolescence is a particularly emotional time, filled with moments of exhilaration, triumph, angst, and despair. Unfortunately, there are precious few opportunities for adolescents to deal with these emotions that accompany their ultra-sensitive experience of the world in their traditional academic writing. It is my belief that youth, who are at once vulnerable and invincible, would connect to the ideals, outlooks, and processes of the Romantic and Surrealist writers; they may be more likely to engage writing and produce more engaged writing under these circumstances.

SLAVE NARRATIVES

I spoke at length in chapter 3 about the importance of literacy in the African-American tradition; a tradition that dates back to the institution of slavery. Even though African-American slaves were officially denied the right to learn to read and write, many were able to seek out instruction or teach themselves, and this act became significant as literacy emerged as a vehicle to contemplate freedom. Literacy, specifically writing, also became a vehicle for slaves to use texts to make sense of their own experiences while also being able to "document" and share their narratives of dehumanization and triumph. Out of this tradition and context emerged an entire genre of literary production known now as the "slave narrative." The most popular narratives are those written by Frederick Douglass, Harriet Jacobs, and Sojourner Truth, but literally hundreds of these written narratives survive. These narratives are important to us today for a variety of reasons. For one, they stand out as the only surviving texts written by African-Americans themselves that describe the institution of slavery. In that way they are not simply "African-American" texts; rather they exist as the only authentic collective memory and history for the nation of this despicable yet defining institution of racial and social relations. Equally as significant, though, these texts exist as representatives of an important genre of writing as care for the self. Many (including myself) would argue that these authors were not just writing to share their horrors with others; most of these texts were not even published during the lifetimes of the authors. The present-day African-American literary theorist and cultural critic Henry Louis Gates Jr. collected and published many of these slave narratives. For Gates, these slave narratives existed as a way for the authors to write themselves into being (Gates, 2002).

Gates offers a powerful heuristic for analyzing the autobiographical narrative of the marginalized and oppressed as a political act of self-definition. When one considers the totalizing narratives of oppression in which these authors existed, which included even the United States constitution, it makes sense that they would need to find conscious ways to will themselves into being, because technically they did not exist as humans, as subjects in the philosophical sense of the term. Writing for the self and for posterity served to acknowledge both their existence and the realities of that existence, in the act of production, in the meta-awareness of reality engendered, in the permanence of the documentation, and in the pedagogy of distribution, which all served to give being to the authors and to others implicated in these narratives.

This becomes particularly important for members of subaltern groups who have been excluded from mainstream and historical discourses (Guha, 1982). The slave narrative served as a way for slaves to codify, memorialize, and make apparent a problematic way of life that, although prevalent, remained on the outskirts of the American conscience. Outside this vibrant yet subordinated genre, those with the sanctioned "power" to articulate slavery were those who, by definition, were removed from its realities. This exclusion within the discourse of contemporary American thought also ensured a certain silence and "softening" of the horrors of the institution. The published slave narrative, then, existed as both a pedagogical and a political discourse genre. At an even more foundational level, however, these narratives were referential biographies first and foremost for the authors, who, through these narratives, were able to articulate even to themselves their own subjectivity, their authentic painful and triumphant existence. There are parallels in the slave narratives to the *écriture féminine* of Hélène Cixous: both are instances of writing that affirm presence in the absence of presence; they are models of sentient writing that is both witness and testimony to the empowered alternative existence. Feminine writing and slave writings are writings of the Other for the Other; they are writings, though, and as such they are texts to be studied and engaged; they are texts that, by their very existence, affirm the author and the realities of which the author writes.

An obvious application can be found in the proliferation of spoken word poetry in urban classrooms and community centers across the country. As its practitioners will attest, the spoken word poem is often narrative and it is often autobiographical and, in explicitly pedagogical contexts, it is used by urban youth to make their stories exist through the telling to others, both those "others" who are implicated in the same sociohistorical conditions and those others who are concerned and empowered enough to act against those totalizing conditions. These spoken word authors, then, write their lives as poetic texts that can be read and reread, in order to be critiqued, discussed, and even rewritten in the process of rewriting the world. The authentic spoken word poem, like the slave narrative, is existential and self-referential even as it historicizes and problematizes the past and present. Both are excellent genres to promote self-reflection and self-healing in urban literacy pedagogy.

In the hierarchy of literary writing in secondary instruction, the autobiographical narrative is seen primarily as a prelude to more distanced, objective, and "academic" expository writing that ostensibly exists at the top of the K-12 academic literacy heap; it is via expository writing that Advanced Placement and Honors students demonstrate their merit as literate intellectuals. Rarely, if ever, are students asked to write autobiography or fiction to demonstrate such intellect even though our many of our most prized cultural texts are actually fiction or autobiography.

There is a need for literacy educators and researchers to reconsider the role of reflexive autobiographical narratives in the literacy pedagogy and production of urban adolescents. Students need to be provided with opportunities to articulate, embrace, and analyze their own lived experiences as part of their development as writers, intellectuals, artists, and potential agents of change. The autobiographical narrative has literary appeal, pedagogical imperative, and a central role to play in pedagogies of care for the self.

CHE GUEVARA'S MOTORCYCLE
DIARIES AND OTRA VEZ

What is so special about the writing of Che Guevara and the political diary? Even though Che's two travel diaries *The Motorcycle Diaries* (Guevara, 2003) and *Otra Vez* (Guevara, 2001) were posthumously published and disseminated worldwide, they were originally written as diaries, stories with an audience of one, Che himself. It is often said, and he admits as much himself, that the trips through Latin America transformed his life. The first trip forced him to ask questions about oppression of poor and indigenous peoples. He also recognized the potential for unity amongst the various populations of the

Americas. From the second trip, which would lead him to Mexico City and into the circle of Fidel Castro, he would never return.

Both of these trips were trips of self-discovery for Che as well as the discovery of a continent. I would argue that in addition to his explorations and conversations with people, that Che's diary writing also played a significant role in his emergent consciousness. These self-authored, self-audienced texts allowed Che the time and space to process what he was learning about the people's of the continent and about himself as a young man, as a traveler, and (especially in *Otra Vez*) as a budding revolutionary thinker.

TEACHING CRITICAL LITERACY AS CARE FOR THE SELF

What must we do as critical literacy educators to teach critical literacy as care for the self? When does it make sense to use classroom assignments to promote writing in genres such as the personal memo or the diary entry? How can we assess assignments that, by definition, we are not supposed to read? All of these are interesting and important questions that do not have easy answers; particularly in the current structure of schools that is heavily dependent on standardized practices and assessment. Critical literacy, though, should not necessarily be beholden to the current structure of schools. Conceptualizing critical literacy as care for the self stretches literacy educators in important ways. It forces us to rethink the multiple purposes of our literacy pedagogies and also re-theorizes the role of audience in composing in having opportunities for students to compose to a primary audience of one: themselves.

What makes writing as care for the self a practice in critical literacy? As I quoted him in chapter 2, it was Socrates who said that the unexamined life is not worth living. Critical theory challenges us to question the production of knowledge as a set of value-laden, ideological activities. Usually, its conceptual and theoretical tools have been used to examine the external world, particularly in search of social, racial, gender, and economic oppression/repression. Far more rarely are we asked to use these tools to examine ourselves explicitly. Writing as care for the self offers the opportunity for students to use writing to question and clarify perceptions, values, attitudes toward the world in a space that is safe, yet inherently pedagogical. Without fear of external judgment, students can critically analyze and transform their own thinking.

Writing as care for the self is also critical in its potentially emancipatory nature. Without fear of censorship or punishment, students are free to express themselves in a language and manner that is totally their own. Emancipatory writing also leads toward emancipatory thinking and, in the philosophizing of Freire, emancipatory action. I argue for the spaces for free-flowing unedited unread prose as an act of transgression against the myriad constraints and social norms that are placed on budding writers and thinkers. If we are truly interested in promoting spaces of transformation, we also must allow for students to write in these types of ways. This means more than a sloppy copy or an unedited draft; this is about writing as a practice of freedom and self-exploration that may be the key to individual and social transformation as well as innovative textual production.

Critical Literacy as Social Praxis

The previous chapters have mostly focused on the pedagogy of critical literacies as a pathway to academic achievement, traditional and new media literacy development, and identity development. This chapter, though, looks at the potential role of literacy pedagogy in social transformations. As urban literacy educators and researchers, we must acknowledge that the real change we imagine may not be possible within the system as it is currently construed. So, while we work to help students to gain access to literacies of power and access, we must also consider the implications of our work with students, families, and communities as it relates to dismantling the systems and structures that have caused all of the problems in the first place. In that vein the chapter first turns toward the Freedom Schools of the Civil Rights Movement and the Cuban Literacy Campaign, two successful mid-twentieth-century social movements that paid explicit attention to a pedagogy of critical literacy. I examine these two movements in hopes that they shed light on the characteristics of literacy education in the context of social change. Drawing from the principles of these two movements, I will then examine two contemporary research projects in which teens utilized critical qualitative research as a tool for social change. I will conclude with a discussion of a pedagogy of critical literacy as social praxis with urban youth.

THE FREEDOM SCHOOLS OF THE
CIVIL RIGHTS MOVEMENT

In 1960, nearly a full century after the culmination of the Civil War and the abolition of slavery with the Thirteenth Amendment, eighty-six percent of African-Americans in Mississippi lived below the national poverty line.

What's more, despite the fact that Mississippi's population was over forty percent African-American, fewer than five percent were registered to vote (Kasher, 1996). Those who were registered to vote often were faced at the polls with "literacy" tests. That is, if poll workers felt that African-Americans were unable to read and interpret sections of the constitution, then they would be denied the right to vote. Now, in the racist climate of the south in the 1960s this meant that even literate blacks could be denied the right to vote while illiterate whites seemed to pass these same tests. The implications, however, were clear: literacy was seen as fundamentally tied to civic life. Indeed, literacy in this example was a prerequisite to participation in the electoral process, one of the basic rights of citizenship in our republican democracy. Now, it had already been documented by the US Supreme Court in 1954 that African-Americans in the South attended segregated and underfunded, under-resourced schools that often prevented them from attaining similar literacy levels as members of other ethnic groups. The low literacy rates contributed not only to low income and civic disengagement, they also limited the ability of blacks to effectively engage in professional life and activism, and, by default, their basic empowerment on the political, social, and economic levels.

Toward these ends, civil rights workers descended on Mississippi to develop Freedom Schools. Similar to the work of Freire and the Cuban Literacy Campaign, the community-based education was tied to literacy and numeracy development, but the curriculum began first and foremost with the real experiences of poor blacks (and poor whites) in Mississippi at that time (Williams, 1987). Many would argue that it was the centering of the Freedom School curriculum around issues of social and racial justice that led to its success and the success of the grassroots mobilization that resulted from that campaign. One measurable impact is the percentage of African-Americans registered to vote in the state of Mississippi, which rose from 16.3 percent in 1964 to 66.5 percent in 1969 (Kasher, 1996).

The Freedom Schools are an important site of study for several reasons. First of all, they are further evidence of the argument made by Perry (2003) that literacy has always been tied to freedom in the African-American tradition, which debunks many deficit theories which proclaim that African-Americans are not concerned about education or are unaware of the benefits of a literacy education. Second, this example exists as further evidence of the interrelationship between non-school literacy campaigns and social movements in the 1960s. It is ironic that the Freirian and Cuban literacy campaigns are more highly recognized by critical theorists in the United States than our own contemporary domestic movements, such as the Freedom Schools. Nevertheless they each reinforce the relationship between critical literacy education, individual empowerment, and social change. Finally the Freedom School example is important in that it shows the potential of literacy campaigns to change the shape of our nation politically, socially, and economically. And although this example focuses in on the rural poor, I argue that such a movement would prove similarly powerful with contemporary urban populations as well. Even further, I contend that there are elements of these out-of-school campaigns that can and should inform in-school literacy instruction for urban youth.

THE CUBAN LITERACY CAMPAIGN

In 1959 Fidel Castro stood unabashedly before the general assembly of the United Nations and pronounced that, within a year, he would make his fledgling revolutionary republic fully literate. Arming a group of young *brigadistas* from the city with passion, commitment, and a kit of pedagogical literacy tools, he was able to fashion the impossible. *Campesinos* in the countryside began to acquire the literacies of power that Castro and his advisers felt was so crucial to maintaining a revolutionary identity in the heart of the Americas, where they were surrounded by the United States and its Latin American colonies (UNESCO, 1965). Within the year, after the interventions of this army of youthful pedagogues, Fidel Castro was receiving hundreds of thousands of letters written with newly literate hands that were making their ways from the streets and farms of Cuba to the capital in Havana. Happy hands that were writing letters of acknowledgment and thanks. The deed was done; the task had been accomplished; the nation was literate, and the revolution would continue.

Over forty years later, the revolution does continue. Though it has more than its share of critics in the West, Cuba remains an independent socialist republic in the heart of the Americas, just ninety miles off the coast of the United States, its sworn enemy these last four decades. The Cuban people have survived invasions of armies and of spies. They have endured the social sanction and economic blockades imposed by the United States. They have even handled the fall of the mighty Soviet Union and the end of the communist counter-narrative to the US capitalist imperialism. Through all of this, the tiny island nation of eleven million souls (less than one-third the population of California by comparison) has maintained a fierce independence and spirit of revolution that in retrospect more than justifies the youthful sprit of *el jefe* and his seemingly impossible boast. Not only has the revolution maintained its energy in the midst of hardships and threats from its nearby neighbor and exiled citizens; Cuba has also maintained extremely high literacy rates.

UNESCO reports the adult literacy rate in Cuba to be over ninety-seven percent. It is also a nation that boasts more doctors per capita than the United States. A formerly agrarian colony producing sugar for the powerful in the West has transformed itself into a modern revolutionary country. How have they been able to accomplish this when their counterparts throughout the world have struggled and failed with similar literacy efforts (Kozol, 1979)? How was the nascent revolutionary government of Cuba able to theorize literacy pedagogy as social praxis? What has been the significance of the literacy movement in Cuba to promoting social praxis in this country and throughout the southern Americas? How might such an examination shed light on our own emerging grounded theories of literacy education as social praxis with urban adolescents? These and more questions I will tackle as I attempt to make sense of the purpose, the process, and the praxis of the Cuban literacy campaign.

The first important aspect of this movement is its purpose and its explicit commitment to literacy instruction as a revolutionary activity. Certainly the acquisition of literacy skills was important to modernizing the economy, allowing the nation to compete with its fellow citizens around the world. But literacy was, first and foremost, a duty of an engaged and responsible citizen. For the literate *brigadistas*, some as young as the pre-teen years, being called upon to teach literacy to older *campesinos* in the countryside was a responsibility of citizenship. For the *campesinos*, humbling themselves to learn from children, working in the evenings and on weekends at the end of already back-breaking toil, and submitting themselves to the excruciating task of actually learning to read were all inextricably linked to a promise to Fidel and a larger commitment to the Cuban revolution. Literacy was an individual activity, but it was situated within a much larger social practice for much larger social purposes. I argue that, without these larger social contexts, the movement would not have been nearly as successful as it was.

The process of the literacy movement was very much centered in the work of scholars such as Paulo Freire who believed in humanizing, dialogic pedagogies that drew upon the everyday lived experiences of the people. The *campesinos* and other illiterate populations in Cuba were not to be considered as illegitimate or ignorant populations; as deficits, or people in need of enlightenment. By contrary the *campesinos* were to be respected, even revered for the service that they provided to the country. By the same token, these populations were not to be talked at, lectured to, or taught through alienating and irrelevant curricula. The *brigadistas* were instructed to engage in conversations with *campesinos*, to respect the vast funds of knowledge that they already possessed, and to center the literacy instruction within matters of everyday importance to these populations.

Finally, there was a clear praxis to this literacy instruction. All Cuban citizens understood that literacy was not only needed to promote national development, but literacy was a form of national security. Literacy praxis was fundamentally tied to decolonizing the mindsets in a region where every nation was treated like a US colony (and many still are under the yoke of the United States or desperately attempting to remove themselves). Literacy praxis entailed critically accessing information about the world that would call into question many of the predominant beliefs in the country and throughout the region about economics, government, and culture. For example, becoming literate meant reading and coming to terms with the history of the nation and its relationships with imperial powers: its role as a tool of capitalist production. Becoming literate also meant coming to understand the revolutionary history of the nation and the reading about the lives and works of people such as José Martí and Simón de Bolívar: personages rarely mentioned in colonial education because of their revolutionary visions for the people.

Becoming literate functioned as praxis because citizens were able to engage the works of Karl Marx and his critique of capitalism, the predominant economic system of the West (Marx, 1983). Reading Marx would expose these citizens to an alternate discourse to the free market capitalist doctrine that was preached indirectly via US education and popular culture that emanated from the United States. Cuban citizens also used newly acquired literacy to become public pedagogues and public producers. Literacy was a commodity to be shared with other citizens in a practice that functioned as practice. Not only was this a skill to re-engage the world, it was knowledge used to re-engage with fellow citizens in a remaking of the world. Finally, critical literacy praxis enabled Cubans to serve as public producers of knowledge, creating their own newspapers, literature, art, and culture that served as a counter to other information being produced by Cuba's enemies. Literacy served as social praxis in enabling its citizens to function as public intellectuals and to create cultural texts that engendered the revolutionary proletariat culture that Gramsci envisioned (Gramsci, 1985).

What is so amazing about this movement is how successful it is and also how it debunks so much of what we think we know about effective literacy pedagogy. For starters, we are talking about very under-resourced learning environments. Although I would never advocate for taking money away from schools, it is important to see how educators can be successful in environments where there are not a great deal of economic resources. Additionally, we often talk about the importance of qualified teachers, which is a valid concern among educators, administrators, and researchers in the field. However, in the Cuban literacy campaign, many of the workers were trained in a relatively short amount of time and most did not have formal certification as teachers, yet they served as extremely effective literacy educators. This forces us to ask ourselves tough questions about what we mean by qualified teachers and what we mean by formal training.

Finally, the Cuban revolutionaries were adamant about the interrelation between an overt political ideology and the work of literacy education. Too often we are concerned to avoid the discussions of politics or ideology in education; which we attempt to pass off to our students as a neutral enterprise (Apple, 1990). Critical literacy education cannot or should not fall into this trap. Although we do not want to indoctrinate students, it remains important to relate the development of literacy skills with advocacy for justice and change. Often the lack of motivation in schools is attributable to a lack of perceived relevance of school activities (Wigfield and Eccles, 1992, 2000). If students see academic literacy learning as "acting White" (Fordham and Ogbu, 1986) or as not related to their everyday lives, they will be far less inclined to invest themselves in the work in schools. On the other hand, if students can be made to see how the acquisition of empowering literacy skills can help them in their struggle against inequitable material conditions, they might be more willing to engage in the work of school.

In both examples, the civil rights workers and the Cuban citizens understood the acquisition of literacies of power as part of their revolutionary duty. Everyday people were willing to make tremendous sacrifices and engage in tremendous acts of courage to become "literate" in the traditional sense of the term. Many adult citizens with very little formal education overcame their apprehension and ultimately became empowered users of the word in the context of struggling for social justice and human rights. What a powerful message to send to students: that the development of literacies of power can play a role in the transformations of their schools and communities! What is even more powerful is to include opportunities for students to use their critical literacies to advocate for change on a local and global level. With that in mind we return to the summer research seminar to examine two projects that allowed urban adolescents to do just that.

A CRITICAL PUBLIC HISTORY OF SCHOOLING IN POST-BROWN LOS ANGELES, 1954–2003

In the summer of 2003 the seminar focused on *Oral Histories of the Educational Experiences in Post-Brown Los Angeles from 1954–2003*. We began with the premise that young people who attended substandard schools for many years generally understood that they had been given a raw deal. They knew that teachers were supposed to be well prepared and care for their students. They knew that water fountains should work and bathrooms should be open and safe. They knew that they should receive their textbooks at the beginning of each term. And they knew that none of these conditions existed at their schools. Yet, because these students had not been educated about how these conditions came into being, they didn't have a language to explain why their schools were the way they were and how they might be different. Further, given the absence of a context for collective dialogue and collective agency, they were alienated from any sort of engaged praxis around these issues.

As organizers of the seminar, we felt that the young people needed a sense of history to understand that the present is not inevitable and the future is full of possibilities. We operated under the belief that these young people forge their deepest understandings through practice (Lave and Wenger, 1991). That is, the students would learn most about the nature of present conditions and of possibilities of alternate futures through a collective engagement of the issues at hand; in this case, through engaging the history of public schooling in urban Los Angeles, focusing on the post-*Brown* era.

We felt that when students make public history—which would include conducting interviews, examining historical records, and analyzing census data—they could see what it means to construct an historical narrative. First of all, such a process would allow them to look at how the lived experience of everyday people is shaped by and in turn shapes structural conditions in the economy and legal system. As young people placed themselves and their families in this historical narrative, they would forge a deeper understanding of who they were and the society they live within. And when this history calls on them to study people like themselves who have joined the struggle for education on equal terms, they would begin to imagine an identity as historical agents. By writing public history, young people could come to see themselves as *authors* of the future.

Second, engaging in a critical public history would also allow the students to see how historical research is conducted, and, in turn, bring to their attention the subjective elements of historical narrative. When examining archives and other artifacts, they would gain firsthand knowledge of the myriad decisions historians make when creating these narratives. They could, through examining their own decision-making, come to understand how important details get left out depending on the needs and beliefs of the historian as agent and author. With respect to the research on the historical experiences of students of color in Los Angeles schools, they could ask pertinent questions about why sources they located and analyzed had not been included in dominant historical accounts of schooling in their city.

However, they would not only have this new understanding of the "holes" in dominant historical narratives. They would also develop the tools and gain access to the artifacts that would allow them to express their critiques through the presentation of counter-narratives in the form of legitimate historical research. In this way the process was critical in that it involved those not customarily associated with historical research and in that it explicitly critiqued the traditional ways of constructing historical narratives of the experiences of marginalized groups. Further, the process can be considered as public because it involved authentic members of the public in the process of research and in that it was research intended to inform and contribute to the public discourse about race, education, and civic life in urban Los Angeles.

We saw many overlaps between the project of critical public history and our project of critical literacy. As educators, we were very much aware of the literacy practices that such research would entail. We felt that, as with the Freedom Schools and the Cuban literacy campaign, our students would rise to the literacy challenges of critical public history as they envisioned their practice as part of a larger movement of social action. Toward these ends, each of the five student research teams focused on one of the post-*Brown* decades in Los Angeles. In their research teams, the students collected oral history interviews and examined statistical databases such as the US Census and educational achievement indices. Further student research groups accessed available archives, where they encountered other historical artifacts such as yearbooks, newspaper articles, and photographs from the periods they set out to study. Finally, the students created research reports, PowerPoint presentations, and short films. As with the other summer seminars, these student research products were presented to multiple public, administrative, and professional audiences; they were also placed on websites that were available to multiple publics.

There were many important outcomes associated with students engaging as critical public historians, outcomes that inform our discussions of critical literacy, academic development, and social praxis. First and foremost, these urban adolescents created history. Each research group created a compelling and well-articulated narrative that added to the body of work available to scholars and advocates wanting to know more about the educational experiences of students of color in Los Angeles. The student reports were presented to representatives of the educational establishment with power to make changes in schools. These reports were published on websites and presented at youth summits and professional conferences.

What's more, these student-researchers added scholarly research to the historical archives. Around this time, a local library in the city had begun amassing a huge archive on the people's history in neighborhoods in the city that had primarily served people of color for some time. The students accessed these archives as part of their investigations, but they were also able to embellish these archives, which, unlike their university counterparts, were free and open to the public. Each student group contributed its PowerPoint presentations, reports, and short films, but they also contributed all of the raw footage from the oral history interviews, as DVD-ROMs, to the archive. This raw footage would then become available to future generations of public and professional historians.

Finally, these student research groups became involved in history-making research, which itself exists as a form of social praxis. In articulating the foundations of a new research method, critical public history, students participated in an explicit critique of the academy structures that prevent the active participation of everyday citizens in the making and recording of historical narratives. The research itself also contributed to contemporary conversations about the state of education in the city. In the context of the fiftieth anniversary of the *Brown* decision, the research conducted by the students became important as districts throughout the nation began to evaluate their own efforts to achieve equity and integration in the schools. Particularly, the students were able to show how Los Angeles public schools were becoming increasingly segregated with time. Many of the schools in the central neighborhoods of the city, for example, were more integrated at the time of the *Brown* decision than they were at the time of the research conducted half a century later!

Rarely do we consider the role of critical research in social praxis. Usually we associate more overt forms of activism, marches, rallies, or even cyberactivism campaigns with social praxis. Even the previous examples of the Freedom Schools and Cuban literacy campaign conform to our prevailing aesthetic of revolutionary action. In this work, I am advocating for a larger view of social action that incorporates activist and action-oriented scholarship. In a world where citizens are inundated with information designed to constrain and configure social thought, we must consider critical knowledge production as a revolutionary action and the critical knowledge producers as revolutionary actors. As the saying goes, the pen, or in this case the keyboard, may be mightier than the sword.

Certainly, there were important outcomes of this project at the level of individual student development. As critical literacy educators we are rarely afforded the opportunity to focus solely on social action at the expense of individual skill development, so I would like to speak briefly to important historical lessons and literacy skills learned while participating in the critical public history project. First of all, students complicated their view of race relations in their city. The narratives of racial integration were not nearly as one-sided as many imagined. In the oral history interviews that students conducted with people who had attended central city and Westside schools in the 1950s and 1960s, for instance, our students were repeatedly told that the schools were fairly integrated spaces with little overt racial hostility. Since this information disconfirmed many of the working hypotheses that the students held, the initial tendency was to ignore the information as nostalgia and erroneous recall. However, when students examined demographic data and high school yearbooks, they noticed that these schools were indeed more ethnically diverse and showed signs of indeed being integrated, when students looked at participation in clubs and activities. The student research groups were forced to acknowledge that there was a tale of neither unequivocal hatred nor unlimited progress.

The student researchers also uncovered many disconfirming narratives of agency and resistance. As co-directors of the project, my colleague John Rogers and I both operated under the assumption that students were not exposed to the histories of resistance in their schools and communities. This assumption was confirmed as students expressed their surprise that a long and vibrant tradition of student action and resistance existed in their city schools. Without being exposed to the legacy of activism and advocacy in history classes, young people are implicitly taught to believe that the present is an unfortunate yet inevitable reality. They are also implicitly taught that change is caused by people much older and with much more power than they currently possess. Our students were able to learn, however, that many people their age had created powerful counter-movements in the very neighborhoods and schools where they were now conducting research. As an example, through the seminar students were acquainted with the student-led Chicano blowouts in 1968. Some of the active participants in that movement, themselves high school students at the time, participated in the oral history interviews and met with student researchers.

Students developed sophisticated research skills during this process as well. I have already talked at length in chapter 5 about the skills developed during the summer research seminars, but some of the unique skills related to historical research include archival analyses and analysis of census and educational achievement databases.

CRITICAL CIVIC LITERACY IN THE
ELECTION CAMPAIGN, 2004

In the summer of 2004, the seminar focused on Urban Youth, Political Participation, and Educational Reform. Students explored: a) what it means for urban youth to participate powerfully in civic life; b) how urban youth can learn to participate in such ways; and c) what civic lessons young people now learn in and outside of urban schools. The students, who were placed into small research teams, talked with youth, educators, community leaders, and elected officials about: a) issues facing young people in the local community; b) how young people should participate in civic life; and c) what skills are needed for such participation. Each team conducted research at a high school site and a community center in a local neighborhood. The teams also developed research tools for examining civic education in a school. These tools included survey instruments (see Table 9–1), interview and focus group questions (or protocols), and rubrics for examining books and other curricula.

As with other seminars, students produced individual texts and group texts. These texts ranged from standard written documents to iMovies and PowerPoint presentations. Individually, students produced fifteen hundred-to two thousand-word essays dealing with their journeys to becoming critical researchers and the implications of their seminar work for engagement in their schools and communities. Student research teams produced PowerPoint presentations, research reports, and a public presentation, which showcased the tools that they developed along with their research findings. Further, the students produced five-minute iMovie documentaries (discussed in chapter 7) and materials for an electronic journal targeted toward urban teachers and parents.

Each team, as I mentioned, conducted research at a high school site and a community center in a local neighborhood. The teams also developed research tools for examining civic education in a school. These tools included survey instruments, interview and focus group questions (or protocols), and rubrics for examining books and other curricula. Throughout their participation in the seminar young people demonstrated complicated academic and critical literacies as they participated as critical sociologists. They also re-appropriated tools of social science research and developed new ones to better serve their needs as scholar-activists. Further, and for the purposes of this chapter, these students used research to participate civically through presentations, writing, and using research to organize students and parents for action. Analysis of interviews, seminar discourse and student writing reveals that they saw

TABLE 9–1

Youth Engagement and Civic Literacies Survey

	Strongly agree		Agree somewhat		Strongly disagree

SECTION ONE: CONCEPTIONS OF CIVIC ENGAGEMENT

	Strongly agree		Agree somewhat		Strongly disagree
I consider voting as political activity	1	2	3	4	5
I consider reading as political activity	1	2	3	4	5
I would consider writing as political activity	1	2	3	4	5
I would consider writing poetry as political activity	1	2	3	4	5
I would consider community service as a political activity	1	2	3	4	5
I would consider protesting as political activity	1	2	3	4	5
Knowing how to research is important for engaged citizenship	1	2	3	4	5
Knowing how federal, state, and local government works is important for engaged citizenship	1	2	3	4	5
Knowing how to speak publicly is important for engaged citizenship	1	2	3	4	5
Knowing how to use the Internet is important for engaged citizenship	1	2	3	4	5
Knowing how to program a website is important for engaged citizenship	1	2	3	4	5
Knowing how to use a digital camera is important for engaged citizenship	1	2	3	4	5
Knowing how to edit digital video is important for engaged citizenship	1	2	3	4	5
I understand politics	1	2	3	4	5
I feel it is my responsibility to participate in politics	1	2	3	4	5
I am an active citizen	1	2	3	4	5

	Strongly agree		Agree somewhat		Strongly disagree
I believe that all students should be involved in their community	1	2	3	4	5

SECTION TWO: YOUTH CIVIC PARTICIPATION

	Strongly agree		Agree somewhat		Strongly disagree
I am aware of local organizations that challenge inequality in my community	1	2	3	4	5
I am very involved in community activities and organizations	1	2	3	4	5
I participate in protests against issues that affect me in negative ways	1	2	3	4	5
I have organized protests against issues that affect me in negative ways	1	2	3	4	5
I am involved politically in issues that affect my school	1	2	3	4	5
I teach others about how to be involved politically	1	2	3	4	5

SECTION THREE: WHERE YOUTH LEARN TO PARTICIPATE CIVICALLY

	Strongly agree		Agree somewhat		Strongly disagree
I learn to participate civically from my teachers at school	1	2	3	4	5
I learn to participate civically from my parents and guardians at home	1	2	3	4	5
I learn to participate politically from watching television	1	2	3	4	5
I learn from artwork how to act politically	1	2	3	4	5
I learn to participate politically from listening to music	1	2	3	4	5
I learn to participate politically from watching film	1	2	3	4	5
I learn to participate politically from the Internet	1	2	3	4	5
I learn to participate civically from organizations in the community	1	2	3	4	5

TABLE 9-1

Continued

	Strongly agree		Agree somewhat		Strongly disagree
I am encouraged to participate in political life at school	1	2	3	4	5
My parents support me and go with me to community meetings for social issues	1	2	3	4	5
SECTION FOUR: THE PURPOSE OF CIVIC EDUCATION					
Civics Education should teach students about the rules of government	1	2	3	4	5
Civics Education should deal with local community concerns and issues	1	2	3	4	5
Civics Education should teach students how to organize and protest	1	2	3	4	5
SECTION FIVE: LITERACY PROFILE					
I am able to read academic books	1	2	3	4	5
I am able to read newspapers and magazines	1	2	3	4	5
I am able to read the media	1	2	3	4	5
I know how to write a letter or e-mail to a public official	1	2	3	4	5
I know how to surf the Internet	1	2	3	4	5
I know how to create a web page	1	2	3	4	5
I know how to use a digital video camera	1	2	3	4	5
I know how to edit digital video	1	2	3	4	5
I was taught politics at school	1	2	3	4	5

	The Business	Bomb	Straight	Wack	Not the Business
How would you rate your community?	1	2	3	4	5
How would you rate your local school environment?	1	2	3	4	5
How would you rate your teachers and your local schools?	1	2	3	4	5

Open-ended questions:
How do you define being political?

In your opinion, what kind of citizen does your school produce?

What school do you attend?

What is your race/ethnicity?

What is your age/grade?

Are you enrolled in U.S. Government?   Yes   No

Have you taken U.S. Government?   Yes   No

themselves as enabled and as agents of change. Toward this end, let's look at a few of the texts produced by the students in this seminar space. First, we will visit the introduction of one student report, which numbered forty-two manuscript pages in length:

> It is often taught that with time, comes progress and change. If this holds true, then why is it that South L.A. students are finding themselves facing the same struggles and the same disparaging conditions that students in the 1960's faced? Struggles that students demonstrated against by walking out, protesting, and demanding that political figures take action. If these students supposedly invoked progress, then why is it that these same schools, forty years later, are still facing issues with overcrowded classrooms, under funded programs, and overall, are failing to educate their students? Have these students failed themselves by not voicing out, or is it that the world failed them by not listening?
>
> During the summer of 2004, a research group composed of high school students from [they mention various schools and neighborhoods throughout the city] embarked on the task of discovering ways students are involved politically in their community. Through careful examination of the current curriculum, we discovered that educational institutions are failing to instruct their students in how they can demonstrate against unjust situations; they are effectively not being taught how to voice their opinion, and thus are not taught how to act politically. With these current situations in mind, the group sought out to answer: 1) What does it mean to be political in South L.A.? 2) What skills and tools do young people need to be effective in their civic engagement? and 3) Why is it important for youth to study critical civic literacies? To uncover the answers to the questions posed above, we implemented the use of critical research that included: Surveys, personal interviews, demographic studies, research on school curriculum, research on local grass roots organizations, and the study of previous research data.
>
> This research is significant because 1) Throughout history, systematic forces have gone through efforts to marginalize people of color, and through our work we hope to give a voice to the voiceless. 2) Through our work we hope to unveil the current social and educational inequalities that exist in the [x] community and 3) We hope to show educators what changes can be implemented into current school culture and curriculum so that students feel like they can engage politically.

This introductory passage is enlightening for several reasons. First, it shows what students are capable of as writers when they are working on a project that is meaningful to them and when they have mentoring and assistance. Second, it shows the sophistication of the research process itself. These young people created and carried out a multi-method research project that incorporated complex anthropological and sociological tools to understand the civics curricula in local schools and neighborhoods. Finally, and for this chapter most importantly, the opening paragraphs provide a sense of the direct link that the students are making between research and transformative action.

In other places I have argued that, when members of historically marginalized groups gain access to tools of critical participatory research, they naturally employ these tools to benefit their neighborhoods and communities (Morrell, 2004a). This example is a case in point. In the last two sentences the research group makes explicit that they hope to shed light on current inequalities, but that they also hope to communicate directly with educators about strategies they can use to add more critical elements to traditional civics curricula that might lead to more empowering relationships between urban adolescents and civil society.

In addition to implicating schools and educators in the problem and the solution, the student researchers also turn toward an examination of the role of media as a pedagogical institution that imparts its own civics curriculum:

> The media plays an essential role in the community when it comes to youth participating civically. The disappearance rate of Central High school from freshmen to senior year is staggering. It appears that so many youth are not interested in college. Why is that the case? The youth watch television and pay attention to the mainstream ideas of the mainstream media. The youth pay attention to those sitcoms where they see minority families who are rich and successful. The schools practically brainwash and manipulate students, when they hear the phrase brainwash, students can't really connect that terminology with the school's actions. According to a number of television programs, they define to the viewer that the act of brainwashing deals with having the brainwashed person act as a zombie that has no control of what he or she is doing. In reality, the act of brainwashing is an act of manipulation. The media portrays, through movies, self-defeating resistance as the way to go, that it is the life. The media establishes all these gang movies that manipulate the viewer by showing them aspects of gangs that look interesting to youth. The media gives them the mindset that college is not that important because they get the image that there are a lot of successful brown and black minorities when in reality there aren't. If the media presented the community with the marginalized information of brown and black minorities, then the minorities would be influenced to go to college in spite of the system.

The student group implicates the media industries in the problems that they have uncovered in the course of their investigation. In an analysis reminiscent of the work of pioneers in cultural studies such as Gramsci and Adorno, the students point toward the harmful narratives of urban youth that are proliferated through television and film. These harmful narratives serve to create and legitimate stereotypes among the dominant sectors of society but according to this analysis, they also *teach* young people how to be. This is an extremely important point for media and cultural theorists studying urban adolescent populations: that young people gain an aesthetic and a value system via their interactions with dominant media genres.

Building on the work of older generations of media theorists, however, the student groups also see the media as a potential site of critical knowledge exchange. As I discussed in chapter 7, when youth become critical media producers, they play a role in reshaping the media curriculum in powerful ways. In the last sentence of this excerpt from the group report, we see the students suggesting that they have information that, if presented through the proper media channels, could play a role in reshaping this curriculum and, consequently, changing what and how young people learn about themselves as beings and as potential intellectuals and informed civic agents.

TEACHING CRITICAL LITERACY AS SOCIAL PRAXIS WITH URBAN YOUTH

The two historical movements along with the pair of contemporary examples underscore the importance of providing spaces for young people to become critical researchers and critical literacy educators as a part of the development of their own critical literacies. With respect to the Cuban and Civil Rights campaigns, young people were placed in very important positions of knowledge disseminators and public pedagogues. This positioning allowed them to develop their own literacy skills even as they also helped others to do so and, in the process, bolstered their respective fledgling movements. With respect to the two examples from the summer research seminar, students were able to develop their own academic and critical literacies as they were placed in positions of authentic public intellectuals involved in the project of knowledge production. We should learn from these powerful examples that young people are often capable of far more than we generally give them credit for. Teens and young adults have played foundational roles in all of our important social movements in the last half-century. We ignore that blatant reality in our curricula and pedagogies to our own peril. Indeed we must ask ourselves why so little information is available in schools on the history of social movements in general and on the involvement of young people in these social movements. The second lesson concerns the relationship between social praxis and academic literacy development. One of the successes of all of the movements mentioned in this chapter is that they were able to effectively situate literacy learning within a larger context of collective action for social change. Rather than viewing social justice work as a distraction from the real work of schools, it might just provide the framework and the motivation that will compel students to overcome their justifiable skepticism with dominant literacies and dominant institutions in a way that will allow them to develop the literacy skills that they need to function as citizens, as intellectuals, and as committed activists.

I must also repeat that these ideas are not all that new or strange. In chapter 2 I argued that the relationships between literacy education and engaged citizenship are as old in the Western tradition as Plato's *Republic*. We also have examples in the early twentieth century from the work of the pragmatist philosopher and educational architect John Dewey that support the situating of educational practice within children's exploration of and intervention in their own social worlds (Dewey, 1990). In fact, much of the learning theory that I've drawn upon for this book has been consistent in its emphasis on learning through practice. The practices in schools, however, have been more focused on behavior modification than authentic learning via authentic participation in meaningful practice. Again, the huge discrepancies between what we know to be effective practice and what we actually do raise the questions: Why do we put forth a seemingly apolitical curriculum that is presented via pedagogies more bent on social control than learning? What purposes can this serve? What impacts does this have on the project of critical literacy education in urban schools? What would it mean to think otherwise and start from scratch in remaking urban schools and classrooms to fit our vision of critical literacy education? It is to the final chapter and these larger questions that we must now inevitably turn.

A Vision of Critical Literacy in Urban Education

> Can you imagine a world in which nobody any longer asked the philosophic questions, nobody was philosophical? It would be a world in which nobody penetrated below the facts of everyday life to think about what is real, true, valuable, just and meaningful in human life. It would be a world of mechanical men and women, and children moving among physical objects, a world in which we would have become hollow ... going through meaningless motions and our speech would be empty chatter. (Lavine, 1984, p. 5)

This concluding chapter considers how the preceding theoretical framing and empirical research points toward a radical model of critical literacy education in urban schools. I begin by making the case that what is needed in critical literacy education are spaces that allow for the training and positioning of urban teachers and students as critical philosophers. Karl Marx reproached his predecessors in philosophy for their unwillingness to intervene in everyday life and challenged future philosophers to become engaged activists as well as intellectuals. This chapter considers what that might look like in urban teacher development and in K-12 classroom instruction.

Second the chapter offers a concrete vision of what critical literacy praxis might look like in urban education at the primary, middle, and secondary levels including curricula, pedagogies, and activities in which students and teachers might engage. In addition I consider how this vision communicates with current national standards for literacy education. Clearly this work stands as a critique of those standards but, as I also take an approach that is both critical and pragmatic, I do attempt to offer suggestions for ways to think about guidelines and assessments within a critical literacy education paradigm. Those of us who work in today's schools cannot wait for standards to change themselves before we begin this very necessary project. While we advocate on a macro-structural level, we must also work diligently to create innovative and empowering learning spaces in our literacy classrooms. One could even argue that it's the careful documentation of the practices such as the ones that I have presented throughout the book that could serve to convince stakeholders and power brokers of the need to make radical changes in literacy standards and assessments.

The book concludes where it begins, by situating the work of critical literacy education in urban schools within the larger framework of a project that I identify as Universal Critical Literacy. I contemplate how this might be different from what is recommended by UNESCO and other international organizations, which work to achieve a basic literacy for all. Although this is certainly a noble and worthwhile goal, I argue that it may not be enough to fundamentally empower individuals and collectives in our age. Toward this larger critical project, I consider how urban literacy teachers play a role in this process both in and outside classroom spaces and how as citizens and as members of a larger humanity we are all charged to participate in such a movement and the various roles we might play whether we are positioned as educators, researchers, scholars, public intellectuals, policymakers, or community citizens interested in social and educational justice.

TEACHERS AND STUDENTS AS
CRITICAL PHILOSOPHERS

Socrates is purported to have called philosophy down from the heavens and turned its attention to human affairs in the city and in the household. Plato viewed philosophy as an activity concerned with virtue and citizenship and warned against ivory tower intellectuals who were irrelevant to social issues. Wittgenstein too referred to philosophy not as a discipline but as an activity, and regularly discouraged his students from reading classical philosophers, of which he read very little. The existentialists, de Beauvoir and Sartre, also sought to recover philosophy for the everyday person and wrote novels and plays for consumption by the larger public. During the twentieth and twenty-first centuries, when philosophy has been relegated to disciplinary status and controlled by university departments of philosophy, I revisit these age-old questions of the nature of philosophy and of the work of the philosopher. Central to this discussion are three questions:

1. Who philosophizes?
2. Why is philosophizing still an important activity?

3. How can philosophizing by teachers and students help to accomplish progressive educational and social goals with respect to critical literacy?

I argue that teaching the works of classical, contemporary, and multicultural philosophers and "doing philosophy" are excellent ways for literacy teachers to help their students develop academic competencies and skills for critical citizenship. A premise of this argument is that a 2500-year tradition of scholarship has been lost to America's high school students who do not read Plato, Aristotle, or even contemporary philosophers from the African-American, postmodern, feminist, or postcolonial traditions. What is lost from their absence? What can be gained from their inclusion? How can the incorporation of philosophical texts help to accomplish the multiple goals of primary and secondary critical literacy instruction?

I make the argument that philosophy is meant for real people to deal with real problems of everyday life. Philosophy needs to be retaken from the hallowed halls of the university back to people in the real world who can use it. There is no better place for the study and use of philosophy than in literacy classrooms. I ultimately argue that, when teachers and students become philosophers or students of philosophy, powerful literacy learning can follow. I am generally concerned about the element in our society that distinguishes, even dichotomizes between thought and action, or dialogue and action; that is, that there is a difference between those who talk or think and those people who actually do. This manner of thinking is problematic for several reasons. First, it presupposes that thought and dialogue are not actions and, in doing so, negates the important work of philosophers, intellectuals, poets, novelists, and musicians who have used language to proliferate ideas that essentially change the way we see ourselves in the world. Their words, in a Bakhtinian sense, create possible worlds for us to see. Freire once wrote that speaking true words presupposes action. I would go one step further to suggest that thinking, speaking, or writing true words is a form of action. Revolutionary thoughts, conversations, and texts are the source of all transformative action. For what can be done without first being conceived or given language? Negating or ruling out thinking or speaking takes away the foundations of the big ideas that often lead to self- and social transformation.

Freire's notion of praxis encompasses the dialectic relationship between thought and action. Dialogue or thought that is not followed by action is labeled by Freire as verbalism. Action, on the other hand, that is not preceded by thought is merely activism. Freirian praxis has been an essential organizing concept for contemporary critical educators. However, I believe that it also contributes to problematic assumptions of thought and dialogue as non-actions. It is also contrary to the true revolutionary moment, which occurs when ways of thinking and speaking change. All other actions are postscript.

A second frustration with this reasoning is that it separates those who think from those who do. To me, this leads to the alienation of the producers of words, who, in a Marxian sense, become alienated from the words and ideas that they produce. To the extent that "the people" are encouraged to act without participating as intellectuals, they are alienated from their potential selves; used as pawns in a struggle or elicited as foot soldiers in battle to follow orders or even give their lives for causes they scarcely understand. Further, such ideas are limiting to the production of future words that presuppose future actions when the producers of words are not respected.

True revolutionary change of the self or the social necessarily begins with critical literacies. That is, how people come to interpret, deconstruct, produce, and distribute language and texts that name and ultimately destabilize existing norms and power relations in the cause of promoting change. The philosophic quest is very consonant with this process of change, because philosophy has always concerned itself with the very big questions about existence, about what it means to know and how one can truly know, what it means to act as a citizen, and what an ideal society looks like, to name a few. Developing the tools to interrogate these questions and revisiting the thoughtful scholars who have shared their processes with us over the millennia is an important starting point for critical literacy praxis. It is no accident that many of the scholars who have informed this work (including Paulo Freire) were trained philosophers.

This idea of revolution beginning at the level of language is antithetical to much of the "revolutionary" language to which I have been exposed. Much common thought treats those who think and write as if they are engaged in non-activities; as if throwing a stone or marching through streets is more important than a rigorous internal dialogue, a repositioning of oneself to the world of words and ideas, writing a poem, or facilitating transformational classroom conversations.

Within the critical language and literacy approach that I am advocating, people are empowered to encounter and subsequently produce and distribute texts on their own terms. This allows subjects to first acknowledge how they want to exist in the world and how they want to access texts and organizations. My approach to critical literacy is much more concerned with how individuals learn to access and produce language than whether and how they participate in any individual organization. After all, who can say that any participant in a social cause is truly critical if they have not engaged in any of the difficult intellectual work related to this cause or organization? Participation in an individual organization may work against the principles of critical literacy in that subjects are asked to subordinate their individual interests to the will of the group; to question is heresy. One need look no further than many Marxist revolutionary groups to understand this principle. How is an anti-capitalist organization that does not allow dissent from its members an example of critical praxis? Education within these organizations often resembles the very banking education that Freire critiques in *Pedagogy of the Oppressed* in that workers, party members, etc. are socialized into a prevailing ideology. Critical literacy does not begin with or subordinate itself wholly to a cause or ideology. Rather, it seeks to develop agents who are more critical consumers of causes and ideologies. Many of our best spokespersons about the dangers and the workings of dogmas and ideologies have been our philosophers. Exposing students at all levels to these thinkers and their ideas can also help them to develop these tools, which are an important component of being and becoming critically literate.

I recognize that any learning is necessarily situated in a sociocultural context and I also agree with poststructuralists such as Foucault who suggest that it is impossible to exist outside of the realm of ideology. Thus any learning of critical language and literacy will necessarily involve causes and ideologies, though, I would argue, in a radically different relationship. I also understand that there may appear to be a disconnect between critical literacy as an individual relationship with the world and the critically literate person, the citizen-philosopher, as engaged in collective agency. However, I do not see a contradiction between a focus on the individual and a commitment to the social. In fact, I would argue that only a true philosopher-citizen can act meaningfully in social movements. It takes a person who has a sense of themself, yet a commitment to social change, to act with confidence within organizations, institutions, and movements. That is, the citizen-philosopher can make informed decisions about how much she is willing to accept, how she will engage information that is presented to her, whether, when, and how much she will subordinate her interests to those of a larger collective, and when it may be time to leave one collective in search of another. The critically literate citizen-philosopher is also poised to produce or create collectives that exist in very different ways from what we are used to associating with the term. In our time, it is important to articulate ways that individuals can become selectively involved in collective actions without subordinating themselves wholly to an ideology or dogma.

Urban schools stand as one important site of engagement for young people and adults interested in using language and texts to advocate for equity and justice in the world. Within the framework of creating competent and compassionate literate citizen-philosophers, I would like to expand on the examples included in the previous chapters to offer a vision of what critical literacy education can look like inside classrooms where the basic educational transactions take place. I believe it important that I argue up front that possibilities for critical literacy exist across the K-12 spectrum and across subject matters. These practices or ideas are not just appropriate for secondary English teachers, although there are many applications to that age group and subject matter that have already been explained in great detail throughout the book. Literacy education, and therefore critical literacy education, should be considered as a K-12, cross-subject matter project in the urban schools. We are literacy educators all; none of us is exempt, but then again none of us is excluded from this special task.

A VISION OF CRITICAL LITERACY
EDUCATION IN URBAN SCHOOLS

Critical Literacy across the K-12 Educational Spectrum

It is unfortunate that the few theorists and educators interested in critical literacy tend to focus on adolescent and adult learners when elementary students are a population also in need of such pedagogy. These urban elementary students, youth who are in their formative years, when they develop their identities as people, as intellectuals, and as citizens, are bombarded with advertisements via print and visual media; they spend countless hours watching television and playing video games (Gee, 2003); and they are just being introduced to the power of the written word as emergent readers and writers. Those young students who come from ethnically, linguistically, and socioeconomically marginalized groups, as many urban youth do, have their languages and cultures implicitly assaulted as soon as they set foot on school campuses. If they do not survive these onslaughts, we will not see them in our secondary classrooms, or we will have inherited a stoic and jaded generation near the edge and almost completely out of hope.

What better time than elementary school to introduce students to the power of literacy, the ideology of literacy, and the multiplicity of literacy? As young students are learning decoding and comprehension skills, they can also learn that not everything they read in books is true. Through the teaching of critical comprehension, students can learn to respectfully challenge the very texts they are working to understand. One could argue that this represents a more sophisticated form of comprehension than simply uncovering and reciting the "facts" of texts. Of course these literacy skills of decoding, comprehension, summary, and analysis are all interrelated as the latter depend on the mastery of the former; but there is no reason that elementary-age students cannot learn to simultaneously comprehend, summarize, and interrogate the various texts they confront in schools and society.

For those critics who would argue that early elementary students are too young to understand esoteric critical theory, we are reminded of the psychologist Jerome Bruner, who claims that any concept can be taught to students of any age through a spiraling curriculum that attends to their developmental stages (Bruner, 1996). Perhaps brainstorming effective approaches to critical literacy instruction at the elementary level will force us to be more precise about what we actually mean by the term. It would also force us to acknowledge the implicit dangers of "uncritical" literacy, or education that operates under the assumption that literacies are neutral technologies that consist only of acquiring discrete decoding, comprehension, and composition skills.

For other critics who would argue that the ideas behind critical literacy are too "adult" and would make premature, disillusioned, and nihilistic cynics out of our happy and innocent children, they need only to analyze for themselves the media texts to which these children are exposed. Young children are incredibly resistant and can fill a room with smiles and laughter even under the most dire of circumstances; but they do not need adults to hide from them the truth about the injustice in the world. Adult literacy educators need only look closely at youth themselves to understand the cynicism that cohabits with that youthful exuberance. I hope, however, that I have also successfully presented cases of critical literacy education that are much more concerned with instilling legitimate reasons for hope than they are with stoking the fires of despair. I would further argue that the ends of critical literacy are just and good, and in the interest of all of our students at all ages and stations along the educational continuum.

We would be better served to help our children to acquire a textual power and agency that would exist as a superior antidote for cynicism than a denial of reality outside of the classroom or even the realities of many schools and classrooms. The best way for us to demonstrate respect is not to destroy their innocence, but to honor their brilliance and perceptiveness; to tap into their natural curiosity about words and the world while constantly being aware of the consequences of our failure to act. Jawanza Kunjufu (2004) talks about young black boys developing negative attitudes toward teachers, school literacy, and societal institutions as early as the fourth grade in response to their maltreatment. These attitudes do them great harm in limiting their resolve to navigate the problematic gatekeepers to their future. We know that students are tuning out of school in the middle and upper elementary grades. They may still watch Disney, but they are nobody's fool.

So what might this critical literacy education look like in urban elementary classrooms? I've already mentioned briefly what it might mean in terms of teaching reading of texts as they are traditionally defined, but there are many other types of texts that warrant critical readings. Certainly reading media texts needs to be an important component of any critical literacy education for urban primary students. This includes texts ranging from cartoons, to commercials, to movies and television shows, to video games, to popular music, to Internet websites targeted at young children. Although they may not be ready for Hegel, Marx, or Fanon, or terms such as ideology, hegemony, or dialectic, literacy teachers can engage students in conversations about value systems, about interests, about power, about privilege, about how knowledge is constructed, and about what makes any text believable. Students can use basic analytic techniques to make sense of how media texts portray populations of color, those who are poor; how they position women, how they characterize developmentally disabled, and practitioners of non Judeo-Christian religions. Elementary classrooms are also ideal spaces to analyze how media texts promote attitudes towards violence and habits of consumption.

Whether dealing with the consumption of traditional or new media texts, critical literacy education has implications for the core texts to be selected for study. Children need to be exposed to texts that are critical of dominant value systems; they need to be given texts that provide counter-histories and counter-narratives in general; and they need to read texts that are culturally affirming, culturally relevant, and culturally responsive. Certainly these additional criteria explicitly challenge the content of texts, but they also challenge the genres of texts that should be foundational to urban elementary literacy learning. Students should have access to more postcolonial and multicultural literature, but their curricula should also entail informational non-fiction texts from philosophy, literary theory, and the social sciences. If these texts do not yet exist that translate the ideas of these disciplines for elementary students, then it is our responsibility as criticalists and scholars to create these texts and to develop textbooks and other curricular materials that represent these ideas and approaches. I would be remiss at this point if I didn't mention the wonderful work that is happening in elementary literacy classrooms across the world (see, for instance, the scholarship of Mary Cowhey, Barbara Comber, Glynda Hull, Jodene Kersten, Marjorie Orellana, James Damico, and Vivian Vasquez and websites such as rethinkingschools. org). But I am not off the mark in my assessment that these practices are far from mainstream in conversations about literacy curricula and pedagogies in urban elementary classrooms.

Educators and policymakers need to keep these thoughts in mind when developing reading lists and grade-level benchmarks; moving beyond discussions of readability and award-winning titles to also consider the potential of texts to foster the critical literacy development of students. It should be noted, however, that students can and should bring to bear a critically informed and culturally responsive reading toward any text that they confront. For this reason dominant texts need to remain at the heart of instruction, though these texts may be taught differently within a critical framework.

Of course critical literacy education needs to extend beyond what students read; students also need to gain power over the texts that they create. Thus, student textual production needs to be privileged within an urban elementary critical literacy pedagogy. Elementary youth will still require instruction in the basic structure of the written language including vocabulary, grammar, and usage, but this instruction might be situated within different contexts; where students are encouraged to create and disseminate authentic and meaningful written and new media texts as expressions of freedom, as celebrations of culture, and as contributing artifacts to the ongoing struggle for equity, humanity, and justice.

Toward these ends, urban elementary students might be asked to design critical media education curricula that they can teach to their peers or to younger students; they may be trained as investigative journalists or social science researchers, or as critical social historians collecting archival information on their families, their cultures, and their communities. These students may start and edit literary magazines, school newspapers, or online journals that allow them to share their ideas with a larger public; they can enter essay contests, they can write persuasive letters to local, state, and national politicians; they can create community-focused brochures and newsletters; and they can write poems, plays, and short stories in which they express their unique and important ideas about the world.

Critical Literacy Education Across the Subject Matter Areas

Many of the ideas that would work in elementary education would also apply to the teaching of middle and secondary students. They too need to critically comprehend the multiple texts they read; they too need exposure to traditional and new media texts; and they too need multiple opportunities to operate as critical producers and disseminators of texts. What's important is that we view critical literacy education as an enterprise that extends across the content areas and one that ties literacy praxis to academic achievement, professional preparation, and civic engagement. What I will focus on in this segment is an articulation of a theory of literacy for civic engagement along with a vision of what a radical literacy education might look like across the content areas in urban middle and secondary classrooms.

In their 2004 journal article Westheimer and Kahne identify three models of citizenship ranging from a personally responsive citizen, through a participatory citizen, to a justice-oriented citizen that not only takes care of him- or herself and participates in the electoral process but also joins or initiates struggles for social justice. Westheimer and Kahne contend that social studies education needs to become more concerned with creating spaces for the development of justice-oriented citizens. There is certainly merit to this proposition and the justice-oriented citizen represents a marked improvement over the personally responsive citizen. However, in the scope of the study the content area is limited to social studies, as if that were the only discipline responsible for the preparation of engaged citizens. Expanding upon the work of Westheimer and Kahne, I argue that we need model of transformational civic engagement (and critical literacy development) that extends across all of the content areas. It is toward this model that I now turn.

Critical Literacy and the Social Studies Curricula

There is really no excuse for thinking of a social studies curriculum outside of a framework of critical literacy. Unfortunately many of the teachers in these courses, who have great ideas for how to engage their students, are saddled with textbooks that teach about history and government as a set of facts to be ingested and regurgitated. US history, for example, is a march from colonial times to the Cold War in eighteen to twenty chapter segments with chapter tests and a monthly unit exam. American government, then, is a course that teaches about the rules of American government. Students learn how seats are apportioned in congress, what the electoral college does, the intent behind the Bill of Rights, etc. In other years students are marched through the Europeanized version of world history, complete with conquest and domination. What does this sanitized fact-firing frenzy get our students? How do these facts, in and of themselves, make a more engaged and humane citizenry?

Social studies can and should be a place where students actually engage the social. Where they learn about their place in the world, and where they tackle difficult questions about the nature of government, the economy, the protection of minority rights in a democracy, the genesis of social movements, etc. Students should also have spaces to learn about their own world as they also learn about the worlds of the past and the distant. I have already shown a few examples of what this can look like in the context of history and government curricula, but its important to restate that any social studies class can incorporate a critical literacy framework and remain consonant with the intent of the disciplines they borrow from and the intent of the state and national standards in these subject areas.

With respect to American and world history, its important for teachers to expose students to the narrative of history; that they learn to understand that histories are narratives constructed by individuals who do the best they can to arrange the facts that are available to them to tell coherent narratives about past societies. But these individuals are human and come with their own predispositions and biases that are often reflected in these texts. One only need to look at the difference in how British and American historians tell the historical narrative of the Revolutionary War, for example. When teaching about the narratives of history, teachers can also expose students to the various methods of historical research. As in the project I described in chapter 9, students can visit archives, conduct interviews, and actually "do" historical research as a way of learning about history. Of course they would still need to consult secondary sources and other historical scholarship, but it would have more meaning were students to see themselves as fledgling historians.

Finally teachers can allow spaces for students to engage and interrogate existing historical narratives as they uncover hidden relationships between ideology and history. What would a reading of turn of the (twentieth) century historians' portrayal of African-Americans and Native Americans reveal about the ideology of the people they were writing for and writing to? How might contemporary historians from these ethnic backgrounds evaluate the same original sources? What other sources might they consider when constructing their historical narratives? Teachers can actually make original sources available to students to have them perform their own analyses.

Again, I don't want to write as if none of this is happening. Many history textbooks include original sources, for instance. However these practices are far from the norm. Most high school students do not have the opportunity to visit archives, they do not have the opportunity to produce original historical scholarship, and they do not juxtapose competing historical narratives of the same events. All of these practices, I argue, would increase student motivation while developing core academic competencies and critical sensibilities.

There are similar implications for the teaching of American government courses. In our summer seminar work, we correlated instruction in American government classes with implied models of citizenship. When drawing from a model of personally responsible or participatory citizenship, it seems enough to teach students about the rules of government—the idea being that students who know how government works are more inclined to be voters, the primary act of citizenship according to this model. However, there are other ways of being a citizen, such as Westheimer and Kahne's justice-oriented citizen or even more activist models of citizenship such as the participants in the Freedom Schools or the Zapatista movement.

Social studies educators can develop curricula with more of a focus on grassroots organizing and local politics, which make the most sense for those who are going to become activist-oriented citizens. In conversations about the constitutional conventions and apportionment, there is rarely space to talk about how school board members are elected, who the city council members are, or what the mayor intends to do with the local schools. Social studies classrooms can change these practices by having students involved in creating or participating in campaigns, even at the level of improving conditions in their schools and communities. They would be far ahead of most adults, for instance, if they understood how various local, city, state, county, and federal municipalities intersected to circumscribe and regulate their daily existence. Who, for instance, controls the buses and subway trains? Exactly what role does the federal government play in urban schools? Who oversees the police department? Who controls the jails? Understanding how government works across each of these levels and figuring out ways to become involved across each of these levels is an excellent strategy for helping students to become truly motivated to learn about the workings of government.

There are also plenty of opportunities for high-level reading, writing, research, and speaking that go along with these models of citizenship. If students were to become involved in an issue of importance to them, for example, they would need to understand how various municipalities intersected; they could also think about different ways to lobby policymakers across each of these domains. They would need to conduct research in order to figure out who these people actually are and what they could do to intervene in the problem. Education is a good example of an issue that students could attack. Those students interested in a campaign to improve the conditions of urban schools might end up speaking, directly or indirectly, with school administrators, district administrators, school board members, district superintendents, mayor's offices, county boards of education, state secretaries of education, the governor's office, state assembly representatives, representatives to the House, senators, or even the office of the president.

Even once these powerbrokers are located, further reading, research, and writing are required.

Of course there are other possibilities when considering the intersections between critical literacy and social studies outside of the customary history and government courses. While it's important to work inside the box of these staple courses of secondary social studies curricula, we should also argue for spaces where young people can apply the tools of anthropology and sociology to explore their own cultures and communities. It's possible to imagine courses at the primary and secondary levels in which students have the opportunity to conduct ethnographic fieldwork in their neighborhoods or in which they are able to engage in the types of sociological inquiry that are described in earlier chapters. My vision would also include spaces for courses on law, ethnic studies, and political science, philosophy, comparative governments, and ethnic studies.

Critical Literacy and Language Arts Curriculum

I have already talked at length in chapter 4 about the intersections between critical literacy and the stated goals of traditional language arts education. I will add to that only by encouraging literacy researchers and educators to stay on the offensive in advocating for the entire language arts curriculum to be situated within a larger context of critical literacy. As I continually examine standards documents at the district, state, and national level, I see no incongruence between the stated goals of these documents and the mission of critical literacy education. As a collective, these documents call for students to be exposed to multiple genres of literature, to use multiple reading strategies to decode these texts and to draw upon multiple literary tools to interrogate these texts. Further, these standards documents call for opportunities for students to produce sophisticated texts across multiple genres that include expository essays, poems, plays, short stories, autobiographical narratives, advertising campaigns, letters, and, in some cases, electronic and multimedia texts.

Why is it not possible, then, to be fully complicit with these standards documents and to frame the language arts curriculum entirely within a context of critical (and multimodal) literacy? These standards documents allow room for educators to engage in multicultural, Marxist, feminist, and postcolonial criticisms of dominant literary texts; to introduce multicultural and anti-colonial literatures into the traditional curricula; to bring in multimodal artifacts and media studies as a form of cultural analysis; and to encourage new media production in the form of web pages, weblogs, newsletters, and film documentaries, to name a few. Finally, there is sufficient room in a standards-based language arts curriculum for critical essay writing, poetry, and playwriting.

Critical Literacy and Foreign Language Curriculum

Most of this work has operated under the assumption of critical literacy in urban schools as a practice that solely occurs in the English language. Given that we offer foreign language courses, that we find our classrooms becoming increasingly linguistically diverse, and that we are becoming increasingly implicated in a global economy, its important to at least briefly consider the potential of a critical literacy curriculum in foreign language coursework. What would it look like, for instance, if all students were required to be fully bilingual and biliterate before graduating from the K-12 educational system? What if foreign language instruction involved cultural history and politics, literary analysis, study abroad (why do we not have more opportunities and resources made available for students to spend time experiencing life outside the United States?), and the study of philology, linguistics, sociolinguistics, language colonization, dialect, and history of language?

Allowing students to gain a high level of proficiency in other languages would enable them to read complex works, translate intellectual works into English, and even create literary works in other languages. Imagine the intellectual work behind creating a play to be performed entirely in another language, especially if there is a large community population fluent in this language. This would provide a perfect context for drawing upon community expertise and creating intellectual and artistic work with the immediate community as the primary audience. We are limited, sometimes, only in our ability to dream!

Critical Literacy and the Math and Science Curricula

Far too seldom do literacy educators and scholars examine critical literacy education in the context of mathematics and science curricula. Specifically we too seldom examine and articulate the myriad literacies associated with critical practice within the disciplines. Even as state credentialing agencies are requiring all students to take literacy courses and accreditation bodies are requiring all disciplines to discuss their outcomes related to literacy, our primary examples of critical literacy education are still situated largely within language arts and social studies. Not only do we ignore much valuable work that has been done by our colleagues in math and science education (Brown, 2004; Gutstein, 2005), but we also concede valuable ground and leave students and teachers with the impression that critical literacy is valuable for only half of the core subject areas. I urge scholars and practitioners to continue to imagine connections between these disciplines and the project of critical literacy. Two examples of what shape this work may take are critical activist research for urban environmental justice and the role of literacy in statistical research for educational and social justice.

Science activists have recently explored and expounded the concept of environmental racism, particularly using the tools of scientific inquiry to investigate how impoverished urban communities of color are forced to bear the brunt of environmental waste that accompanies capitalist production. Some examples of how K-12 urban science teachers have situated their curricula within this crusade include students measuring toxicity levels in soil to developing research reports, creating environmental education and recycling programs, and creating and managing urban gardens on school campuses. Important reading, writing, and research skills are associated with this work as well as literacies for citizenship and social action teaching young kids how to expose injustice in their neighborhoods while also advocating for the future health of the planet.

In being apprenticed as activist-researchers of the physical, natural, and social sciences, students also come across quantitative research methods that force them to develop mathematical reasoning skills. For example, in conducting critical research for educational justice during a summer seminar, students accessed census data and other statistical databases to uncover trends in demographic shifts and corresponding achievement of ethically marginalized students throughout the city. Students also developed and scored a survey on attitudes toward civic engagement and civic education that they distributed to five hundred students throughout the city. Math educators interested in critical literacy can help their students to understand the computational and mathematical aspects of scholarly writing as incentives to get K-12 students to read and write as they use mathematical skills to advocate for equity and justice. Activities and research methodologies can be modified up or down the educational spectrum for students of various ages. There are also various ways that K-12 math educators can help students consider how to write/represent their research projects to teachers, parents, and peers.

WHAT IS REQUIRED OF US?

There are many implications for literacy praxis that emerge from the lessons and case studies of the previous chapters. One I have stated repeatedly, but it doesn't hurt to repeat (repetition is reinforcement): critical literacy should be theorized as the textual productions that surround individual liberation and social praxis. Toward these ends, students need opportunities to produce multiple authentic texts in multiple authentic genres for multiple authentic purposes. The purposes of the textual productions should intersect with themes of critical literacy: exploration of the self in relation to social contexts; an examination of marginalized/oppressed social contexts and relations; discourses of exclusion; agency; resistance; and change. Students need to understand the 2500-year tradition of language, production, and empowerment. They also need opportunities and publishing presses that are receptive to these kinds of books. Students' textual productions should consist of multiple genres including research papers, persuasive essays, poems, short films, plays, posters, video montages, speeches, ad campaigns, websites, blogs, etc. Creating spaces for the meaningful productions of these texts is not enough. I argue that a responsibility of critical educators is to locate and generate sites of exchange and distribution of these texts including online journals, literary magazines, film festivals, and conferences.

A significant portion of the literacy revolution also entails fighting against curricular and testing regimes that draw upon a concept of a single, autonomous conception of literacy. Wherever we find ourselves positioned—whether on departmental committees, curricular committees, in teacher education courses, or on commissions for regional and national organizations—we need to articulate a vision of adolescent literacies that incorporates local, indigenous, popular cultural, and new media texts. This stands as a challenge to critical literacy educators at all levels not only to advocate for student textual production and distribution, but also to become textual producers and distributors themselves. We need more teacher-produced action research that documents what the practice of critical literacy might look like in urban secondary contexts. We need university-based researchers to argue for the legitimacy of critical research within the academy. These researchers are charged with developing questions and methodologies that challenge problematic, reproductive pedagogies while developing conceptual and empirical pieces that point toward empowering literacy practices among urban adolescents. As researchers, we must not stop with the successful production and distribution of our own texts; we too must become advocates and activists for the issues we research and write about with so much passion and diligence. What does this mean? For one, it means thinking about the relationship between research and policy; brainstorming strategies for distribution of research artifacts to educational policymakers at every level ranging from principals and curriculum specialists to elected officials at the local, regional, state, and national levels. This means that literacy researchers and practitioners need to become acquainted and proficient with the language of policy. It also means that we may need to challenge or extend our preferred genres of representation. Although this book may be perceived as a valuable pedagogic or research tool, I may be better served by producing and editing a short or feature-length documentary film that carries the potential of sharing these same ideas via visual images with larger popular and policymaking audiences. I may also need to consider developing short policy briefs that I can share with sympathetic officials.

The former slave and abolitionist Frederick Douglass is noted as saying that power concedes nothing without a demand. As critical literacy educators we need to imagine collectively what it means to make demands of institutions and governments. When does it make sense to protest in the streets? When do we need to campaign or advocate for political candidates and parties? When do we need to advocate or demand for the toppling of one system of government in favor of another? When do we need to put our jobs and livelihood on the line? When do we need to consider putting our lives on the line for our beliefs? How much does the literacy revolution matter? If it is as important as I think it is, then it might cost everything; but then there may be everything to gain.

I have been accused of being a dreamer before (a charge I do not consider an insult) but I teach and research and write as I imagine a world much different from the one we experience today. I imagine change, true change, complete change, as possible; even as imminent. I imagine the foundational role of critical literacy praxis in the remaking of the world. In fact, I believe that universal critical literacy would be the greatest revolution of all. For universal critical literacy is the prerequisite to the global revolution of indigenous and marginalized peoples. This is an approach to praxis that focuses on the development of a skill set and a stance toward knowledge and the world rather than adherence to any given ideology, party system, or aesthetic. A universal critical literacy would make everyday citizens better consumers and producers of political movements; and that may be the key to the change we so desperately need in our urban centers, and in the world at large.

That to me as a teacher, scholar, writer, activist, and human, is a cause worth living (and dying) for. The road is long and full of challenges. But life is long and full of possibilities. This, I know, is my road and my life. As I look, though, at the vibrant classrooms at North High School with young women and men interrogating academic texts and a world of contradictions; as I reminisce about the teens roaming through the streets of Los Angeles with cameras and notebooks as critical researchers, or I recall the conversations of youth engaged in sophisticated content analyses of media artifacts; when I imagine the Internet-mediated struggles of the Zapatista Liberation Army or countless other organizations struggling under the radar screen for social justice; when I imagine hackers, café writers, musicians, filmmakers, teachers, scholars, novelists, critical journalists, artists, and poets, and the people they write for and with—I am reminded that the revolution is not as far off as it sometimes seems. We are too many; we are embattled. We are filled with too much love. The causes are too righteous and too important. Our wills and our texts are simply too strong.

And so I urge us to walk, march, read, write, film, sing, dance, tattoo, and paint with a sense of urgency but with pride, unity, and resolve through the peaks and the valleys, the triumphs and the tragedies with that greatest and self-defining of human characteristics: hope.

TOWARD A UNIVERSAL CRITICAL LITERACY

One of my stringent critiques of education and educational scholarship (in which I include myself) is our limited scope of vision and action. Most teachers and professionals are credentialed without having to read any literature written more than a century ago; most curricular plans and standards exist at the level of the school district or the state; the federal government is a relative minor player in education compared to most other industrial nations, where the educational system is nationalized. And very little of our scholarship or practice is explicitly informed by the work of our contemporaries abroad. Certainly there are exceptions with Lesson Study coming from the Japanese and the rise in positions being offered for International and Comparative Education, but it only tempers the critique; it does not make it null and void. Ultimately, there is a lack of connection between progressive movements in schools and larger social movements on a global scale. Can an international social movement, however, actually begin in schools? Can the critical literacy education in America's urban schools serve as the foundation for an international critical literacy movement? What would such a movement look like and how might it be different from international literacy movements currently sponsored by organizations such as the United Nations? These are important questions to consider as we move forward with this most important task.

NOTHING IS INEVITABLE

In one of my favorite quotes, the noted Canadian media theorist Marshall McLuhan claims that "Nothing is inevitable as long as there is a willingness to contemplate what is happening." I admire this quotation both for its optimism, but also for its process. First and foremost, we must understand that any reading of history shows us that the only constant is change; and any reading of the history of social movements shows us that people have continually overcome greater obstacles than those we currently face in literacy education. Second, we must think about our process of change. McLuhan recommends contemplation, a word with many layers of meaning and connotation. It primarily means to think deeply and to be aware of one's own thinking. In this book we have thought deeply about the histories of literacy education and critical thought and their bearing on our current challenges in literacy instruction. Contemplation also means being "in" and "with" time. In other words, if we contemplate we are also forced to think about our moment; to consider what needs change and how we, as everyday citizens, as teachers, as public intellectuals, and as agents can change it. I have also in this book tried to include myriad examples of the ways that educators can work with urban youth in our time to develop academic and critical literacies. Contemplation is important because it forces us to think carefully about our conditions and then to think deeply about alternatives to those conditions. Once we imagine alternatives, we begin to understand the possibilities for transformation, for making the world anew, even if in our case we are talking about the world of the classroom. That is a large enough goal, which will ultimately have a large impact on the remaking of the world. Contemplation, our collective contemplation, can make these things happen. I am also reminded of the words of another important scholar of a bygone era; Paulo Freire contends that to imagine new ways of being is to already begin to act differently upon the world. In other words we must not only contemplate, we must act. That is our best—and only—hope.

Appendix

Description of Data Collection and Analysis

The data that I collected include:

- **Field notes:** Whether I was the classroom teacher (at North or South High School) or the lead teacher in the seminar I made a point of recording observational notes on the activities in the classroom. Obviously, for the lead teacher or co-teacher, taking notes during class can be quite difficult, but I developed several strategies to assist with the note-taking. First, there were many activities when students were working independently on projects that would allow me time to jot down a few notes. I was also able to write while the students themselves were writing. For instance, during the film-watching episodes in my English classes or during the critical journaling periods of the seminar, I would use those opportunities to record my own notes of classroom activities. Additionally, when class time became too hectic for note-taking, I would find time immediately after work to record notes either on the laptop computer or in my notebook. I found that I could recreate fairly accurate notes if I did so within a twenty-four-hour window after class. Often in the evenings I had greater clarity and distance from the day's events to record more accurate field notes. Even when I was able to record notes during class, I would often augment these notes during the evening.

  By far, the most effective strategy for recording notes entailed recording class sessions with a digital video camera. During the class sessions at South High and during the six summer seminars, I set up a camera on a tripod to record the class events. When I had more time, I would go back to the digital videotapes to record my field notes. Certainly there are tradeoffs to taking notes from digital video, but there are still possibilities for full-time educators to acquire excellent observational data on their classroom activities.

- **Interviews with students:** As part of the larger data collection for the South High Futures project, we conducted interviews at the end of each semester asking students about their experiences attending a bimodal school. We also asked students about their experiences becoming critical researchers and agents of change. During the summer seminar, we conducted closing interviews with the students where they were asked to reflect on their seminar experiences. Finally, I would occasionally conduct interviews with students following units at North High.

- **Interviews with teachers and adults:** I also talked with teachers and university faculty members who had significant contact with the students. Particularly, I wanted to talk to university faculty involved with the summer seminars to get a sense of their perception of how the students made use of the language and tools of the academy as they learned to become social science researchers. Like Deborah Meier (1995), I used these interviews with subject matter experts as another examination of the quality of student work, which I could then triangulate with my own observations and analyses of student work products.

- **Informal conversations with students:** Merriam (1998) asserts that informal conversations and observational notes may be more appropriate ways to gather ethnographic data than formal interviews. For teachers or others with close relationships to students, formal interviews may seem too staged or arbitrary. Though I did use formal interviews on occasion, my preferred method of obtaining direct information from students involved informal conversations before or after class, conversations during group work, or chats while out in the field. I also used email and AOL Instant Message to communicate with students away from class. Chapter 6 presents data from the rich virtual community that we established in the South High Futures Project in particular.

- **Analysis of student work:** The majority of my data analysis involved examining student work. Over the years I saved and photocopied volumes of student-generated products including essays, journals, notebooks, research reports, and original poetry. I recorded and analyzed student conversations and formal presentations. I also examined student-created research tools such as interview and observational protocols, and surveys distributed to students, teachers, parents, or media personnel. Finally, I collected student-created media artifacts such as iMovies, PowerPoint presentations, email communications, and websites.

*   **Analysis of achievement data:** With the Futures students at South High, I collected academic achievement data to understand the relationship between the Futures Project and student performance in non-Project courses. The project with which I was working ultimately collected data on GPA, standardized test scores, graduation rates, college acceptance, and college-going rates. We also surveyed student participants in the summer seminar to learn about their graduation status and college attendance decisions.

DATA ANALYSIS

To make sense of the data I employed a four-part analysis that develops from new literacy studies, semiotics, critical discourse analysis, and ethnic studies. I developed this analytic framework to understand the various empowering literacies associated with the curricula and pedagogies (interventions) described in the middle data chapters. I drew upon a new literacy studies framework in order to understand reading and writing (and digital literacy production) in sociocultural context (Barton and Hamilton, 2000). I drew upon the conceptual–methodological work of Barton and Hamilton, who discuss the processes by which researchers uncover literacy practices from documenting literacy events. The idea of employing ethnographic fieldwork to document the literacy event first appeared in the work of Shirley Bryce Heath (1983). Heath sought out to understand the various cultural interactions mediated by print in out-of-school contexts. I drew upon the expanded definition of literacy that included new media texts to code for cultural interactions (literacy events) mediated by traditional and new media texts in order to understand the literacy practices of urban adolescents in school and in out-of-school contexts.

I also drew from Norman Fairclough's (1995) critical discourse analysis (CDA) to make meaning of the literacy praxis of these adolescents. Particularly, I was interested in Fairclough's conception of critical language awareness, in which everyday citizens, via a critical language education, gain an understanding of the relationship between language, ideology, and power. As Fairclough does, I also believe that there is an intimate relationship between people's critical awareness of language and their own language capabilities and practices (Fairclough, 1995, p. 227). Related to critical language awareness is the work of James Gee (1999), who advocates making students social theorists of social languages. Both Gee and Fairclough see an importance in youth developing a reflexivity and understanding of languages as ideological, socially situated cultural practices, and as key constituents in the configuring social thought. As Fairclough states, "it is mainly in discourse that consent is achieved, ideologies are transmitted, and practices, meanings, values, and identities are taught and learnt" (1995, p. 219). The critical discourse analysis of Gee and Fairclough is closely related to poststructuralist ideas that meaning is constructed through language or discourse (Foucault, 1972).

I drew upon the work of critical linguists (Fairclough, 1995; Gee, 1996; Mills, 1997) and poststructural language philosophers (Foucault, 1972), but I went further in my conception of critical language pedagogy and praxis to theorize and create spaces in which youth not only engaged in analyzing discourses of power, but saw themselves as producers of critical discourse. To gain a sense of the development of critical language awareness and critical language praxis, I coded for reflexivity about language in conversations, writing, and media artifacts and I also coded for use of empowering language across all of these activities and products as well.

Although the combination of new literacy studies and critical discourse analysis offer powerful analytic tools for theorizing and making meaning of adolescent literacy practices, I recognized that I was missing an important component of my analytic toolkit. Most of my analytic tools were heavily linguistic, even though I recognized that many empowering youth literacy practices (both consumption and production) were centered upon new media technologies, in which the image and not the word predominates. I needed an analytic coding scheme that would allow me to make sense of the urban adolescents' critical media consumption and production. For assistance, I turned to the field of semiotics.

The French poststructuralist literary scholar Roland Barthes defined semiology as the study of signs (Barthes, 1975b), which would include linguistic, print, and media images. Along with other scholars of his period, Barthes was concerned with the use of sign systems by corporate elites to maintain ideologies of capitalism and oppression. Through semiotics, he was able to identify dominant hegemonies being reinforced through sign systems in popular culture ranging from cereal boxes to public wrestling to the haircuts of actors in films (Barthes, 1967).

Barthes felt that, with an understanding of semiology, critical citizens could become better consumers of mass society. I wholly agree with this proposition. I also agree that students can use knowledge of semiology to intentionally construct and manipulate images to create countercultural thought. Toward these ends I draw from semiology to code for all interactions students have with media images, whether they are consuming dominant images or they are using desktop editing software to manipulate images and disseminate their own media texts. This expansive view of literacy comports with the work of contemporary scholars such as Gunther Kress (2003) who speak to the turn in literacy from the linguistic toward the semiotic in the new media age.

Finally, I needed a coding scheme for literacy praxis among urban adolescents that adequately dealt with race and ethnicity. The work of media and cultural studies theorized literacy as cultural practice, but there is very little mention in this work of the relationships between race, ethnicity, and literacy. Certainly as far back as the work of Labov in the 1970s and Heath in the 1980s we understood the racialized nature of literacy learning inside and out of schools, but little work was done to explore empowering practices in schools that acknowledged the racialized nature of academic literacy acquisition. To address this theoretical gap, I drew heavily from ethnic studies, multicultural education (Banks, 1996; Nieto, 1992; Sleeter, 1996), and critical race theory (Delgado and Stefancic, 2001).

I became particularly interested in the intersections between literacy praxis and ethnic affiliation: how did the students, through literacy pedagogy, become more aware of themselves as racialized, ethnic beings? Further, I wanted to understand how critical literacy praxis translated into the language of racial critique and ethnic affiliation, in which students used their critical faculties to call into question racial ideologies while also affirming their ethnic identities and even developing a pan-ethnic solidarity with other groups who found themselves marginalized within the same imperialist economic conditions. Finally, I borrowed from critical race theory the idea of counter-story telling. I wanted to document how students used their critical literacy skills not only to deconstruct problematic racial and ethnic narratives, but also to recreate empowering racial and ethnic counter-narratives to be shared with wide audiences.

This four-part analysis, taken as a whole, offers a thorough, complementary, and comprehensive set of tools to investigate the literacy practice and performance of urban adolescents in and outside classrooms that considers literacies as multiple, that favors reflexivity, that honors changing technologies, and that recognizes the students as racialized, ethnic beings.

Bibliography

Adorno, T. (2002). *The culture industry.* London: Routledge.

Alim, H. S. (2006). *Roc the mic: The language of hip-hop.* New York: Routledge.

Althusser, L. (2001). Ideology and Ideological state apparatuses. In V. B. Leitch (Ed.). *The Norton anthology of theory and criticism.* New York: W. W. Norton and Company, 1483–1508.

Alvermann, D. (2001). *Effective literacy instruction for adolescents.* Executive summary and paper commissioned by the National Reading Conference. Chicago: National Reading Conference.

Anderson, B. (1991). *Imagined communities: Reflections on the origins and spread of nationalism.* New York: Verso.

Andrews, W. L. (Ed.) (1989). *Six women's slave narratives.* Oxford: Oxford University Press.

Anyon, J. (1981). Social class and school knowledge. *Curriculum Inquiry,* 11, 1, 3–42.

Anyon, J. (1997). *Ghetto schooling: A political economy of urban educational reform.* New York: Teachers College Press.

Apple, M. (1988). *Teachers and texts: A political economy of class and gender relations in education.* New York: Routledge.

Apple, M. (1990). *Ideology and curriculum.* New York: Routledge.

Applebee, A. (1974). *Tradition and reform in the teaching of English: A history.* Urbana, IL: National Council of Teachers of English.

Appleman, D. (2000). *Critical encounters in high school English: Teaching literary theory to adolescents.* New York: Teachers College Press.

Aristotle (1991). *The art of rhetoric.* New York: Penguin.

Aristotle (1997). *Poetics.* Mineola, NY: Dover Publications.

Aronowitz, S., and Giroux, H. (1991). *Postmodern education.* Minneapolis, MN: University of Minnesota Press.

Ashcroft, B., Griffiths, G., and Tiffin, H. (Ed.) (1995). *The post-colonial studies reader.* New York: Routledge.

Atwell, N. (1998). *In the middle: New understandings about writing, reading, and learning.* Portsmouth, NH: Boynton/Cook Heinemann.

Audi, R. (1999). *The Cambridge dictionary of philosophy.* Cambridge: Cambridge.

Bakhtin, M. M. (1981). *The dialogic imagination.* Austin, TX: University of Texas Press.

Bakhtin, M. M. (1986). *Speech genres and other late essays.* Austin, TX: University of Texas Press.

Banks, J. (Ed.) (1996). *Multicultural education, transformative knowledge, and action: Historical and contemporary perspectives.* New York: Teachers College Press.

Barthes, R. (1967). *Mythologies.* New York: Hill and Wang.

Barthes, R. (1975b). *Elements of semiology.* New York: Hill and Wang.

Barthes, R. (1975a). *S/Z: An essay.* New York: Hill and Wang.

Bartolome, L. (1994). Beyond the methods fetish: Toward a humanizing pedagogy. *Harvard Educational Review,* 64, 173–94.

Barton, D. (1994). *Literacy: An introduction to the ecology of the written language.* Oxford: Blackwell.

Barton, D. (2000). Researching literacy practices: learning from activities with teachers and students. In D. Barton, M. Hamilton, and R. Ivanic (Eds.). *Situated literacies: Reading and writing in context.* New York: Routledge, 167–179.

Barton, D., and Hamilton, M. (1998). *Local literacies: Reading and writing in one community.* London: Routledge.

Barton, D., and Hamilton, M. (2000). Literacy practices. In D. Barton, M. Hamilton, and R. Ivanic (Eds.), *Situated literacies: Reading and writing in context.* London: Routledge, 7–16.

Baudrillard, J. (1994). *Simulacra and simulation.* Ann Arbor, MI: University of Michigan Press.

Baudrillard, J. (2001). *Impossible exchange.* New York: Verso.

Baudrillard, J. (2003). *Screened out.* New York: Verso.

de Beauvoir, S. (1949/1989). *The second sex.* New York: Vintage.

Bell, D. (2001). *An introduction to cybercultures.* New York: Routledge.

Benson, C. (2002). *Writing to make a difference: Classroom projects for community change.* New York: Teachers College Press.

Best, S., and Kellner, D. (1991). *Postmodern theory: critical interrogations.* New York: Guilford.

Bhabha, H. (2004). *The location of culture.* New York: Routledge.

Bizzell, P., and Herzberg, B. (Ed.) (2001). *The rhetorical tradition: Readings from classical times to the present.* Boston: Bedford/St. Martin's.

Blackburn, S. (1994). *Dictionary of philosophy.* Oxford: Oxford University Press.

Bonnycastle, S. (1996). *In search of authority: An introductory guide to literary theory.* Peterborough, ON: Broadview Press.

Bourdieu, P. (1990). *The logic of practice.* Cambridge: Polity Press.

Bowles, S., and Gintis, H. (1976). *Schooling in capitalist America: Educational reform and the contradictions of economic life.* New York: Basic Books.

Boyd, T. (1997). *Am I Black enough for you: Popular culture from the 'hood and beyond.* Bloomington, IN: Indiana University Press.

Bradley, L. (2001). *This is reggae music: The story of Jamaica's music.* New York: Grove Press.

Breton, A. (1972). *Manifestoes of surrealism.* Ann Arbor, MI: University of Michigan Press.

Brown, B. (2004) Discursive identity: Assimilation into the culture of science and its implications for minority students. *Journal of Research in Science Teaching,* 41, 8, 810–834.

Bruner, J. (1996). *The culture of education.* Cambridge, MA: Harvard University Press.

Buckingham, D. (2003). *Media education: Literacy, learning, and contemporary culture.* Cambridge: Polity Press.

Castañeda, J. (1998). *Compañero: The life and death of Che Guevara.* New York: Alfred A. Knopf.

de Castell, S., and Luke, A. (1983). Defining 'literacy' in North American schools: Social and historical conditions and consequences. *Journal of Curriculum Studies,* 15, 373–389.

Cochran-Smith, M., and Lytle, S. (1993). *Teacher research and knowledge.* New York: Teachers College Press.

Cole, M. (1996). *Cultural psychology: A once and future discipline.* Cambridge, MA: Harvard University Press.

College Board (2005). *2005 college-bound seniors.* City, ST: College Board.

Collins, R. L., Ellickson, P. L., McCaffrey, D. F., and Hambarsoomians, K. (2005). Saturated in beer: Awareness of beer advertising in late childhood and adolescence. *Journal of Adolescent Health,* 37, 1, 29–36.

Comber, B., and Simpson, A. (Ed.) (2001). *Negotiating critical literacies in classrooms.* Mahwah, NJ: Lawrence Earlbaum Associates.

Conference on College Composition and Communication (1974) Students' right to their own language (special issue). *College Composition and Communication,* 25.

Cooper, C. (2004). *Sound clash: Jamaican dancehall culture at large.* New York: Palgrave Macmillan.

Cope, B., and Kalantzis, M. (Ed.) (2000). *Multiliteracies: Literacy, learning, and the design of social futures.* London: Routledge.

Cuddon, J. A. (1999). *The Penguin dictionary of literary terms and literary theory.* London: Penguin.

Culler, J. (2000). *Literary theory: A very short introduction.* Oxford: Oxford University Press.

Cushman, E. (1998). *The struggle and the tools: Oral and literate strategies in an inner city community.* Albany, NY: SUNY Press.

Cushman, E., and Morrell, E. (2005). *Critical approaches to English education: Sites for pre-service teacher training.* Paper presented at the annual meeting of the American Educational Research Association, Montreal.

Cushman, E., Kingten, E., Kroll, B., and Rose, M. (2001). *Literacy: A critical sourcebook.* Boston: Bedford/St. Martin's.

Dagbovie, P. (2005). Of all our studies, history is best qualified to reward our research: Black history's relevance to the hip hop generation. *Journal of African-American History*, 90, 3, 299–323.

Darder, A. (1991). *Culture and power in the classroom: A critical foundation for bicultural education*. Westport, CT: Bergin and Garvey.

Darling-Hammond, L. (1998). New standards, old inequalities: The current challenge for African-American education. (Ed.) *The state of Black America report*. Chicago: National Urban League.

Darling-Hammond, L. (2000). *Solving the dilemmas of teacher supply, demand, and standards: How we can ensure a competent, caring, and qualified teacher for every child*. New York: National Commission on Teaching and America's Future.

Davis, A. (2003). *Are prisons obsolete?* New York: Seven Stories Press.

Delgado, R., and Stefancic, J. (2001). *Critical race theory: An introduction*. New York: New York University Press.

Delpit, L. (1988). The silenced dialogue: Power and pedagogy in educating other people's children. *Harvard Educational Review*, 58, 3, 280–298.

Denzin, N. (1997). *Interpretive ethnography: Ethnographic practices for the 21st century*. Thousand Oaks, CA: Sage.

Dewey, J. (1900/1990). *The school and society & the child and the curriculum*. Chicago: University of Chicago Press.

Docker, J. (1994). *Postmodernism and popular culture: A cultural history*. New York: Cambridge University Press.

Douglass, F. (2001). *Narrative of the life of an American slave, Frederick Douglass: Written by himself*. New Haven, CT: Yale University Press.

DuBois, W. E. B. (1982). *The souls of black folk*. New York: Signet.

Durham, M., and Kellner, D. (Ed.) (2000). *Media and cultural studies: Keyworks*. place: Blackwell Publishers.

During, S. (Ed) (1999). *The cultural studies reader*. London: Routledge.

Eagleton, T. (1983). *Literary theory: An introduction*. England: Blackwell.

Eagleton-Pierce, M. (2001). The Internet and the Seattle WTO protests. *Peace Review*, 13, 3, 331–337.

Edgar, A. (1999). Ideology. In A. Edgar and P. Sedgwick (Ed.). *Key concepts in cultural theory*. New York: Routledge, pp.

Elbow, P. (1973). *Writing without teachers*. Oxford: Oxford University Press.

Escobar, A. (2000). Welcome to cyberia: Notes on the anthropology of cyberculture. In D. Bell and B. M. Kennedy (Ed.). *The cybercultures reader*. New York: Routledge, 56–77.

Escobar-Chaves, L. S., Tortolero, S. R., Markham, C. M., Low, B. J., Eitel, P., and Thickstun, P. (2005). Impact of the media of adolescent sexual attitudes and behaviors. *Pediatrics*, 116, 303–326.

Fairclough, N. (1989). *Language and power*. London: Longman.

Fairclough, N. (1992). *Discourse and social change*. Cambridge: Polity Press.

Fairclough, N. (1995). *Critical discourse analysis: The critical study of language*. London: Longman.

Fanon, F. (1963). *The wretched of the earth*. New York: Grove Press.

Fanon, F. (1965). *A dying colonialism*. New York: Grove Press.

Fanon, F. (1988). *Toward the African revolution*. New York: Grove Press.

Farley, C. (1999). Hip-hop nation: There's more to rap than just rhythms and rhymes. After two decades, it has transformed the culture of America. *Time*, 153, 5, 55–65.

Feinstein, A. (2004). *Pablo Neruda: A passion for life*. New York: Bloomsbury.

Fine, M. (1991). *Framing dropouts: Notes on the politics of an urban high school*. Albany, NY: SUNY Press.

Fine, M., and Weiss, L. (1998). *The unknown city: The lives of poor and working class young adults*. Boston: Beacon.

Fordham, S., and Ogbu, J. (1986). Black students' school success: Coping with the burden of acting white. *Urban Review*, 18, 3, 176–206.

Foucault, M. (1972). *Archaeology of knowledge*. New York: Pantheon.

Foucault, M. (1997). *Ethics, subjectivity, and truth*. P. Rabinow (Ed.). New York: New Press.

Foucault, M. (2002). *The order of things: An archaeology of the human sciences*. London: Routledge.

Freire, P. (1970). *Pedagogy of the oppressed*. New York: Continuum.

Freire, P., and Macedo, D. (1987). *Literacy: Reading the word and the world*. New York: Bergin and Garvey.

Freire, P. (1997). *Teachers as cultural workers: Letters to those who dare teach*. Boulder, CO: Westview.

Fromm, E. (1965). *Escape from freedom*. New York: Avon Books.

Gallagher, C. W. (2002). *Radical departures: Composition and progressive pedagogy*. Urbana, IL: NCTE.

Gates, B. (1996). *The road ahead*. New York: Penguin.

Gates, H. L. (2002). *The classic slave narratives*. New York: Signet Classics.

Gates, H. L., and Andrews, W. L. (Ed.) (2001). *Slave narratives*. New York: Library of America.

Gee, J. P. (1996). *Social linguistics and literacies: Ideology in discourses*, 2nd edn. London: Taylor & Francis.

Gee, J. (1999). *Learning language as a matter of learning social languages within discourses*. Paper presented to the annual meeting of the American Educational Research Association, Montreal, Canada.

Gee, J. P. (2000). The new literacy studies: From 'socially situated' to the work of the social. In D. Barton, M. Hamilton, and R. Ivanic (Ed.) *Situated literacies: Reading and writing in context*. London: Routledge, 180–196.

Gee, J. P. (2003). *What video games have to teach us about learning and literacy*. New York: Palgrave/Macmillan.

Geertz, C. (2000) *Local knowledge: Further essays in interpretive anthropology*. New York: Basic Books.

George, N. (1998). *Hiphopamerica*. New York: Penguin.

Gilroy, P. (1993). *The Black Atlantic: Modernity and double consciousness*. Cambridge, MA: Harvard University Press.

Giroux, H. A. (1988). *Teachers as transformative intellectuals*. New York: Bergin & Garvey.

Giroux, H. A. (1996). *Fugitive cultures: Race, violence, and youth*. New York: Routledge.

Giroux, H. A. (2001). *Theory and resistance in education: Toward a pedagogy of the opposition*. New York: Bergin and Garvey.

Glaser, B. G., and Strauss, A. L. (1967). *The discovery of grounded theory: Strategies for qualitative research*. New York: Aldine de Gruyter.

Golden, J. (2001). *Reading in the dark: Using film as a tool in the English classroom*. Urbana, IL: NCTE.

Goodman, S. (2003). *Teaching youth media: A critical guide to literacy, video production, and social change*. New York: Teachers College Press.

Gramsci, A. (1971). *Selections from the prison notebooks*. New York: International Publishers.

Gramsci, A. (1919/1985). *Selections from cultural writings*. Cambridge, MA: Harvard University Press.

Gramsci, A. (1991). *Selections from cultural writings*. Cambridge, MA: Harvard University Press.

Greenberg, E., Jin, J., Boyle, B., Hsu, Y., and Dunleavy, E. (2007). *Literacy in everyday life: Results from the 2003 National Assessment of Adult Literacy*. U.S. Department of Education. Washington, DC: National Center for Education Statistics.

Guevara, C. (2001). *Back on the road: A journey through Latin America*. New York: Grove.

Guevara, C. (2003). *The motorcycle diaries: Notes on a Latin American journey*. New York: Ocean Press.

Guha, R. (Ed.) (1982). *Subaltern studies I: Writings on South Asian history and society*. Delhi: Oxford University Press.

Gutstein, E. (2005). *Reading and writing the world with mathematics: Toward a pedagogy for social justice*. New York: Routledge.

Gutting, G. (2001). *French philosophy in the twentieth century*. Cambridge: Cambridge University Press.

Habermas, J. (1981). *The theory of communicative action I: Reason and the rationalization of society*. London: Heinemann.

Habermas, J. (1987). *The theory of communicative action II: Lifeworld and style*. Cambridge: Polity Press.

Hakim, A.B. (2001). *Historical introduction to philosophy*, 4th edn. Upper Saddle River, NJ: Prentice Hall.

Hall, S. (1999). Cultural studies and its theoretical legacies. In S. During (Ed.), *The cultural studies reader*. New York: Routledge, 97–112.

Hall, S., Morley, D., Chen, K. H. (1996). *Stuart Hall: Critical dialogues in cultural studies*. London: Routledge.

Heath, S. B. (1983). *Ways with words: Language, life, and work in communities and classrooms*. Cambridge: Cambridge University Press.

Hegel, G. W. F. (1979). *Phenomenology of spirit*. Oxford: Oxford University Press.

Hegel, G. W. F. (1999). *Science of logic.* Amherst, NY: Humanity Books.

Hill, J., and Gibson, P. C. (Eds.) (2000). *Film studies: Critical approaches.* Oxford: Oxford University Press.

hooks, b. (1994). *Teaching to transgress: Education as the practice of freedom.* New York: Routledge.

Hughes, B. (2004). Opposite intended effect: A case study of how over-standardization can reduce the efficacy of teacher education. *Teacher Education Quarterly*, 31, 3.

Hymes, D. (1974). *Foundations in sociolinguistics: An ethnographic approach.* Philadelphia: University of Pennsylvania Press.

Jacobs, H. A. (2000). *Incidents in the life of a slave girl.* New York: Signet Classics.

James, C. L. R. (1963). *The Black Jacobins: Toussaint L'Ouverture and the San Domingo revolution.* New York: Vintage.

Kant, I. (1788/1993). *Critique of practical reason.* Upper Saddle River, NJ: Prentice Hall.

Kant, I. (1781/1998). *Critique of pure reason.* Cambridge: Cambridge University Press.

Kant, I. (1790/2005). *Critique of judgment.* New York: Barnes and Noble Books.

Kasher, S. (1996) *The civil rights movement: A photographic history.* New York: Abbeville Press.

Kastman Breuch, L. M. (2003). Post-process pedagogy: A philosophical exercise. In V. Villanueva (Ed.). *Cross-talk in comp theory: A reader.* Urbana, IL: NCTE, 97–126.

Kellner, D. (1995). *Media culture: Cultural studies, identity, and politics between the modern and the postmodern.* New York: Routledge.

Kent, T. (Ed.) (1999). *Post-process theory: Beyond the writing-process paradigm.* Carbondale, IL: Southern Illinois University Press.

Kincheloe, J., and McLaren, P. (1998). Rethinking critical theory and qualitative research. In N. Denzin and Y. Lincoln (Ed.), *The landscape of qualitative research.* Thousand Oaks, CA: Sage, 260–299.

Kirtchev, C. A (1997). *A cyberpunk manifesto.* www.dvara.net/HK/cyberpunk_manifesto. ASP, retrieved November 10, 2004.

Kozol, J. (1979). *Children of the revolution: A Yankee teacher in the Cuban schools.* New York: Delta.

Kozol, J. (1991). *Savage inequalities: Children in America's schools.* New York: Perennial.

Kramnick, I. (ed.) (1995) *The portable Enlightenment reader.* New York and London: Penguin.

Kress, G. (2003). *Literacy in the new media age.* London: Routledge.

Kunjufu, J. (2004). *Countering the conspiracy to destroy black boys.* Jawanza Kunjufu.

Kurlansky, M. (2003). *1968: The year that rocked the world.* New York: Ballantine Books.

Labov, W. (1972). *Language in the inner city: Studies in the Black English vernacular.* Philadelphia: University of Pennsylvania Press.

Ladson-Billings, G. (1994). *The dreamkeepers: Successful teachers of African-American children.* San Francisco: Jossey Bass.

Langer, J. (1995). *Envisioning literature: Literary understanding and literature instruction.* New York: Teachers College Press.

Langer, J. (2002). *Effective literacy instruction: Building successful reading and writing programs.* Urbana, IL: NCTE.

Lankshear, C., and Knobel, M. (2003). *New literacies.* place: Open University Press.

Lankshear, C., Peters, M., and Knobel, M. (1996). Critical pedagogy and cyberspace. In H. A. Giroux, C. Lankshear, P. McLaren, and M. Peters (Ed.), *Counternarratives: Cultural studies and critical pedagogies in postmodern spaces.* New York: Routledge, 149–188.

Laureau, A. (2000). *Home advantage: Social class and parental intervention in elementary education.* Lanham, MD: Rowman and Littlefield.

Lave, J., and Wenger, E. (1991). *Situated learning: Legitimate peripheral participation.* Cambridge: Cambridge University Press.

Lavine, T. Z. (1984). *From Socrates to Sartre: The philosophic quest.* New York: Bantam Books.

Lee, C. (1992). *Signifying as a scaffold for literary interpretation: The pedagogical implications of an African American discourse genre.* Urbana, IL: NCTE Press.

Lee, C., and Smagorinsky, P. (2000). Introduction. In C. Lee and P. Smagorinsky (Ed.), *Vygotskian perspectives on literacy research: Constructing meaning through collaborative inquiry.* New York: Cambridge University Press, 1–18.

Light, A. (1999). *The vibe history of hip-hop.* New York: Three Rivers Press.

Lipsitz, G. (1994). History, hip-hop, and the post-colonial politics of sound. In *Dangerous crossroads: Popular music, postmodernism, and the poetics of place.* New York: Verso, 23–48.

Loewen, J. (1995). *Lies my teacher told me: Everything your American history textbook got wrong.* New York: Touchstone.

Loomba, A. (1998). *Colonialism/postcolonialism: The new critical idiom.* London: Routledge.

Lyotard, J. (1984). *The postmodern condition: A report on knowledge.* Minneapolis: University of Minnesota Press.

Macey, D. (2000). *The Penguin dictionary of critical theory.* London: Penguin Books.

McLaren, P. (1989). *Life in schools: An introduction to critical pedagogy and the foundations of education.* New York: Longman.

McLaren, P. (1997). *Critical pedagogy and predatory culture: Oppositional politics in a postmodern era.* New York: Routledge.

McLaren, P. (2005). *Capitalists and conquerors: A critical pedagogy against empire.* Lanham, MD: Rowman and Littlefield.

MacLeod, J. (1987). *Ain't no makin' it: Aspirations and attainment in a low-income neighborhood.* Boulder, CO: Westview.

McLuhan, M. (1964). *Understanding media: The extensions of man.* New York: Signet.

McLuhan, M. (1966). *The medium is the massage: An inventory of effects.* Toronto: Penguin.

McLuhan, M. (1967/2003). *War and peace in the global village.* Toronto: Penguin.

McNeil, L. (2000). *Contradictions of school reform: Educational costs of standardized testing.* New York: Falmer.

Mahiri, J. (1998). *Shooting for excellence: African American and youth culture in new century schools.* New York: Teachers College Press.

Manley, M. (2004). Reggae and the revolutionary faith . . . The role of Bob Marley. In H. Bordowitz (Ed.). *Every little thing gonna be alright: The Bob Marley reader.* Cambridge, MA: De Capo Press, 216–224.

Marcuse, H. (1961). *Soviet Marxism: A critical analysis.* New York: Random House.

Marcuse, H. (1964). *One dimensional man.* London: Routledge and Kegan Paul.

Marx, K. (1976). *Capital: Volume 1.* New York: Penguin.

Marx, K. (1983). A contribution to the critique of political economy. In *The portable Karl Marx.* New York: Penguin.

Marx, K. (1988). *The Communist manifesto.* New York: W. W. Norton and Company.

Marx, K., and Engels, F. (1988). *The German ideology.* New York: International Publishers.

Mastronardi, M. (2003). Adolescence and media. *Journal of Language and Social Psychology,* 22, 1, 83–93.

Meier, D. (1995). *The power of their ideas: Lessons from America from a small school in Harlem.* Boston: Beacon.

Merriam, S. B. (1998). *Qualitative research and case study applications in education.* San Francisco: Jossey-Bass.

Mills, C. W. (1959). *The sociological imagination.* Oxford: Oxford University Press.

Mills, S. (1997). *Discourse: The new critical idiom.* London: Routledge.

Moll, L. (2000). Inspired by Vygotsky: Ethnographic experiments in education. In C. Lee and P. Smagorinsky (Eds.), *Vygotskian perspectives on literacy research: Constructing meaning through collaborative inquiry.* New York: Cambridge University Press.

Morrell, E. (2002). Toward a critical pedagogy of popular culture: Literacy development among urban youth. *Journal of Adolescent and Adult Literacy,* 46, 1, 72–77.

Morrell, E. (2004a). *Becoming critical researchers: Literacy and empowerment for urban youth.* New York: Peter Lang.

Morrell, E. (2004b). *Linking literacy and popular culture: Finding connections for lifelong learning.* Norwood, MA: Christopher-Gordon.

Morrell, E. (2005). Critical English education. *English Education,* 37, 4, 312–322.

Morrell, E., and Duncan-Andrade, J. (2002). Toward a critical classroom discourse: Promoting academic literacy through engaging hip-hop culture with urban youth. *English Journal,* 91, 6, 88–94.

Morrell, E., and Rogers, J. (2007). Students as Critical Public Historians: Insider Research on Diversity and Access in Post *Brown v. Board* Los Angeles. *Social Education,* volume, issue, pp.

Morrison, T. (1993). *Playing in the dark: Whiteness and the literary imagination.* New York: Vintage.

Murray, D. (1972/2003). Teach writing as process not product. In V. Villanueva (Ed.) *Cross-talk in comp theory: A reader.* Urbana, IL: NCTE, 3–7.

Muspratt, S., Luke, A., and Freebody, P. (Ed.) (1997). *Constructing critical literacies.* Creskill, NJ: Hampton.

National Research Council (2005). *Advancing scientific research in education.* Committee on research in education. Lisa Towne, Laures L. Wise, and Tina M. Winters (Ed.).

Center for Education, Division of Behavioral and Social Sciences and Education. Washington, DC: The National Academies Press.

Neel, J. (1988). *Plato, Derrida, and writing.* Carbondale, IL: Southern Illinois University Press.

Neruda, P. (1950/1993). *Canto general.* Berkeley: University of California Press.

Neruda, P. (1977). *Memoirs.* New York: Farrar, Straus, and Giroux.

Neruda, P. (1978). *Passions and impressions.* New York: Farrar, Straus, and Giroux.

New London Group (1996). A pedagogy of multiliteracies: Designing social futures. *Harvard Educational Review,* 66, 1, 60–92.

Nieto, S. (1992). *Affirming diversity: The sociopolitical context of multicultural education.* New York: Longman.

Noguera, P. (2002). *City schools and the American dream.* New York: Teachers College Press.

Oakes, J. (1985). *Keeping track: How schools structure inequality.* New Haven, CT: Yale University Press.

Oakes, J., and Rogers, J. (2006). *Learning power: Organizing for education and justice.* New York: Teachers College Press.

O'Connor, D. K. (1999). Socrates and the Socratics. In R. Popkin (Ed.). *The Columbia history of Western philosophy.* New York: Columbia University Press, 23–32.

Perry, T. (2003). Freedom for literacy and literacy for freedom: The African-American philosophy of education. In T. Perry, C. Steele, and A. Hilliard, *Young, gifted, and black: Promoting high achievement among African-American students.* Boston: Beacon, pp. 11–52

Piccone, P. (1998). Introduction. In A. Arato and E. Gebhardt (Ed.). *The essential Frankfurt school reader.* New York: Continuum.

Quartz, K., et al. (2003). Too angry to leave: Supporting new teachers' commitment to transform urban schools. *Journal of Teacher Education,* 54, 2, 99–111.

Richter, D. H. (1998). *The critical tradition: Classic texts and contemporary trends.* Boston: Bedford/St. Martin's.

Robbins, R. (1999). Introduction: Will the real feminist theory please stand up? In J. Wolfreys (Ed.). *Literary theories: A reader and guide.* New York: New York University Press, 49–58.

Robinson, T. M. (1999). The Sophists. In R. Popkin (Ed.). *The Columbia history of Western philosophy.* New York: Columbia University Press, 20–23.

Rogoff, B. (1991). *Apprenticeship in thinking: Cognitive development in social context.* Oxford: Oxford University Press.

Ronfeldt, D., Arquilla, J., Fuller, G., and Fuller, M. (1998). *The Zapatista "social netwar" in Mexico.* Santa Monica, CA: RAND, MR-994A.

Rosenblatt, L. (1978) Efferent and aesthetic reading. In *The reader, the text, the poem: A transactional theory of the literary work.* Carbondale, IL: Southern Illinois Press, 22–47.

Rosenblatt, L. M. (1995). *Literature as exploration.* New York: Modern Language Association.

Russell, A. (2005). Myth and the Zapatista movement: Exploring a network identity. *New Media and Society*, 7, 4, 559–577.

Said, E. (1979). *Orientalism*. New York: Vintage.

Said, E. (2003). *Reflections on exile and other essays*. Cambridge, MA: Harvard University Press.

Sardar, Z., and Van Loon, B. (2000). *Introducing media studies*. New York: Totem.

Sartre, J.-P. (1964). *Nausea*. New York: New Directions.

Sartre, J.-P. (1984). *Being and nothingness*. New York: Washington Square Press.

Sartre, J.-P. (1989). *No exit and three other plays*. New York: Vintage.

Sartre, J.-P. (1992a). *The age of reason*. New York: Vintage.

Sartre, J.-P. (1992b). *The reprieve*. New York: Vintage.

Sartre, J.-P. (1992c). *Troubled sleep*. New York: Vintage.

Sartre, J.-P. (1993). *Essays in existentialism*. New York: Citadel Press.

Sartre, J.-P. (2000). *Modern times: Selected non-fiction*. London: Penguin Classics.

Sartre, J. (2001). *Basic writings*. S. Priest (Ed.). New York: Routledge.

Saussure, F. (1915/1966). *Course in general linguistics*. New York: McGraw-Hill.

Schirmacher, W. (Ed.) (2000). *German 20th century philosophy: The Frankfurt school*. New York: Continuum.

Scholes, R. (1998). *The rise and fall of English: Reconstructing English as a discipline*. New Haven, CT: Yale University Press.

Scholes, R. (1986). *Textual power: Literary theory and the teaching of English*. New Haven, CT: Yale University Press.

Shor, I. (1992). *Empowering education: Critical teaching for social change*. Chicago: University of Chicago Press.

Sleeter, C. (1996). *Multicultural education as social activism*. Albany, NY: State University of New York Press.

Smagorinsky, P., and Whiting, M. E. (1995). *How English teachers get taught: Methods of teaching the methods class*. Urbana, IL: NCTE.

Smith, A. (2003). *The wealth of nations*. New York: Bantam Classic.

Smitherman, G. (1999). *Talkin that talk: Language, culture, and education in African America*. New York: Routledge.

Spady, J., Alim, S., and Meghelli, S. (2006). *The global cipha: Hip hop culture and consciousness*. place: Black History Museum Press.

Spivak, G. (1999). *A critique of postcolonial reason: Toward a history of the vanishing present*. Cambridge, MA: Harvard University Press.

Steele, C., and Aronson, J. (1995). Stereotype threat and the intellectual test performance of African-Americans. *Journal of Personality and Social Psychology*, 69, 5, 797–811.

Strauss, A., and Corbin, J. (Ed.) (1997). *Grounded theory in practice*. Thousand Oaks, CA: Sage.

Street, B. (1984). *Literacy in theory and practice*. Cambridge: Cambridge University Press.

Street, B. (1995). *Social literacies: Critical approaches to literacy in development, ethnography, and education*. London: Longman.

Strinati, D. (1995). *An introduction to theories of popular culture*. London: Routledge.

Towne, L., Wise, L. L., and Winters, T. M. (Ed.) (2004). *Advancing scientific research in education.* Washington, DC: National Academies Press.

Truth, S. (1997). *Narrative of Sojourner Truth.* New York: Dover Thrift Editions.

Villanueva, V. (2003). The givens in our conversations: The writing process. In V. Villanueva (Ed.). *Cross-talk in comp theory: A reader.* Urbana, IL: NCTE, 1–2.

UC/ACCORD (2004). *California opportunity indicators: Informing and monitoring California's progress toward equitable college access.* www.ucaccord.org, retrieved July 7, 2005.

UNESCO (1965). *Report on the method and means utilized in Cuba to eliminate illiteracy.* Havana, Cuba: UNESCO.

UNESCO (1975). *Final report for international symposium for literacy.* Persepolis, Iran: UNESCO.

UNESCO (2005) *UNESCO and Education.* Paris, France: UNESCO

United States Department of Education (2002). *Overview of elementary and secondary public school districts: School year 2001–2002.* Washington, DC: National Center for Education Statistics.

United States Department of Education (2005). 'National Assessment of Educational Progress' The Nation's report card: Reading 2005. Jessup, MD: Ed Pubs.

Vasquez, V. (2004). *Negotiating critical literacies with young children.* Mahwah, NJ: Lawrence Earlbaum.

Villanueva, V. (Ed.) (2003). *Cross talk in comp theory: A reader,* 2nd edn. Urbana, IL: NCTE.

Volosinov, V. N. (1973). *Marxism and the philosophy of language.* Cambridge, MA: Harvard University Press.

Vygotsky, L. (1962). *Thought and language.* Cambridge, MA: The MIT Press.

Vygotsky, L. (1978). *Mind in society.* Cambridge, MA: Harvard University Press.

Walker, A. (1984). *In search of our mother's gardens: Womanist prose.* New York: Harcourt Harvest Books.

Weis, L., and Fine, M. (2004). *Working method: Research, critical theory, and social justice.* New York: Routledge.

West, C. (1993). *Race matters.* New York: Vintage Books.

Westheimer, J., and Kahne, J. (2004). What kind of citizen? The politics of educating for democracy. *American Educational Research Journal,* 41, 2, 237–269.

Wigfield, A., and Eccles, J. (1992). The development of achievement task values: A theoretical analysis. *Developmental Review,* 12, 265–310.

Wigfield, A., and Eccles, J. (2000). Expectancy–value theory of achievement motivation. *Contemporary Educational Psychology,* 25, 68–81.

Wilhelm, J. (1997). *You gotta BE the book: Teaching engaged and reflective reading with adolescents.* New York: Teachers College Press/NCTE.

Williams, J. (1987). *Eyes on the prize: America's civil rights years 1954–1965.* New York: Viking.

Williams, R. (1995). *The sociology of culture.* Chicago: University of Chicago Press.

Williams, R. (1998). The analysis of culture. In J. Storey (Ed.), *Cultural theory and popular culture: A reader.* Athens, GA: University of Georgia Press, 48–56.

Williams, R. (2003). *Television*. London: Routledge.

Wilson, W. J. (1996). *When work disappears: The world of the new urban poor*. New York: Vintage.

Witkin, R. W. (2003). *Adorno on popular culture*. New York: Routledge.

Wittgenstein, L. (2001a). *Tractatus logico-philosophicus*. London: Routledge.

Wittgenstein, L. (2001b). *Philosophical investigations*. Oxford: Blackwell.

Woodson, C. G. (1933/1990). *The miseducation of the Negro*. Washington, DC: Africa World Press.

Yetman, N. R. (Ed.) (2001). *Voices from slavery: 100 authentic slave narratives*. Mineola, NY: Dover.

Yetman, N. R. (Ed.) (2002). *When I was a slave: Memoirs from the slave narrative collection*. Mineola, NY: Dover Thrift Editions.

Zinn, H. (1995). *A people's history of the United States: 1492–present*. New York: Harper Perennial.

Index